DEATH BY ENCHANTMENT

By the same Author
WHICH WITCH?

DEATH BY ENCHANTMENT

AN EXAMINATION OF ANCIENT AND MODERN WITCHCRAFT

BY

JULIAN FRANKLYN

G. P. PUTNAM'S SONS
NEW YORK

FIRST AMERICAN EDITION 1971

COPYRIGHT © 1971 BY V. KEEBLE

Library of Congress Catalog
Card Number: 78–152769

DEDICATED
TO
VIOLETTA
WHO IS
ENCHANTING
IN A DIFFERENT WAY

List of Illustrations

following page 118

Preface

No one has ever written an unbiased book on Witchcraft although some have claimed to have done so. No matter how normally fair-minded and just a person may be, in making a study of witchcraft he must incline either to Montague Summers who believed too much, or to Notestein who believed nothing at all.

There is no new material on the old cases: one must be guided by the court records of trials, and by the contemporaneous booklets, which latter may or may not be available.

All that the modern writer can do is re-tell the old tales putting emphasis on the particular aspect of the case that he thinks either supports his thesis or illustrates his present point, but in doing even this much he, being human, must himself be the slave of his own beliefs.

If his study of the case has convinced him of the guilt of Dames Chattox and Demdike then he cannot avoid emphasizing what vile old hags the ladies were. On the other hand, your hard-headed materialistic non-believer is going to condemn the accusers, the witnesses and the justices.

The present writer, while making no claim to be unbiased, has, he hopes, succeeded in avoiding the mistake of letting his emotions and beliefs take command of the situation. When an accused hag of evil intentions is maltreated he does not offer excuses for the persecutors; when victims of witchcraft are clearly hysterics putting on an act he does not fail to condemn the victim and exonerate the accused.

He is aware of the findings of modern psychologists in relation to witch phenomena and, within the compass of his understanding of the claims made, reveals the 'rational' and 'compassionate' attitude they adopt, but, he does not permit himself to be 'blinded by science': he does not take the attitude that modern science must be right, and that psychology has solved the age-old problem. Psychology has done no such thing. It has, most certainly, let light in and has illuminated a few superficial points, but the dark cavern of goety * remains, in the main, dark and dangerous.

It is not this author's intention to moralize, nor is he qualified to do so, but he concludes by expressing the hope that this book will have the effect of enlightening those who think witches are to be found in fairy-stories only.

JULIAN FRANKLYN

* Magic effected by the aid of demons.

Chapter One

JUSTIN, the Christian apologist, wrote, 'God committed the care of men and all things under Heaven to angels whom he set over these', however, only God himself is perfect. Angels, in spite of their being superior to mankind, are not entirely free from faults, and the manifest evil that mars this world was brought about by angels who 'transgressed the Divine appointment and by sinful intercourse with women produced offspring who are demons [who] subdued the human race to themselves [and] sowed among men all manner of wickedness.'

Athenagoras, writing on the fall of angels, lays emphasis on one in particular, named Satan who is chief and leader of all demons hostile to God.

Tertullian states that the angels were given free will as mankind was, and he asserts that the fall of the former was occasioned by their being corrupted in the ambitious exercise of free-will, so that they became the progenerators of all evil, and fathers of the host of demons. He acknowledges Satan as the chief—the Prince of Darkness, the Father of lies—and he attributes to the machinations of demons all disease and disasters.

Lactantius explains that God created, before the Creation recorded in Genesis, a spirit like Himself, called the Logos, and then another who, of his own free will, abandoned the Divine, generated evil, assumed the name of Satan and, of his hatred for and jealousy of God in this sublime goodness, strove (and incessantly strives) to win for himself the worship of mankind. Satan's power is, however, limited: although he can tempt, and incite human beings to sin, he cannot affect their free will or reduce their spiritual awareness.

Thomas Aquinas teaches that the devil, who was the greatest of all the angels, desired to be as God and, through his pride and envy, he engendered his own degradation. He was not, at his creation, an evil spirit, for God does not create evil, but by the exercise of his free-will he became evil, and is the cause of the subsequent fall of lesser angels by his inciting them to rebellion.

The Roman Catholic Church still accepts the reality of the devil and all his imps but has somewhat modified the ideas expressed on the matter by early theologians. The Catholic conception of the existence of good and bad angels was retained by Protestantism after the Reformation, and not abandoned until well into the eighteenth century when 'rationalization' was extended from secular to sacred ideas leading to the growth of atheism, the reduction of general piety, and an increased toleration of evil behaviour, as well as its expression in literature. 'Rationalization' culminated in the diabolical triumph manifested as the French Revolution. The early nineteenth century saw the re-acceptance, by Protestantism, of the belief in good angels, and by the colder, more dismal and denunciatory non-conforming sects of both good and evil spirits with a decided preference for the Evil One, hellfire, and eternal damnation.

The devil, the arch-enemy of God, the chief demon or fiend, became identified with the serpent of Genesis: he was Prince of the power of the air: he was Beelzebub, Abaddon, Apollyon, Leviathan, Asucodeus, Behemoth, Belial and Lucifer. Pagan conceptions become grafted on to the main-stem of the devil-idea, hence his likeness was that of the Greek god Pan, hence the devil's horns and cloven hooves; but he was also a black-man, a giant, a lion, a serpent, a bull, a wolf, a scorpion, even an army on the march. The devil might appear in the form of a woman, a 'monk, a priest, or even as a good angel.

Witchcraft and Satanism were inseparable, and with the growth of science in the nineteenth century the belief in both waned. In the twentieth century, this age of enlightenment, electrification and mechanization of the very means of life, no one, not even a modern, undisciplined, mundane-minded, sophisticated child, believes in either the devil or the witch, and the last sixty years has seen more and greater evil at work in the world than the sum total of all that was deplorable in the previous hundred and twenty years.

Dr Ernest Jones says* 'In a psychological study we must start from the assumption that the Devil is a creation not of heaven,

* *On the Nightmare*. Hogarth Press, 1931.

as the theologians still teach, but of the human mind. . . . Our first problem, therefore, is to ascertain which* components of the instinctual life constitute the source of the belief in the Devil.

'This question evidently belongs to the series of those that have to do with anxiety emotions. The whole history of the Devil is one of constant dread. . . . As a starting point for our investigation may be taken a remark of Pfister's,† in which the Devil is traced back to "infantile experiences of fear" in the life of the individual. Since the origin of infantile terror is not known it naturally suggests itself to one to investigate the descriptions of the belief in the Devil in the light of this new knowledge. This procedure has led me to formulate the following conclusions, the evidence for which will presently be brought forward: *The belief in the Devil represents in the main an exteriorization of two sets of repressed wishes, both of which are ultimately derived from the infantile Oedipus situation: (a) The wish to imitate certain attributes of the father, and (b) the wish to defy the father; in other words, an alternating emulation of and hostility against the father.*‡ Both sources contain repressed material; the latter obviously does, and even the former differs from the early piety which later expresses itself in the belief in God, through being more directly concerned with admiration for the darker "evil" side of the father's nature and activities. In this respect the Devil personifies the Father, while in the other he personifies the Son: he thus represents unconscious aspects of the Son-Father complex, sometimes the one side being the more prominent, sometimes the other. The corresponding female Oedipus situation also contributes material of no less importance.

'The idea of evil supernatural powers, although perhaps not absolutely universal, is exceeding widely spread among ruder peoples, and was so with the civilized peoples of antiquity. On investigating specific instances more closely, however, it is striking to note how very rarely these powers were *purely* § evil in nature. With almost the sole exception of the Persian Ahriman, described in the Vedida section of the Zend-Avesta, one may say that before the advent of Christianity there was no definite conception of a supernatural being professionally devoted to evil.'

---

* Dr Jones's italic.
† Leader of the Zurich School of Psychoanalysis.
‡ Dr Jones's italic. § Dr Jones's italic.

Dr Jones gives a brief summary of the ambivalence of numerous pagan gods and he points out that the Satan of the Old Testament was not wholly evil, but was a servitor of God. He continues: 'Discredited by the failure of its prophecies (the end of the world at 1000 A.D. and numerous other dates) and by moral and ecclesiastical scandals, torn by internal political and religious dissensions, its very existence threatened by powerful heretical sects, the condition of the Church in the twelfth century was such as called for the most desperate measures. To attribute all its difficulties to the activity of the Devil, and in this way to distract people from contemplating its weakness by terrifying them with an external danger, one moreover with which the Church knew itself competent to deal, was a device at which it eagerly clutched; it is one to which Governments in embarrassment have seldom failed to have recourse. The people, in abject misery at their social conditions, devastated with pestilence and war and, in consequence of their misfortunes saturated with the sense of sinfulness, fell an easy prey to the Church's teaching. Indeed, these teachings at moments overreached themselves, for the people, in despair at the obvious failure of God and the Church to relieve their misery, greedily absorbed the doctrine of the wonderful powers of the Devil, so that not a few took refuge with him; probably the definite nature of the bargain driven in the well-known facts appealed to them more than the unending and often inefficacious prayers to Saints. The extent of the belief in the Devil's influence on even the most trivial everyday happenings was so colossal that one cannot read the records of the time without thinking that Europe was being visited by a mass psychoneurosis of an unusually malign type.'

The foregoing somewhat copious quotations reveal that theology teaches there is a devil and a host of demons, and that psychology teaches there is no devil, nor are there any demons. Neither the one discipline nor the other can prove its contention. The layman is left to exert the free-will which he possesses to believe that there either is or is not a devil: however, the layman who is intellectually alert, and who can profit from experience, may discover in the procession of the years that the extreme point of view he so passionately defended in his youth cannot, in justice to himself, be rigidly retained. The extremist teaching of theology must be watered down with libations of psychology, the ultra-mundane aspects of psychology that overwhelm the spiritual qualities of man must be softened by the sound, age-old guidance for life given by theology, and the devil, disguised either as priest or doctor, is himself now the spiritual, now the medical adviser, who advocates the total elimination of the other if the sufferer is to be saved: but both priest and doctor, and the devil himself would unite in accepting Dr Ernest Jones's conclusion that in the twelfth century Europe was sick of a mass psychoneurosis.

Eric Partridge concludes an essay entitled *The Language of Witchcraft and Magic*,* with these words: 'After an eclipse lasting throughout most of the eighteenth and nineteenth centuries, Satan has returned to European literature; by (say) 1900, he had been laughed out of existence. He remained "an exploded myth" until the war of 1914–18, when people began to doubt their doubts. The war of 1939–45 virtually reinstated him. Two such world-scarring, soul-blasting wars are perhaps attributable only to one of two forces: either to Satan or to an incredible stupidity in mankind; or, of course, to that stupidity employed by Satan as an invincible weapon. The Catholic Church has, I'm told, never ceased to warn its members against the formidable patience and the well-nigh infinite resourcefulness of Satan, the Great Adversary. It is, therefore, natural that novelists of France (for instance, Mauriac) and Britain (Graham Greene) have put Satan back, not on a pedestal, but where he can be seen and watched. For, as that macabre poseur, but true poet, Baudelaire, said:

> The Devil's best trick is to persuade us that he
> does not exist.

Every cultural period has its architectonic: all the trends of an age assume a contour conforming to the pattern of the whole, and it was eighteenth-century rationalization that produced John Wilkes (1727–1797). His political activities and his advocacy of the freedom of the press were probably sincere, and may have been beneficial, but his personal life, his moral character, and his social relationships, severely censured by Dr Johnson, were deplorable.

Among Wilkes's public works was that of reorganizing the militia, and while engaged on this mission he made the acquain-

* To be found in A *Charm of Words*, Hamish Hamilton, 1960.

tance of Col. Sir Francis Dashwood who, in some respects, was a man after Wilkes's own heart. Dashwood initiated Wilkes into his Order of Medmenham Monks, also known as 'the Hell-Fire Club'. The avowed intention of the organization was the very rude and somewhat puerile one of ridiculing the Roman Catholic Church and parodying its rituals, but in practice it was a society of roystering libertines whose amusements were both profane and profligate. Their avowed ridicule of the Catholic Church was expressed, *inter alia*, in devil worship, and at some of their meetings they celebrated a version of the Black Mass.

It is doubtful whether any of those initiated into the society took their Satanism seriously: John Wilkes was one who certainly did not. To him, the meetings were merely occasions for debauchery in which he was a whole-hearted participant. On one occasion he imprisoned in a cupboard* an ape, which creature he released during the celebration of the Black Mass, at the juncture when the devil is invoked.

The biographers of Wilkes are often men who admire his political career, and who therefore do not emphasize his undesirable personal character, with the result that accounts of the incident vary. Either the ape, after careering round the room, perched itself on Sir Francis Dashwood's shoulder and he, calm and dignified, walked over to the window, which he opened, and permitted the animal to escape, this comprising a harmless little practical joke such as was expected from all members of the Hell-Fire Club: or else the creature leapt furiously about terrifying all present (except Wilkes), and Sir Francis Dashwood, on his knees implored the devil to depart, complaining that the present materialization was unexpected, and most unfair, because he (Dashwood) did not believe in the reality of the devil, and never had. This more acceptable, because more likely, version also states that a young man who was present sustained so great a shock that he died.

Whether the ape was the devil or the devil was an ape, whether the devil does or not not exist, Wilkes's practical joke makes it abundantly clear that the devil is a dangerous playmate.

Whether the devil does or does not exist there are periods in history that produce a son of Satan in whom evil becomes incarnate. There is no need to travel far in either space or time to

* According to some versions, 'in a chest'.

produce two outstanding examples: in our own country, Oliver Cromwell; in our own time, Adolf Hitler.

In this age of nuclear fission, of colour television, of supersonic aircraft, space-travel and heart-transplantation no one is willing to believe in a personal devil, and, alas, but few in a personal God.

John Wesley wrote*: 'It is true likewise, that the English in general, and indeed most men of learning in Europe, have given up all accounts of witches and apparitions as mere old wives' fables. I am sorry for it, and I willingly take this opportunity of entering my solemn protest against this violent compliment which so many that believe the Bible pay to those who do not believe it. I owe them no such service. I take knowledge that they are at the bottom of the outcry which has been raised, and with such insolence spread throughout the land, in direct opposition not only to the Bible, but to the suffrage of the wisest and best men in all ages and nations. They well know (whether Christians know it or not) that the giving up of witchcraft is in effect giving up the Bible. With my last breath I will bear testimony against giving up to infidels one great proof of the invisible world; I mean that of witchcraft and apparitions, confirmed by the testimony of all ages.'

By coupling witchcraft with apparitions Wesley demonstrates a broader conception of the meaning of the term 'witchcraft' than is justified by the Church's condemnation of the cult. The kernel of this quotation—'the giving up of witchcraft is in effect giving up the Bible'—is, so expressed, unsound because, in the Bible, there is not recorded a single example of witchcraft as it was known in Christendom from about 1350 to about 1750. Wesley's meaning is however clear enough and abundantly true: if mankind does not fear the devil it does not fear God.

The words 'witch', 'wizard', 'witchcraft' that are to be found a number of times in the English Bible appear only as a vernacular translation: it must be borne in mind that the unicorn and the cockatrice are ensconced in Holy Writ, too.

The witchcraft of the Old Testament was sorcery, psychopractice, and similar activities: 'thou shalt not suffer a witch to live' (Exodus XXII, 18), the text that, in Christian Europe, was made the justification of mass-murder on a huge scale and by

* *Journal*: 25 May, 1768.

methods so horrible that one is left in no doubt of the veracity of
demoniac possession, might have meant simply 'do not patronize
fortune-tellers and others of that fraternity: do not pay them
for their services and so provide them with a livelihood'.

'Witchcraft' is a vague, loose term which, in all parts of the
world is in some degree related to magic, and magic is the measure
of the intellectual and spiritual equipment of the average person
in a community.

At a Christmas party, attended by adults of superior education,
one asked 'any lady present' to lend him a finger-ring. Upon
receipt of the desired object he pulled the outside pocket of his
jacket open and dropped the ring from between nine and twelve
inches above, into it, patted it on the outside two or three times
and then, inserting his hand drew forth a small, velvet bag, closed
with a draw-string and tied. This he handed to the lady who had
lent her ring, and told her to open it which she did, only to find
another bag of the same kind, similarly tied which, opened, revealed another, and so on till half a dozen or more securely fas-
tened bags at last gave up a normal jeweller's ring-box, covered
with imitation leather, having a hinge and a snap fastener. Inside this, which, on emerging from the final bag had been tightly
closed, was found the lady's ring.

Everyone present was gratified at having witnessed a superb,
most skilfully performed conjuring trick, but the company consisted in adult, well-educated Europeans. Had a student from (say)
Melanesia been of the party he, notwithstanding an equally high
educational standard would, while applauding, conventionally,
the conjuring trick, have mutely entertained a profound, awe-
inspired respect for the performer's magicianship.

Dr W. H. R. Rivers says in his work *Medicine, Magic &
Religion* *:

'The concept of magic which at present holds good in sociology
and ethnology is largely influenced by the art called by this name
in our own Middle Ages. The best known form of mediaeval magic
was one in which non-human, spiritual agents took a most important part. These beings acted as the immediate producers of
disease and other effects, the magical character of the proceedings
resting on the belief that the non-human agents had come, in
one way or another, under the power of the human magician.

* Kegan, Paul, Trench, Trubner & Co. Ltd., 1924.

'The magic of many people of rude culture, including those of the area with which I especially deal* differs widely from this in that disease or injury is, in many cases, ascribed to purely human agency, even when to us the real cause of the condition would seem to be obvious. This mode of causation is not merely brought into play to explain cases of illness which have no obvious antecedent, but also those in which what we should call the natural cause is obvious.

'Thus, if a man is killed or injured by falling from a tree in the Island of Ambrim in the New Hebrides, the fall is not ascribed to a loose branch, or to some failure of co-ordination of the movements of the climber, but the accident, as we loosely call it, is put to the account of the sorcerer . . . .

'Similarly, death or injury in battle is not ascribed to the superior skill of the enemy, or to a failure of defence, but it is believed that a sorcerer has directed the missile of the assailant, or has interfered with the defensive motions of the victim . . . .

'A case of snake-bite is not ascribed to the act which, according to our ideas, is natural to a venomous animal, but it is believed that the snake has been put in the path of the victim by a sorcerer, or has been endowed with special powers by a sorcerer; or it may even be held that the animal which has bitten the victim is no ordinary snake, but the sorcerer himself in snake-like form.'

Sorcery and witchcraft are not one and the same thing. Witches were sorcerers but sorcerers were not necessarily witches. Sorcery is age-old and universal, witchcraft does not antedate 1350 and many authorities would declare this to be a century too soon.

Sorcery is the ability believed to be possessed by qualified persons to control nature for good or ill either with or without the aid of superhuman entities: to cure, by the use of charms, minor ailments: to influence by potions, the object of a person's love: to foretell the future, and to induce good fortune.

Witchcraft is the similar magical practice inverted to secure a disastrous end, by persons who are believed to have entered into a contract (generally signed with their own blood) with the devil whom they elevate to omnipotence, worship, and revere before the Trinity.

Thus, witchcraft is a heresy. A deliberate rejection of God

* Melanesia.

and the Church; a rejection of good and a dedication to evil. Witchcraft was a crime of conscience, a declaration of enmity towards God. Witches were condemned by the tribunals for sin rather than for crime.

Before the Church had formalized demonological definition of witchcraft every village possessed its sorcerer or Sibyl, to whom the population applied for aid at need, and no doubt derived much benefit from charms supplied to destroy warts, and vegetable simples designed to cure coughs. The qualified physicians, down to mid-nineteenth century, could do very little more.

It was not until the fourteenth century that the ecclesiastical authorities began to take notice of sorcery. In 1310 the Council of Treves forbade the practice of divination and healing, and the concoction of love-potions. Punishment for breach was, at worst, excommunication. Witchcraft was not yet established.

The Church was compelled to proceed with caution, for the possession of magical powers was not contrary to its teaching: most of, if not all, the saints had worked miracles, hence, the heretical aspect of witchcraft received special attention.

The earliest trials in which the heretical nature of witchcraft was emphasized were conducted at Carcassonne in Southern France, and from there spread to Toulouse between the years 1330 to 1335. By 1350 about a thousand persons had been indicted for witchcraft of whom six hundred were burned. This was but a beginning.

Sorcery was no longer an innocent occupation: its practitioners were no longer respectable, and their activities, being part of the devil's dominion, could not be *pro bono publico*. In this reorientation the Christian world became sociologically* inferior to the pagan world.

In primitive society the shaman, or witch-doctor, is not merely a tolerated magician who may be consulted or employed for good or ill by any member of the community who has the means of paying the fee, but he is a superior, essential, respected official without whose mediation between man and the spirits both private and public disaster would be encountered at every crisis.

Shamanism is the term applied to any social system in any part of the world, where either an official magician, or one in private practice, has a far-reaching influence over the lives of the people.

*The emphasis is on 'sociologically'; no reference is here made to religion.

The term is derived from the religious belief and practice of the ethnic groups inhabiting Northern Siberia and Asia. According to their ideas all the forces of nature, and every aspect of life is under the control of a spirit, and the decisions of these powers may be influenced by the arcane activities of the shaman who uses the rhythms of his magic drum and his mystical chants to bring the appropriate spirit under control and force it to do his bidding. The shaman is the priest and is the guardian of the people.

In other cultural areas the shaman is less of the priest and more of the doctor—W. H. R. Rivers's title, *Medicine, Magic and Religion*, is most apt, for this trilogy is indivisible, nor can the investigator be sure where one ceases and the other begins.

Government officials, such as district officers in areas under European supervision, condemn the shaman or witch-doctor as a conscious charlatan and trickster, battering on the credulity of the unsophisticated tribesmen whom he bleeds white. The tribesmen, however, hold an altogether different opinion, and in the most Europeanized 'native' states, the detribalized tribesmen, not only wearing trousers and toppers, but possessing motor-vehicles and television sets, sometimes even having been educated in a European University, call, in secret, upon the shaman at every turn of the wheel of time: birth, marriage and death, seed-time and harvest. The lambing and the calving seasons cannot be left to the vagaries of the controlling spirits, or to the evil spells paid for by one's enemy in an adjacent village. The shaman must persuade or bully the spirits of the universe, must force them to send the rain at the right time, must out-manoeuvre the enemy by counter-magic.

Whether the shaman is a prosaic villain and cheat, performing his antics with his tongue in his cheek; or whether he is sincere, a believer in his own powers, a master of hypnosis with such occult attributes as clairvoyance, clairaudience, and, perhaps, mediumistic sensitivity, the fact remains that his power and influence is greater than the government's. He can cure where European medicine has failed, he can kill from afar off by casting a death-dealing spell. As soon as the victim is made aware of his having been condemned to death by enchantment he will sink down and die—European medicine, injections, psycho-therapy will not save him.

Belief in, fear of, spirits is ineradicable. Funerary rites at all stages of culture—including our own—are primarily connected with fear of the ghost of the departed. If the whole of mankind (including those who do not believe in ghosts) fear the released human spirit, how much more greatly do they dread spirits not of human origin and form, spirits whom they conceive as demons from a darker sphere where the devil rules supreme!

One cannot reconcile good and evil, God and the Devil, white and black; each is an antithesis of the other, but in the Middle Ages when the ordinary man was expected to accept the miracles performed by saints and the sorceries of the witches, he could not always distinguish a sharp line of demarcation, and while he was overtly a communicant Christian, he did not hesitate, at need, to have recourse to the reputed magician of the locality.

In Europe there is no record of attempts to bind into a logical system both demonology and Christianity, but that is precisely what has been achieved in Haiti, the home of Voodoo, or, more correctly, Vodun. To the man in the street, 'voodoo' is the name of an originally African system of incantation, magical rites, and psychological terrorism by which the Negroid population of the island is kept in a state of subjection bordering on slavery: an attempt to emancipate oneself from the dominance of the magicians is punished by them. The rebellious man becomes, by their conjurations, a zombie, a creature neither living nor dead, without soul, without will, and without emotions, a kind of mystically controlled robot.

This idea of the nature of Vodun is, in common with most other popular understandings of esoteric matters, very far from the truth. The word, which comes from West Africa means 'God'.

The Republic of Haiti celebrated, in 1954, the one hundred and fiftieth anniversary of its independence. The Negro population was introduced into the island as long ago again, and notwithstanding their basic African theological conception, they have, for the whole of that time, been subject to Catholic religious discipline. The Haitian spiritual belief is that God the Father created the universe, in the ruling and organization of which He is assisted by His Son, Jesus Christ and the Holy Ghost. A simple attitude with which no Christian, irrespective of sect, would wholly disagree, although the conception is materialistic in its form, rather suggestive of a shopkeeper whose family constitutes the staff.

The Haitian, however, does not end his creed with the simple Trinitarian belief he adds to his pantheon the *loa*, or gods who accompanied his ancestors from Africa; beneficent spirits willing to help in the conduct of the universe by attaching themselves to men who, by their aid are rendered better people: healthier, happier, more industrious.

When a young person becomes 'possessed' of a *loa* his behaviour may be crude, even violent, reminiscent of poltergeist phenomena. To restrain this pagan spirit he must receive baptism. The possessed youth is confined in a room for three days during which the family and friends gathered outside sing and pray using Catholic prayers. On the third day lamps are kindled, a banquet of chicken and rice is prepared, and the Vodun priest, often a blood-relation of the initiate, enters the room and performs the act of baptism in the normal way: by pouring out libations of water over the possessed youth's head. This done, the initiate becomes a 'horse' and is 'mounted' by the *loa* by whom he will be guided through life, but familiarity with this pagan spirit does not make the Haitian any less a Christian. H. J. Herskovits, in a book entitled *Life in a Haitian Valley**, says 'Vodun is neither the practice of black magic, nor the unorganized pathological hysteria it is so often represented to be. The gods are known to their worshippers, and the duties owed them are equally well understood. The reward for the performance of these duties is good health, good harvests, and the good-will of fellow-men; the punishment for neglect is corresponding ill fortune. On this basis of belief is erected the ceremonial of worship.'

Vodun is not part of the cultus of the left hand it does not curse and it does not kill. In the system paganism and Christianity form an alliance for the good of the devotees: the Vodun priest is not a shaman. However, there is in Haiti, in addition to the religion of Vodun, a general belief in witchcraft which is, as in other parts of the world, evil, and can be employed to kill by the casting of spells.

A spell is a strong, compelling influence which one person may exert over another in a number of different ways: it may be done by the repetition of an incantation, that is, a set of words, not necessarily having any meaning, that are believed to be fraught with magical power: or by the repeated appearance of a

* Alfred A. Knopf, New York, 1937.

sign, or a symbol at sight of which the victim goes into a second state, loses individuality, and becomes the pawn of the person casting the spell.

In modern parlance to become the subject of hypnosis is to become spell-bound, and because all human beings are both affectible and suggestible, all are subject, more or less, to hypnotic influence. The power of the hypnotist over his victim was revealed in Copenhagen in 1951 when a young man entered a bank and at pistol-point ordered the cashier to hand him all the money from the till. When the command was not instantly obeyed the bank employee was callously shot through the heart, and the manager, who had come upon the scene, was ordered· by the bandit to fill his bag. The manager did not obey the order and he, too, was shot dead. More of the bank's employees might have suffered a like fate had not one of them succeeded in actuating the alarm bells, whereupon the bandit made his escape empty-handed, but a boy of only fourteen years of age followed him in his flight and was able to inform the police of his whereabouts.

The assassin, Pelle Hardrup, upon arrest, showed no fear or emotion, but immediately confessed. In the course of enquiry his close friendship with an older man, Björn Nielsen, was revealed. The latter was a known criminal who had served sentences for offences of numerous kinds from grand larceny to sexual attacks upon young girls.

Hardrup, having been a quisling, had served a sentence in prison where he had met Nielsen. A third party, whose name was not revealed, who had been in prison at the same time, came forward with information: 'The real murderer is Björn Nielsen. I know. The three of us, Björn, Pelle and I were in the same cell. Pelle lives under an hypnotic spell. He is in the complete power of Nielsen. It goes back to old Nazi politics. Nielsen convinced Pelle that he, someday, would be dictator over Scandinavia, leader of the Nordic–Teutonic race and greater by far than Hitler. Nielsen possessed powers of hypnotism and post-hypnotic suggestion. Pelle was an easy subject. During our days in prison he was a walking doll, in a religious-political trance ... whenever Pelle saw the mark X he went into an hypnotic trance and obeyed Nielsen's commands to the last detail ... his eyes became hazy, and he became a slave ...'

It was subsequently proved that the informant was indeed

speaking nothing but the truth: Nielsen was sentenced to life imprisonment, Pelle Hardrup, held to be not responsible for his actions, received treatment in a clinic.* Had Nielsen foreseen this climax he would doubtless have implanted the suggestion that in the event of failure Hardrup turned the gun upon himself.

The foregoing is an extreme case: it is, however, very common for a youth to come under the influence of an older man. Such relationships are usually brought about by some common interest to which the youth aspires and at which the older man excels. There is nothing morbid in the attachment which is, as a rule, of comparatively short duration, but during its course, whether the senior partner is aware of the fact or not, the obsessed youth is not his own master.

On some occasions, however, the older man is himself psychopathic, and will deliberately influence the youth towards evil, expounding some egocentric doctrine and inducing in his victim a morbid philosophy of life. Homosexual practices, being on an entirely physical plane, are the least damaging of effects in such relationships: the most destructive is the maiming of the spirit. The victim of such indoctrination becomes possessed, and remains so for life.

Hypnotism and hysteria are closely allied and examination of the 'evidence' that was taken in the witchcraft trials reveals both of these diabolical forces at work. We have to accept hysteria as a psychogenic disease commanding compassionate treatment, and hypnotism as a force employed by the psychotherapist to a benign and laudable end, but it is an essentially modern concept no older than the twentieth century itself.

The witchcraft epidemic was a cultural hysteria affecting, in greater or lesser degree according to locality, the whole of Christian civilization, and that hypnotism was an active factor in the complex cannot be doubted, for it is not necessary to understand, or even to entertain a theory concerning a force for the force to exist: electricity and atomic energy are both contemporaneous with Creation.

The understanding and control of hypnotism was brought into Europe from India. Dr Rivers says†

* Murder by Hypnosis, by a Police Psychiatrist, as told to Kurt Singer. *Tomorrow*, Vol. 7, No. 4, 1959.

† op. cit.

'. . . the new agent was regarded as a form of magnetism or other physical force. It was only slowly that there came into being the now generally accepted view that the agency through which hypnotism produces its effects is suggestion.'

Hypnotism as a curative factor was employed with the utmost caution, not because its exponents lacked confidence in their theory, but because there was a danger of a doctor being condemned as a charlatan. Mesmer, in the late eighteenth century, had stigmatized 'magnetic' treatment. Again quoting Dr Rivers,*

'Independently, growing out of dissatisfaction with the practical use of hypnotism, a third line of approach was taken by the Viennese physician, Sigmund Freud. It had been found by earlier workers that hypnotism was often the means of reaching experience which had been so completely forgotten that by no effort of the will could it be recalled. . . . Freud found the process of bringing these buried memories to the surface led to the disappearance of hysterical symptoms of long duration and [there was] founded on this experience a theory of hysteria according to which its symptoms are the indirect expression of old mental injuries (traumata), especially those of early childhood.'

Freud later abandoned hypnotism and introduced the analytical method of free association, having postulated the theory of the 'Unconscious'. It is out of this sealed crypt of the mind that there emerge many horrors of hysteria and other forms of mental derangement.

Dr Eliot Slater says, in an *Introduction* to a Report on 'The International Congress on Mental Health' (August, 1949),† 'Even the critics of psychoanalysis will admit that a "revolution" in psychology was begun by the publication of Freud's early papers at the end of the last century. . . . It was above all Freud's discovery that the springs of human action lie deeply buried in functional levels of nervous activity of which the individual himself is unconscious, and the discovery of a method of penetrating to those levels, that have transformed both medical and lay views on the interpretation of human behaviour. Freud began his career as a neurologist, and his neurological experience may have helped to determine the materialism of his approach. But his great work was begun with the treatment of the neuroses; and we can say

* op. cit.
† Printed in *The British Medical Bulletin*, Vol. 6, No. 1.

the movement that stems from him found its beginnings within the confines of clinical psychiatry. . . . It would seem that psycho-analysis finds its most practical fields within the realm of the normal (for it is generally agreed that the neuroses are, to a large extent, merely extreme forms of normal modes of reaction).'

It is important to observe the normality of abnormal behaviour, and to realize that it was in an hysterically deranged period of cultural history that the witch persecutions flourished.

Chapter Two

THE late, learned Montague Summers saw nothing to choose between white and black magic, between sorcery and witchcraft. In his work, *Witchcraft and Black Magic** he says: '... it is mere waste of time and hair-splitting to attempt to draw minute and cavilling distinctions, to chop up words and quibble and sub-divide, to argue that technically and etymologically a sorcerer differs from a witch, a witch from a necromancer, a necromancer from a Satanist. In actual fact and practice all these names are correlative; in use, synonymous. Thus although originally and in its first implication a sorcerer strictly means one who casts lots, and is derived from the late Latin *sortiarius*, *sors* being a lot or chance, our standard authority, *The Oxford English Dictionary* has: "Sorcerer, one who practises sorcery; a wizard, magician", whilst sorcery is, "the use of magic or enchantments; the practice of magic arts; witchcraft".

'Necromancer comes through the Greek, and means one who can reveal future events or disclose secrets by communication with the dead. There has in this word been some confusion of the Greek prefix *Nekros*, a corpse, with the Latin *niger* (*nigr*), black; and in Middle English, that is to say roughly from 1200 to 1500, we have the form "nigromancer", one skilled in the black arts. (*Mancer*, is the Greek *Manteis*, foretelling, divination.)

'Satanist, as is plain, means a devotee of Satan. It is significant, however, and worth remembering that when first employed the word Satanist was equivalent to an atheist, and it is used in this sense by John Aylmer, who was Bishop of London under Queen Elizabeth ...

'To sum up sorcerer, witch, necromancer are essentially all one ... Incidentally, it may be noted that the word "witch", although now popularly, and almost exclusively, intended to

*Rider, 1946.

denote a woman, can be used of a man. . . . Actually "witch" is from the Old English masculine noun substantive *wicea*, "a man who practises witchcraft or magic; a magician, sorcerer, wizard".'

The opposite point of view is maintained by Russell Hope Robbins who, in *The Encyclopaedia of Witchcraft and Demonology** at the entry 'Sorcery' says: 'Sorcery must be differentiated from witchcraft. . . . Sorcery is an attempt to control nature, to produce good or evil results, generally by the aid of evil spirits. On the other hand, witchcraft embraces sorcery, but goes far beyond it, for the witch contracts with the devil to work magic for the purpose of denying, repudiating and scorning the Christian God. The crimes both sorcerer and witch are supposed to commit—that is, the whole range of *maleficia*—appear to be alike, but the motives are distinct. This is the basis on which the Inquisition built up the theory of witchcraft as a heresy—a conscious rejection of God and the Church.'

Paulus Grillandus, Doctor of Laws, and Papal judge in witch trials held in the diocese of Arezzo, Tuscany, who flourished in the early sixteenth century and wrote *Tractatus de Hereticis et Sortilegiis* (Treatise on Heretics and Witches), said, in about 1525, that the civil law did not punish sorcery when it was beneficial, and he gave examples of such benefit including the curing of disease.

Following Grillandus, Francesco Maria Guazzo, an early seventeenth century monk, author of the *Compendium Maleficarum* (Handbook of Witchcraft) which was published in 1608, draws a distinction between natural magic which he holds to be a gift from God, and artificial magic in which results are obtained only by aid of the devil.

Nevertheless the Church disapproved of white magic which was punished by excommunication, and gradually the Church's attitude was adopted by the secular authorities: a healing witch was held to be one who affected cures only by invoking the devil, hence, to be condemned to death no less than the malefic witch by whose spells the illness had perhaps been caused.

Divination, which ultimately came to be considered as a branch of witchcraft, had been condemned by the secular authorities, irrespective of the Church's attitude, not because it was a branch of magic, but because the practitioners were frequently frauds.

* Peter Nevill, 1959.

They claimed that by the exercise of their art they could unearth hidden treasure and so battened on the acquisitiveness and credulity of their patrons. Divination, having been normal procedure in classic paganism, fulfilled all the requirements of a Christian heresy and by the Church was considered to be a branch of witchcraft. Nevertheless, ever since dry agriculture was discovered* the dowser, or water-diviner, has been a useful and beneficial member of a rural community, and simple water-finders are conspicuous by their absence from the witch trials.

It is also noteworthy that healing witches who employed only sympathetic, or else homoeopathic magic, and who distributed only charms and amulets that were not in any way connected with Church ritual, seem to have been tolerated. The first amulet that mankind treasured for its mystical symbolism was the cowrie shell: our primitive ancestors saw in the shell's opening a likeness to the portal through which he had entered this world, hence the shell was venerated as a fecundity charm. Later it was built into a figurine and became representative of the Great Mother goddess.

Cowrie shells, known as 'lucky wedding shells' are still objects of superstition, and the otherwise highly sophisticated, and superstition-free Cockney mother will, if she is fortunate enough to possess such an heirloom, solemnly present it to her daughter on the girl's wedding day.

Another survival of the healing witch's sympathetic magic, not commonly met with in urban, but comparatively frequent in rural areas, is the young married woman's belief that to wear about her neck a 'hag-stone', that is, a flint naturally perforated, will ensure a safe and easy first parturition. Such inoffensive beliefs and remedies were not heretical. The Church's condemnation of the white witch, the declaration that she was in league with the devil and deserving of the same treatment that a convicted malefic witch would receive, arose from the employment of that which was sacred in order to procure a profane end.

The consecrated Host, stolen from churches, was made an ingredient in the concoction of love-philtres, and put to even more profane use. Grillandus says 'in these love-potions and aids to venery there is often set some commixture of the Sacraments of Holy Church, aye, even of the consecrated Host'. Nearly two

* The earliest system of agriculture was by irrigation.

hundred and fifty years after that declaration was penned a piece of the Host, it is on record, was used as a charm to secure victory for a fighting-cock that had been heavily backed.

Holy water was used by witches to baptize the effigies constructed to encompass a person's death by black magic, and early in the thirteenth century Richard, Bishop of Durham, ordered that all fonts in his diocese were to be kept covered and locked, 'the sacred lymph of baptism being constantly stolen to mix and mingle with poisonous potions brewed in midnight cauldrons.'

Faith in the healing quality of holy water, or of sacramental wine, is not in itself a bad trait in the Christian character, nor can it be deemed heretical. There are cases on record of the priest having himself administered these sacramentals for the purpose of healing. Their use as semi-magical pharmacopoeia becomes profane however when they are accepted by the patient or, in the case of a child with whooping cough, the patient's parents, as articles of thaumaturgical potency without reference to their sacred character.

Such sacrilege, rightly resented by the ecclesiastical authorities was not, however, the major offence against religion that was the motive force of the witch trials. The great heresy was the pact, or contract, with the devil which the witches were found guilty of signing. They were traitors to God: deserters from the hosts of heaven: and the Church, the organization of loyal soldiers of Christ in its war against the evil one, executed these renegades in order to thin the ranks of the enemy.

In addition to, in support of and perhaps originally under the compulsion of the Inquisition, the secular authorities avidly persecuted witches. The major interest of the State was not that of allying itself with the Church in the suppression of heresy, but was purely financial: the witch hunt was big business of a very paying nature.

Folklore and the fairy tale have conditioned the modern mind to conceive of a witch as a dirty, decrepit, penniless hag, alone, unwanted, feared by her neighbours and subsisting as best she might in a dilapidated hovel which the cat, the only creature that loved her, made into home. Being friendless she was unfriendly: being undernourished she was irritable. When children at play disturbed with their raucous, concussive penetrating voices her afternoon nap she went to the door a-scolding, called them varmints and imps of hell and expressed the hope that the devil would take them.

If in due course one or more of the children fell ill and perhaps died, then, *post hoc ergo propter hoc,** the sickness or death was the fulfilment of the witch's curse. She was seized by the outraged villagers, and thrown into the horse-pond where, if she, being innocent, did not sink and drown, she was obviously kept afloat by her friend and master the devil and must hang.

Such wretched creatures were certainly to be found in many villages throughout Europe, but not all of the accused who were brought to trial, perhaps not even a majority of them, were grizzled old hags: many were young and beautiful, most were members of peasant families with a steady income and some savings behind them, a surprisingly large percentage were of noble status having both estate and wealth.

The witch, even if acquitted (and that was very rare on the Continent), paid the expenses of her trial, and was not released from prison before the account was fully settled. If (as was almost invariably the case) she was condemned, then all her possessions were escheated to the governing body, generally the civil authorities, but sometimes the ecclesiastical authorities had a share in the spoils. Even the penniless village hag when brought before the justices could prove profitable, the village elders, or else the landlord upon whose estate she dwelt being held responsible.

The big business of the witch hunt provided remunerative employment for many. In addition to the judges, court officials, scribes and messengers, there were the executioner and the torturer—sometimes, but not always, one and the same person—assistants and guards; wood-cutters who, on the Continent, produced the brush-wood and logs for the pyre, the carters who conveyed this fuel to the scene of the burning, the carpenters who erected the scaffold, and other active participants, none underpaid.

As well as those employed in the business, others, such as taverners and innkeepers, had a busy and profitable day when executions took place, their profits accruing not only from the thirst of the crowds who came for the day's entertainment, but

* After that, therefore because of that.

from the banquet enjoyed by the senior officials concerned in the trial, for which repast the victim also paid.

R. H. Robbins, under 'Cost of Witch Trials'* prints some interesting accounts. At Aberdeen, in February 1596 Janet Wishart and Isabel Crocker were executed. The bill is as follows:

Item:

for 20 loads of peat to burn them . . .	40.	0.
for a boll [six bushels] of coal. . . .	24.	0.
for 4 tar barrels	26.	8.
for fir and iron barrels	16.	8.
for a stake and dressing of it	16.	0.
for four fathoms of tows [hangman's rope] .	4.	0.
for carrying the peat, coals, and barrels to the hill	8.	4.
To one justice for their execution . . .	13.	4.

a total of £7. 9. 0. which was at that period a very considerable sum of money.

The even more spectacular account for the slaughter of Margaret Dunhome at Burncastle in 1649 is given in pounds Scots, equivalent to about three shillings and fourpence in the currency of England:

Mone [money due] for Margaret Dunhome, the time she was in prison and was put to death:	£65. 14. 0.
Count given out by Alexander Londdon in Lylestown, in the year of God 1649 years, for Margaret Dunholme in Burncastell:	
Item: in the first [place] to William Currie and Alexander Gray for the watching of her the space of 30 days, each day, 30 shillings	£45. 0. 0.
Item: more to John Kincaid for brodding [pricking] of her	£6. 0. 0.
More for meat and drink and wine to him and his man	£4. 0. 0.
More for cloth to her	£3. 0. 0.
More for two tarred trees [stacks] . .	40. 0.
Item: more for two trees and the making of them, to the workmen	£3. 0. 0.

* op. cit.

Item: to the hangman in Haddington, and fetching of him, three dollars for his expense is	£4. 14.	0.
Item: more for meat and drink and wine for his entertainment	£3. 0.	0.
Item: more for a man and two horses, for the fetching of him, and taking of him home again	40.	0.
More to her for meat and drink, each day, 4 shillings the space of 30 days is . .	£6. 0.	0.
Item: more to the two officers for their fee, each day 6 shillings eight pence is . .	£10. 0.	0.

Summ is 4 score 12 pounds 14 shillings

Ghilbert Lander
(formerly Lauder Bilzaurs)

Taken of this above written sum, 27 pounds Scots, which the said former Margaret Dunholme had of her own:

£92. 14. 0.
27. 0. 0.
———————
65. 14. 0.

It is interesting to observe a slight error in addition—on the right side—the correct total is £88. 14. 0.

These two powerful organizations, Church and State, each had a separate interest in keeping witch-trials in a flourishing condition, but there was yet a third interest that bolstered up the horror. The Church does not, and the State dare not continue to pursue a policy that is unpopular, hence, the general mass of the population desired the continuance of this disgrace to humanity and negation of the Christian doctrine of mercy and love, and of the injunctions to turn the other cheek, and to love one's neighbour as oneself.

Apart from the excitement, and entertainment value of witch hunting, the average man condoned it because of his littleness, his selfishness and greed and his deep, abject cowardice. Both Church and State laid emphasis on the *maleficium* of the witch, her drying-up of cows, her blighting of crops, her distribution of disease and death among her neighbours in order to serve faithfully her master the devil, the object of her worship.

The average man, in order to protect both his pocket and his person gleefully subscribed to the horrible torture and dreadful death of multitudes of helpless, hopeless, innocent women and children.

It is customary to refer to 'witch-trials', and complacently to assume that irrefutable evidence was taken and justice done according to the lights of the period. Nevertheless, records reveal that witches were generally not tried but subjected to an inquisition. In a trial the accused is assumed innocent until proven guilty, is permitted to employ a lawyer to speak in his defence, hears the statements made by witnesses whose veracity and reliability have been investigated by the court, and is acquitted or condemned on the conclusions reached resulting from evidence which, although sometimes circumstantial, is never obviously untrue. In an inquisition the accused is assumed guilty until he has proved his innocence and this he is not permitted to do. He may not, except by special permission which was rarely given, be represented by a lawyer, is unable to protest when traduced by secret witnesses who may be criminals or lunatics and is condemned on presumptive evidence. We have a survival of the system in the inquisitorial powers vested in a British inspector of income tax who has the authority to, and sometimes (apparently solely to impress with his diligence and efficiency a senior officer) does, demand the payment of an extortionate sum which the stricken 'assessed' victim is at liberty to attempt to show is not due from him. A further similarity is in the fact that the victim is paying the salary of his persecutor.

While the virus of anti-witch proceedings was flowing in the bloodstream of Western culture life was darkened by the incessant danger, shared by man, woman and child at every social level, of sudden arrest on a charge of practising witchcraft arising out of information laid by a spiteful, envious, malicious person, himself clearly, if by that act alone, a devotee of Satan, for every informer was well aware that to be charged as a witch was almost certainly to die as a witch. There was no escape, all endeavours to establish innocence were interpreted as confirmation of guilt. The only hope was in the suspension of the proceedings.

Informers were enabled to remain not only anonymous, but

unknown to the prosecuting authority. Reginald Scott, author of *The Discovery of Witchcraft*, the first book written in the English language on the subject, and one in which the current belief in sorcery was ridiculed, and magical ability to shape events was stoutly denied, reveals the iniquity of one of the approved methods of gaining accusations: '. . . a chest is placed in the church into which anyone may freely cast a little scroll of paper, wherein may be contained the name of the witch, the time, place and fact . . . [the chest] is opened every fifteenth day by three inquisitors or officers appointed for that purpose . . . and thus the accuser need not be known.'

Upon receipt of such a sneaking, shamefaced denunciation the local court prepared an indictment; a document couched in Latin, briefly stating the nature of the crime of which the prisoner was accused: '. . . by the damnable arts of witchcraft and sorcery did cast a blight upon the crops of farmer John Brown, and did cause the said farmer's eldest son, William, to fall into lingering sickness whereof in the space of five weeks the said William died . . .'

At that period a criminal trial could not begin until the prisoner pleaded either 'guilty' or 'not guilty', but stubborn silence was no saviour. Pressure was literally brought to bear: the mute defiant was placed prone beneath a board on which pigs of lead (or of iron) were piled, the pressure being increased by the addition to the load of one weight after another till with breaking ribs and displaced organs the prisoner yielded, or was pressed to death. Those indicted on a charge of witchcraft would have been wise to have chosen death by pressure at the commencement of the proceedings.

During the course of the hearing, lack-logic, internally contradictory assertions made by irresponsible people were accepted as veridical evidence. For example, as late as 1663, a man's assertion that when out hunting for rabbits he had followed one round a bush but found on the other side not a rabbit but Mrs Julian Cox, was, without criticism, assumed to be sufficient proof of shape-changing on the part of Mrs Cox, the prisoner.

An outstanding and frequently quoted case in which a number of hysterical juvenile delinquents brought innocent people to their death is that of the Throckmorton children of Warboys, Huntingdonshire, in 1592.

Jane, aged ten, was the first of the household to develop hysterical fits and since the family was of superior social status two doctors, Barrow and Butler, both of Cambridge University, were in attendance.

During one of Jane's fits a neighbour, Mrs Alice Samuels, poor but respectable, called to pay her respects and was accused of witchcraft by Jane. No notice was taken at the time, but hysteria is infectious. Jane's four sisters and seven female servants developed symptoms similar to Jane's and the worried parents began to weaken. Further, Dr Barrow, realizing the futility of such treatment as he was administering, and probably in order to protect his reputation, said he had had previous experience of the malice of witches, and he thought that sorcery was the cause of the children's malady.

Mrs Samuels, who was seventy-six years of age, was sent for and the hysterics behaved exactly as modern science would expect them to behave: they were at once 'strangely tormented', which demonstration Mrs Samuels in the wisdom of years attributed to their 'wantonness', but the children (the eldest was fifteen) continued to accuse her, and the distraught parents urged her to confess.

Mrs Samuels must have been a very kind, sympathetic and cooperative person, for when the hysterics changed their tactics, and threw fits in her absence but not in her presence, she went to live with the Throckmortons, where the little fiends made her life a misery by pretending to see her imp in attendance, and expressing surprise at Mrs Samuels's being unable to see it.

While Mrs Samuels was in residence at the Throckmortons', Lady Cromwell called. She immediately denounced the poor old woman as a witch, seized her by the hair, cut off a lock and advised Mistress Throckmorton to burn it.

Stirred by this indignity Mrs Samuels made a fatal retort: 'Madam, why do you use me thus? I never did you any harm *as yet!*'* After this encounter Lady Cromwell began to be troubled by bad dreams in which a cat offered to scratch all the flesh from her body, as a result of which she went into a decline and about fifteen months after her fatal visit to the Throckmortons, she died.

Meanwhile the Throckmorton children continued their

* Our italic.

hysterical manifestations until old Mrs Samuels, urged by the parents, called upon the children to stop, which they obligingly did, but the effect upon Mrs Samuels who, living so long under the continual strain must herself have been developing symptoms of hysteria, was disastrous: she believed that, after all, she was a witch, and, on the advice of Dr Dorrington, the local parson, she confessed.

The following day, rested and relieved from strain, she withdrew the confession, but on 26 Dec. 1592, before the Bishop of Lincoln, she not only repeated her confession but also revealed the names and nature of her familiars: three dun chickens, Pluck, Catch, and White. These creatures, she said, sucked at her chin, and it was they who carried the disorders to the children. Mrs Samuels declared the chickens were now gone from them, and all three reposed in her belly making her so full that she was like to burst.

Asked from whom she received the familiars she replied that she did not know but, 'put into another chamber', she cried in a loud voice three times, 'O thou divel, I charge thee in the name of the Father, the Son, and the Holy Ghost, that thou tell me the name of the upright man who gave me the divels', and she received the reply 'Langland'.

Meanwhile the Throckmorton children added John Samuels, the husband of the accused, and Agnes, her daughter, to their list of witches, all three being committed to Huntingdon Jail to await the assizes. Agnes, the daughter, for some obscure reason, was allowed bail, and was taken into the Throckmorton household as a kind of nurse to the children, who took full advantage of her presence by again throwing hysterical fits, bowing their bodies till their heads and feet met.

Arising out of old Alice Samuels's 'confession', the hysterics now had a new act added to their performance: they were able to hold conversations with the three dun chickens. Agnes Samuels was continually compelled to release the sufferers from their fits by reciting, 'I charge thee, thou divel, as I love thee, and have authority over thee, and am a witch, and guilty of this matter, that thou suffer this child to be well at this present.'

The Samuels were tried on charges of bewitching to death Lady Cromwell, and causing the Throckmorton children's fits. During the hearing, which lasted five hours, Robert Poulter, Vicar of

Brampton, testified that one of his parishioners, namely, John Langley, having called Mrs Samuels 'an old witch' had twice or thrice narrowly escaped death, had lost a good horse and other cattle to the value of twenty marks, and himself become very ill.

Robert Throckmorton had suffered the loss of many cattle and pigs. At length he made a hole in the ground wherein he burned one of the carcasses and Mother Samuels confessed to being the cause of their death. The jailer testified that his man, who had chained Mother Samuels, was seized with fits and died in five days and that further, his son had fallen sick until he brought the prisoner to the bedside, when the patient had scratched her and immediately recovered.

Sentence of death was passed on all three, but Mrs Samuels, now little short of eighty years of age, pleaded pregnancy 'which set all the company on a great laughing, and she herself more than any other'. Nevertheless, a jury of matrons had to be empowered to examine her. The daughter, Agnes, who also was advised to plead pregnancy, most courageously replied, 'Nay, that I will not do: it shall never be said that I was both a witch and a whore!'

After the execution of these three innocent people, the chief accusers, the Throckmorton children, ceased to experience their hysterical attacks.

In March, 1664, at Bury St Edmunds, Sir Matthew Hale, described as 'the most profound lawyer of his time' (1609–1676), who ultimately (in 1671) became Chief Justice of England, accepted hearsay evidence and the testimony of children who, when detected in falsification by the assistant judge, Serjeant Keeling, were protected by Hale who accepted the most transparent of excuses.

Rose Cullender and Amy Dury, both elderly widows of Lowestoft, were charged by Samuel Pacy with bewitching his children, of whom there were seven, ranging in age from an infant in arms to a young woman of eighteen. In addition, the prisoners were accused of acts of maleficia against Elizabeth and Ann Durant, Jane Bocking, Susan Chandler, and William Durant, to which they pleaded 'not guilty'.

Ann Durant, Susan Chandler and Elizabeth Pacy were brought to Bury St Edmunds to add their quota of accusation, but 'fell into strange and violent fits, screeking out in a most sad manner', after which demonstration they were struck dumb and did not regain their power of speech till after the trial.

One of the chief witnesses, Mrs Dorothy Durant, had hired Amy Dury as a nurse for her infant son William, and the nurse exceeded the terms of her contract by attempting to suckle the child. Mrs Durant was angry and reprimanded Amy Dury, who said 'that she had as good to have done otherwise than to have found fault with her'. That night the infant William seems to have developed the common infantile malady, convulsions, and when Dr Jacobs, of Yarmouth, was consulted (he having the reputation of specializing in the relief of bewitched children) his advice was to hang the child's blanket near the fire all day and at nightfall, examine it for livestock and burn any creature found. An unfortunate toad happened to be there and was held in the fire by the tongs till it made 'a great and horrible noise, and, after a space, there was a flashing in the fire like gun-powder, making a noise like the discharge of a pistol, and thereupon the toad was no more seen'. Dr Jacobs's reputation was, no doubt, considerably enhanced, for the child recovered, but Amy Dury was found with her face and legs burned and remarked to Mrs Durant 'she might thank her for it, but she would live to see some of her children dead and herself upon crutches.'

Following this, Mrs Durant's daughter, Elizabeth, aged ten years, was seized with fits, for which she blamed Amy Dury, who said 'your child will not live long', and two days later Elizabeth died; further, the witness herself, soon afterwards, became lame and was compelled to support herself on crutches in which she had continued for three years.

Edward Durant gave evidence against Rose Cullender. This prisoner had been refused some herrings by Durant's wife after which his daughter, Ann, was seized with an affliction in which she vomited pins, and beheld the apparition of the accused.

Diana Bocking testified on behalf of her daughter, Jane, who, taken with pains in the stomach had vomited pins. She also made snatches in the air and pins were then found in her clenched hands. On one occasion she had told an invisible person that she would not have it, but at length, consenting, a nail was found in her clenched hand. These articles were produced as exhibits in court.

Susan Chandler, eighteen years of age, daughter of one of the women who had examined Rose Cullender for physical signs of her contract with the devil, saw the apparition of the accused accompanied by a great dog, vomited pins, suffered attacks of blindness and dumbness and, being in court, was seized with fits and cried 'Burn her! Burn her!'

Samuel Pacy said his daughter, Deborah, aged nine years, suddenly became lame and so continued for seven days when Amy Dury came to buy herrings, but receiving none she went her way muttering, at which 'very instant of time' Deborah was seized by violent fits, shrieking in a most terrible manner, like unto a whelp. A local physician, Dr Feavor, was called but was unable to diagnose, hence the witness, suspecting Amy Dury of witchcraft, accused her of injuring his child and the accused was set in the stocks. While secured therein she was asked the reason for Deborah Pacy's sickness and she replied, 'Mr Pacy keeps a great stir about his child, but let him stay until he hath done as much by his children, as I have done by mine', in explanation of which she added that she had been forced to open her child's mouth 'with a tap to give it victuals'.

This piece of information was avidly seized upon by Mr Pacy's hysterical children (Elizabeth, aged eleven, though present in court 'could neither see nor speak') who, within forty-eight hours could breathe only with the help of a tap. It was observed that in addition to their attacks of blindness, dumbness, and vomiting of pins, they were unable to read the Bible, finding 'Lord', or 'Jesus', or 'Christ' unpronounceable, but doing very well at 'Satan' and 'Devil'.

Mr Pacy decided that a thorough change might have a beneficial effect and sent his two afflicted daughters to stay with their aunt, his sister, Mistress Arnold, at Yarmouth. She was a woman who evidently had some inkling of the capabilities of children: in giving evidence she said that fearing deceit she had removed all the pins from their clothes. She was, however, unaware of the legerdemain and prestidigitation of hysteria, for the children convincingly produced thirty pins from apparently nowhere.

It was at this juncture Mr Serjeant Keeling expressed the opinion that the evidence was too flimsy to secure a conviction '... admitting that the children were in truth bewitched, yet it could never be applied to the prisoners, upon the imagination only of the parties afflicted.'

Medical evidence was called to confirm the 'fact' of bewitchment. Dr, later Sir, Thomas Browne of Norwich reasoned 'that
in Denmark there had been lately a great discovery of witches,
who used the very same way of afflicting persons, by conveying
pins into them, and crooked, as these pins were, with needles and
nails. The Devil in such cases did work upon the bodies of men
and women, upon a natural foundation (that is) to stir up and
excite such humours super-abounding in their bodies to a great
excess, whereby he did in an extraordinary manner afflict them
with such distempers as their bodies were most subject to as particularly appeared in these children: for . . . these fits were
natural, and nothing else but that they call the mather,* but only
heightened to a great excess by the subtlety of the Devil, co-
operating with the malice of these which we term witches, at
whose instance he doth these villanies.'

The matter was then put to experimental tests. The children
in their fits, apparently unconscious of their surroundings, with
their fists so tightly clenched that a strong man could not open
them would, if touched by the accused, shriek and relax their
hands. When one of them was blindfolded and touched by
another person, it had precisely the same effect. Keeling, supported by Lord Cornwallis, Sir Edmund Bacon and other gentlemen conducting the tests, promptly protested that the children
were practising fraud, but Sir Matthew Hale accepted Mr Pacy's
somewhat lame explanation that if the girl was deceived in
thinking that the witch touched her the effect would be the
same.

The proceedings continued and other evidence of the prisoners'
maleficium was taken. John Soam of Lowestoft, yeoman, recounted how in harvest time he had three carts, which brought
home his harvest. As they were going into the field to load, one of
the carts wrenched the window of Rose Cullender's house, whereupon she came out in a great rage and uttered threats against
Soam. '. . . so they passed into the field and loaded all three carts.
The other two carts returned safe home and back again, twice
loaded that day afterwards. But as to this cart which had touched
Rose Cullender's house, after it was loaded it was overturned
twice or thrice that day. And after that they had loaded it again

* Hysterical conditions were, to some extent, recognized, and thought to
be a disorder of the uterus.

the second or third time, as they brought it through the gate which leadeth out of the field into the town, the cart stuck so fast in the gate's head that they could not possibly get it through, but were enforced to cut down the post of the gate to make the cart pass through, although they could not perceive that the cart did of either side touch the gateposts ...'

This cart, which must have been in a very rickety condition, was hauled home only with a most determined struggle: it could not be got as far as the barn, but had to be unloaded some distance from it and 'they found much difficulty therein, it being so hard a labour that they were tired that first came, and when others came to assist them, their noses burst forth a-bleeding, so they were fain to desist and leave it until the next morning.'

Poor Rose's house seemed to be a target for careless carters. Robert Sherringham told how when, two years earlier, his cart had 'touched' the house, the accused threatened that his horses would suffer. Within a short time all four horses died, and he further experienced loss of cattle and pigs. He was himself attacked by lameness and 'vexed with a great number of lice of extraordinary bigness, and he many times shifted himself.* Yet he was not anything the better but would swarm again with them, so that in the conclusion he was forced to burn all his clothes, being two suits of apparel, and then was clear of them.'

Richard Spencer had but little to say: simply that he had heard Amy Dury declare that the devil would not let her rest until she was revenged upon Cornelius Sandeswell's wife. This good lady was voluble and adequately compensated for Spencer's taciturnity. She recounted that when taking home some geese she met Amy Dury who said the birds would die, and in a few days they did. Further, Amy became a tenant of Cornelius Sandeswell and told her landlord's wife that if they did not 'look well to such a chimney ... the same would fall down.' Amy received a typical landlord's reply, the chimney was new; nevertheless, it fell. It is noteworthy that persons who made accusations against witches had never scrupled in employing them. Ann Sandeswell had asked Amy Dury to go with her and assist in carrying a firkin of fish being delivered by boat. Amy replied 'she would go when she had it', but when Mistress Sandeswell enquired of the boatman for the firkin he replied that 'it could not be kept in the

* Changed his clothes.

boat from falling into the sea, and they thought it was gone to
the devil, for they never saw the like before.'

Sir Matthew Hale, in giving direction to the jury refrained
from repeating the evidence 'lest by doing so he should wrong
the evidence on the one side or on the other . . . they had two
things to enquire after: first, whether or no these children
were bewitched? Secondly, whether the prisoners at the bar
were guilty of it.'

'That there were such creatures as witches he made no doubt at
all; for first, the Scriptures had affirmed so much. Secondly, the
wisdom of all Nations had provided laws against such persons,
which is an argument of their confidence of such a crime. And
such hath been the judgement of this Kingdom, as appears by
that act of Parliament which hath provided punishments pro-
portionable to the quality of the offence. And desireth them
strictly to observe their evidence; and desired the great God of
Heaven to direct their hearts in this weighty thing they had in
hand: for to condemn the innocent, and to let the guilty go free,
were both an abomination to the Lord.'* With such 'guidance'
any twelve just simpletons and true would have returned the
verdict demanded of them. Amy Dury and Rose Cullender were
hanged on Monday, 17 March, 1664.

Apart from the fact of two women going to their death mainly
because of the iniquity of hysterical children, and secondarily
because unsupported assertions and the coincidence of accidents
were admitted in evidence by so eminent a judge, this particular
case is of far-reaching importance—as far as Massachusetts is
from Suffolk—for it was the 'book of the words' on which, thirty
years later, the Salem witch persecutions were conducted.

There are a number of examples of deviated children who,
after having sent to their deaths numerous innocent people,
were themselves exposed. Thomas Darling was one of these.

On 27 February 1596 he had accompanied his uncle, Robert
Toone of Burton-on-Trent into Winsell Wood to hunt hares,
became separated, and found himself alone. A normal boy of
between thirteen and fourteen might, if lost in a wood, develop
after several hours a slight anxiety. There is nothing to suggest

* A *Tryal of Witches* at the Assizes held at Bury St Edmunds for the
County of Suffolk on the Tenth day of March, 1664, before Sir Matthew
Hale, Kt.

how long Thomas Darling was alone, but subsequent events reveal that he became the victim of abject, contemptible fear. On his return home he was suffering from vomiting, ague and hallucinations. 'Look where the green angels stand in the window!' he cried, and he also saw a green cat. A physician was called who, upon failure to rectify the boy's 'light-headedness', came to the conclusion, it subsequently transpired, that the patient was bewitched but at the time he mentioned this conviction to no one.

There was no improvement in Thomas Darling's condition; he fell into violent fits in which he 'roared greviously', bowed his body so that his belly was above his head and feet, and continually repeated prayers in which the adults in his environment joined fervently.

A shrewd neighbour named Jesse Bee, observing that the boy's praying and reading of Scripture seemed to produce the fits, and that he was free of them only when not so engaged, suspected that he was a victim of witchcraft and this opinion was conveyed to his aunt, Mistress Toone.

Thomas Darling, who was present when the suggestion was made, related that while he was lost in Winsell Wood he 'met a little old woman who had a gray gown with a black fringe about the cape, a broad, thrund hat, and upon her face three warts.' In her presence he 'let a scape' that was beyond his control, and this act angered the little old woman. That Thomas Darling did indeed 'let a scape' that was beyond his control is probably true, it being symptomatic of fear, but the presence of the little old woman is open to grave doubt: she was much too glib and sprightly in her retort,

> 'Gyp with a mischief,
> and fart with a bell,
> I will go to heaven
> and thou shalt go to hell.'

This seems very much like an example from a schoolboy's stock of rude rhymes, particularly as the statement contained in the last two lines is contrary to a witch's sentiments. Further, the youth's ability to remember it after but one hearing, and that under adverse conditions, suggests his possessing a superior intellectual ability, while all the other feathers on the wind drift in the opposite direction.

Such indicators were not observed by uncle and aunt Toone,

nor by any of their friends. They immediately cast about in their minds for someone who would fit the description. First choice was 'the witch of Stapenhill', but she was ultimately ruled out in favour of her daughter, Alice Gooderidge. On 8 April Mistress Walkeden, Darling's grandmother, accompanied by Mistress Saunders, another aunt, came on a visit to the Toones. Perhaps on the advice of the grandmother, or perhaps only on account of the strengthening of the family circle, Alice Gooderidge was sent for, and as soon as she entered the room Thomas Darling threw 'a marvellous sore fit'. Dame Gooderidge, sixty years of age, denied that she knew the boy, but he violently scratched her face, and the backs of her hands, 'until blood came out apace'.

Displaying the amazing kindness, gentleness, and submission that seems to accompany people accused and abused in this way, she merely said, 'take blood enough child, God help thee!' in reply to which the boy snarled. 'Pray for thyself, thy prayer can do me no good!'

She admitted being in the wood on the day when Thomas Darling was lost, but she declared she had encountered 'only Sherrat's boy'. On 10 April Robert Toone and Jesse Bee jointly laid a complaint with Thomas Graysley J.P., who instructed the local constable to take into custody both Alice Gooderidge and her mother, Elizabeth Wright, 'the witch of Stapenhill' who had been before him several times on suspicion. Thomas Graysley met Sir Humphrey Ferrers at the Toones' house on 14 April and the prisoners, together with Alice Gooderidge's husband and daughter, were brought before them. The only matter of importance arising from this hearing was that the accused were ordered to be searched for witch's marks. There was found upon Elizabeth Wright 'behind her right shoulder a thing much like the udder of a ewe that giveth suck with two teats, like unto two great warts, the one behind under her armhole, the other a handfull off, towards the top of her shoulder.' She declared that she had been born with this growth. Those who searched Alice Gooderidge reported having 'found upon her belly a hole of the bigness of two pence, fresh and bloody, as though some great wart had been cut off the place.' Dame Gooderidge accounted for it by explaining that she had recently slipped from a ladder and cut herself, but as her clothes were undamaged, and a surgeon reported that the wound 'was like to have been so a long time, for it was not festered, and seemed to be sucken', it was accepted as her witch mark.

To add to her troubles a neighbour came forward and accused her of having bewitched his cow. The animal had broken loose and gone to her house, but Elizabeth Wright had cured the cow on being given a penny for her God. She had effected the cure by kneeling in front of the cow and 'crossing her with a stick in the forehead'.

Alice's husband (Oliver) and her daughter were examined and the cases against them both were dismissed, nevertheless, strangely enough, the latter was held in Derby gaol.

Meanwhile Thomas Darling was keeping his performance of fits alive. The great green cat tormented him by tossing him up and down in a string, and when Elizabeth Wright was brought to him he fell into most violent seizures which continued until she was removed.

Interest in the strange affair began to spread. Mistress Dethicke of New Hall came to behold the spectacle, and two men who were neighbours of Alice Gooderidge, attempting to help her (much to their credit) informed Robert Toone that if he 'would be good to her, she would reveal the whole truth'.

A white witch comes into the story. Widow Worthington of Hoppers, who enjoyed the reputation of successful healing, offered her aid, but Mistress Darling would not agree to such unlawful practice.

Widow Worthington was not the only person offering aid. On 30 April, at the request of a man who claimed to be able to solve the problem, Alice was removed from jail and brought into the boy's presence. She said, kindly, 'God help thee, my child', which he accepted as the signal to put over a very special performance: he threw twenty-seven fits in six hours, 'his neck so wrythen that his face seemed to stand backward'.

The following day (1 May) there was a goodly gathering at the Toones', all come to see the self-recommended man's method of solving the problem and effecting a cure. The method adopted was simplicity itself. Alice was made to don a new pair of shoes and was then set close to the fire so that the shoes became extremely hot.

Alice was not a young woman, and elderly folk generally have some foot troubles, corns and callouses being the least of them.

The unofficial torture was severe enough to induce her to affirm to confess. For this purpose she was taken into another room under the care of Mistress Dethicke, but was unable to speak; 'her wind being stopped'. To assist matters, Thomas Darling was brought in; to him she said, 'Thomas, I pray you forgive me and be good to me', whereupon he fell 'into a marvelous sore fit'. After this Alice would say no more than that she was sorry if she had mistaken him for Sherrat's boy, against whom she had a grievance, he having broken her eggs.

The following day, urged by a number of the 'gentry' who were present she declared, 'I met a boy in the Wood the first Saturday in Lent and passing by me, he called me witch of Stapenhill, unto whom I said, Every boy doth call me witch, but did I ever make thy arse to itch?'

This statement was made much of and the following day she was induced to repeat it, and to add, 'forthwith I stooped to the ground, and the devil appeared to me in the likeness of a little partie coloured dog, red and white, and I called him Minny: seeing that every boy calleth me witch, therefore go thy ways and torment this boy in every part of his body at thine own pleasure, forthwith I strained every part of my own body, enforcing myself to vomit, saying, after this sort vex every part of him. The dog followed the boy to Burton, and as I returned from Winsell (whither I went to buy a groat's worth of eggs) he met me again, telling me he had fulfilled my request, and at my yard's end he departed from me; since when he hath been divers times with me at Darbie gaol, and these two nights at Burton Hall, and continually he scratcheth my head, and scrapeth in the straw. The boy will not mend except you seek for help, you may have help enough.' The poor woman evidently became hoarse: the report explains she would have spoken further but 'something stopped her throat, and she exclaimed "come out thou foul serpent."'

Among callers at the Toones' residence was Mr Hildersham, minister, of Ashby-de-la-Zouche, who was accompanied by several others of his cloth. They were careful to explain that they did not adhere to the Catholic idea of a man's ability to cast out devils, but that they had come to pray. The object of their kindly solicitude was sufficiently overawed to permit them to do so without interruption; nevertheless, no improvement in his condition followed.

He enhanced his performance with fresh hallucinations: a man emerged from his chamber-pot, he saw flames of fire, and witnessed the opening of the heavens which he visited and after embracing the apostles was taken on a conducted tour. Among other sights he was permitted a peep at 'the place of torments where drunkards are hanged by the throat, swearers and filthy talkers by their tongues', which conveys the impression that the apostles sent young Darling sight-seeing in the other place.

On May 27 no less a personage than John Darrell, B.A. arrived. He was a Puritan preacher and the very antithesis of a Catholic priest, but he had taken a leaf from the Catholic book, and did pretty well for himself as a professional exorcist. Darrell was clearly a sorry rogue and he was ultimately exposed by Samuel Harsnett, (1561–1631) who subsequently became Archbishop of York. It seems that Darrell, in dealing with hysterics, persuaded them to cooperate with him in a double act. More than one of his 'patients', including Thomas Darling, thus accused him, but, of course, these emotionally and mentally unstable people are consummate liars, and follow each other's lead.

Darrell diagnosed Thomas Darling's condition to be caused by the boy having become possessed of an evil spirit, and advised exorcism, which he undertook to conduct, as the only means of effecting a cure. A goodly number of people were present, all in a state of nervous excitement, to see John Darrell perform his wonders, and this audience was set to work a-praying to create a sort of dynamo of evil-spirit expelling power for Darrell to direct against the enemy within the boy. In spite of his villainy, this Puritan exorcist displayed a fine sense of 'theatre', and was a competent ventriloquist.

There was heard a thin, small voice which said, 'Brother Glassap, we cannot prevail, his strength is so strong, and they fast and pray, and a preacher prayeth as fast as they.' A voluminous, hollow voice responded, 'Brother Radulphus, I will go unto my master, Beelzebub, and he shall double their tongues.' There came yet a third voice, 'We cannot prevail, let us go out of him, and enter into some of these here!' (This nearly caused the prayer squad to panic.)

Dear little Tommie, if he was indeed conniving with Darrell, had studied his part well: he said one of the devils had left him, he had felt a mouse emerge from his throat. Then came the climax: a further voice spoke saying, 'My son, arise up and walk, the evil spirit is gone from thee, arise and walk.' It must have been most impressive when the invalid, who had about three months earlier lost the use of his legs, instantly obeyed, and walked into town.

Darrell asserted that the evil spirits had been sent into Thomas Darling by Alice Gooderidge who died in prison, but Darling, cross-examined by Samuel Harsnett, confessed that he was himself the author of his experiences.

Soon after the casting-out of his spiritual parasites, Thomas Darling returned to school (where he must have been the hero of the hour to the other boys), and in due course matriculated and entered Oxford but, being a thoroughly bad character, slandered the Vice-Chancellor of the University, for which he was publicly whipped and had his ears cropped.

The latter punishment was meted out to every felon convicted and the mutilation acted as a warning to all with whom he came in contact for the rest of his life. The custom might be reinstituted with great advantage.

Publishers do not (and they never did) publish for posterity. They do (and they always did) publish for profit, and the commercial possibilities in issuing reports of sensational witch-trials were not overlooked. Posterity profits, for when these sensational ephemera have survived they are most valuable sources of information for the modern investigator, but contemporaneously they were not an unmixed blessing. Juvenile delinquents of the period studied them closely and made them the pattern on which to contour their own forthcoming performance.

Thomas Darling of Burton may have read the voluminous report of the Throckmorton girls of Warboys: William Sommers of Nottingham most certainly had. It has been suggested that John Darrell presented copies of the work to his prospective clients but, even assuming this allegation to be true, he was not responsible for its having come to the attention of William Sommers.

This hero was bound apprentice on 7 May, 1593, to Mr Thomas Ponter, musician, of Nottingham, from whose service he absconded. In October, 1597, he was back in Nottingham, where, as we learn from Samuel Harsnett, he 'feigned illness and par-axyms'. John Darrell was called in, gathered a large audience to see him work wonders, and on 7 November the demon was driven by Darrell out of Sommers.

The exorcism was a most spectacular and expertly staged performance in which Darrell preached like an Old Testament prophet and Sommers acted as his demonstrator. The youth, said the preacher, was suffering for the sins of Nottingham: there must be a public fast day, and the citizens must abstain from the company of their wives that night. Darrell detailed fourteen signs of demoniac possession and the victim displayed all of them in turn. He spoke with his mouth wide open and his tongue drawn back into his throat as well as with his mouth firmly closed: he made his frame rigid, 'like iron': he wrestled with five men without perspiring, or shewing signs of physical distress: he gnashed his teeth and foamed at the mouth: among his con-tortions was that of twisting his neck round so that his face was to the rear, (Darrell had told him of the antics performed by Thomas Darling) and also bowing his body, 'his head between his legs, suddenly plucked round like a round brown loaf'.

Darrell now changed the tenor of his address: from the four-teen signs of possession he described the three signs of deliverance, weeping, (Sommers wept copiously); rending the garments, (Sommers tore his to shreds); and lying as one dead, (Sommers laid himself out as a corpse and with fine artistic finish, turned stone cold, and the pulse could not be detected in either his wrists or his temples).

The unclean spirits, Darrell declared, had now gone from William Sommers; there was, however, hinted the exorcist, a possibility of their sneaking back again, and at that juncture he took the collection.

Alas, the demons did return to Sommers, but not until after Darrell had been appointed preacher to St Mary's Church. These demons, said the possessed youth, had been set upon him by the machinations of witches, namely, Mother Higget, Alice Free-man, Thomas Groves, William and Mistress Bend, Widow Boote, two sisters Horseley and his own aunt, Elsie. The psychopathic taint seems to have been a family failing, for Sommers's sister Mary, wife of Robert Cooper, now developed hysterical fits, and joined her brother in accusing Alice (sometimes called 'Doll') Freeman of exercising witchcraft. Later she confessed to having been procured by one Mistress Gray to persecute the woman. No matter how innocent and respectable one was, to be indicted for witchcraft was a terrifying experience: to be searched for the devil's mark, which could not fail to be revealed, even more terrifying, and in this predicament Alice Freeman claimed to be pregnant. When this was reported to Darrell, who was now enjoying the reputation of an oracle, he declared that if she were, then it was a sufficient proof of her having had intercourse with Satan.

Alice Freeman's brother was an alderman and he had not abandoned his sister in her distress. However, a mayor and corporation is a ponderous piece of machinery to set in action, and before it had warmed to its work, there was a sensational development: William Sommers was arrested, charged with witchcraft by Widow Stenland whose husband had died declaring that Sommers had caused his death, bewitching him by treading upon his heel. Sommers was in custody little over an hour before he was released on bail. At a guess one suspects Darrell of providing the security, for Sommers would be likely to save his own skin at the expense of anyone else.

However, the wheels of God grind slow ... and the effort made by Alderman Freeman, receiving impetus from the singularity of Sommers's having been granted bail, moved the worshipful mayor gravely to suspect the integrity of John Darrell. With a view to ferreting out the truth, Sommers was again seized and brought before the mayor and aldermen who, by dint of threats and promises, extracted from him the confession that his behaviour, in which he had been instructed by Darrell, was fraudulent.

Satisfied with their success so far the civic dignitaries permitted Sommers to depart. This was a mistake, because someone impressed upon him that if he had been guilty of fraud he might be hanged. Hence, at the next hearing, conducted by a Commission of enquiry appointed by the Archbishop of York, Sommers withdrew his confession, declaring that he had been persuaded to make it solely to destroy Darrell; that he was indeed possessed, and to prove it he fell into a minor fit with frothing at the mouth.

At the next Assizes Alice Freeman's case came before Chief Justice Anderson and once again where Darrell was concerned Sommers proved a broken reed. Not only did he admit fraud but explained how Darrell had coached him in his impostures and had even arranged for him to travel to Burton, there to take advice and instruction from Thomas Darling. His sister, Mary Cooper, also confessed to having received instruction in simulation from John Darrell.

Alice Freeman was discharged and that fact alone makes this case one of outstanding importance because so very few persons charged with witchcraft escaped so lightly.

The Commissioners of the Province of Canterbury after examining Darrell declared him an impostor. He was unfrocked and imprisoned.

Although the statement that a charge of witchcraft, supported on the flimsiest evidence, and often that of children, led to the ultimate conviction and execution of the prisoner, is, generally speaking, true throughout the Christian world, there is some little satisfaction to be derived from the fact that in England, a witch's chances of being acquitted were higher than elsewhere. C. L'Estrange Ewen, whose contribution to the study of the subject is of the utmost value since he has transcribed court records, finds that in the Home Counties, between 1556 to 1736, of witches tried by regular justices, about eighty per cent escaped the death sentence. This appears very strongly in the St Osyth trial, (1582), as does also the maintenance and employment of familiars, an accusation occurring in early all English witch trials, but the idea does not seem to have recommended itself on the Continent. A statute of 1604 held it a felony to 'consult, covenant with, entertain, employ, feed, or reward any evil and wicked spirit', and any creature that could be found in a house or an outbuilding, including a mouse or a fly, a spider or a beetle, served as a familiar once the accusation of witchcraft had been levelled.

The case was heard by Brian Darcy Esquire, J.P., who had a special technique for extracting confessions: 'For so it is, there is a man of great cunning and knowledge come over lately to our Queen's Majesty, which hath advertised here what a company and number of witches be within England: whereupon I, and other of her Justices, have received commission for the apprehending of as many as are within these limits, and they which do confess the truth of their doings, they shall have much favour; but the other, they shall be burnt and hanged.' Thus reassured there were numerous confessions in the St Osyth case.

Ursula Kemp (alias Gray) indicted with Alice Newman on three heads, namely the bewitching to death of severally, Elizabeth, daughter of Richard Letherdall; Edna, wife of John Stratton and Joan, daughter of John Thornlowe, confessed that about ten or eleven years earlier, being troubled with lameness, she went to 'Cock's wife of Weeley', who told her she was bewitched and gave her a recipe that was calculated to release her from the spell. She was advised to 'take hog's dung and charnell and put them together and hold them in her left hand, and to take in the other a knife, and to prick the medicine three times, and then to cast the same into the fire, and to take the said knife and to make three pricks under a table, and to let the knife stick there: and after that to take three leaves of sage and as much of herb John (alias herb grace) and put them into ale, and drink it last at night and first in the morning . . .'

Following this instruction she derived great benefit, and passed the remedy on to two others who were similarly afflicted and they, too, experienced relief.

Ursula Kemp claimed to maintain four familiars, two male, and two female: the former she used 'to punish and kill unto death', the latter 'to punish with lameness and bodily harm'. It was also part of their work to destroy cattle. 'One he, like a grey cat, is called Tittey, the second, like a black cat is called Jacke; one she, like a black toad, is called Pigin, and the other, like a black lamb is called Tyffin.' These imps she shared with Alice Newman, and last Christmas they had dispatched Tittey to plague Thornlowe's wife. Upon the imp's report that he had executed his mission faithfully, and had 'punished her upon the knee' he 'was rewarded by being allowed to suck blood from the Examinate'. Jacke had similar instructions, and his victim was 'Stratton's wife'. Upon his return 'the spirit did suck of this Examinate upon the left thigh, the which when she rubbeth, it will at all times bleed.' Pigin was not left idle. She was given 'Letherdall's young child' to work havoc upon, and she, too, was rewarded by a sup of Ursula Kemp's blood.

The black lamb, Tyffin, who, as an imp, ought to have known better, talked too much. She told Ursula Kemp that Elizabeth

Bennett, also on trial for bewitching to death, possessed two spirits, one like a black dog named Suckin, the other 'red like a lyon', named Lyerd.

Ursula Kemp had an illegitimate son named Thomas Rabbet, who was eight years of age. He 'testified as to the possession of the four spirits'.

When Elizabeth Bennett's turn came to be examined she complained that the two spirits had forced themselves upon her in spite of her pious endeavours to be free of them. Suckin had pushed her into the oven, causing her to burn her arm. On a later occasion Suckin, accompanied by Lyerd in the disguise of a hare, came and sat beside her when she was milking with the result that the cow snorted, kicked the pail over, and bolted. Unable to rid herself of these very unwelcome imps, she had at length sent Lyerd off on an errand that ought to have satisfied him, namely, that of killing William Byett's beasts, but the imp wilfully ignored the beasts and, concentrating his attention upon Mistress Byett, plagued her to death. Elizabeth Bennett felt justified in taking revenge on William Byett, for he had called her 'old trot, old whore, and other lewd speeches'.

Alice Hunt, also of St Osyth, maintained two familiars 'like unto little colts, the one black and the other white, called by the names of Jacke and Robbin'. The evidence of a child of eight is again taken. Phoebe Hunt testified that 'her mother had two little things like horses, one white, the other black, which she kept in wool in a pot, feeding them with milk out of a trening dish'. This sweet little girl was very observant for she was able to report that 'she had heard her mother bid them go to Hayward of Frowicke'.

At this juncture 'Ursula Kemp testified she had seen one of Hunt's wife's spirits like a ferret'; and that most indiscrete, talkative black lamb of hers, Tyffin, informed her that this ferret-like imp of Alice Hunt's 'had killed six beasts of Hayward of Frowick, afterwards being rewarded by Hunt's wife with a drop of her blood.'

Agnes Heard of Little Oakley had an illegitimate daughter, Agnes Dowsing, aged seven, who gave evidence. 'Her mother had in one box six avices or black-birds, white speckled and all black, and in another box six spirits like cows, as big as rats, having little short horns and they lie upon black and white wool. Examinate received a black and white cow called Crowe, and her brother had a red and white one called Donne. Her mother fed the avices with wheat, barley, oats, bread and cheese, and the cows with straw and hay, and gave them water and beer to drink. The avices had sucked her hands and her brother's legs.'

Dame Bennett tried to relieve herself of the imps' unwanted attentions 'by praying to the Father, the Son, and the Holy Ghost', but they persisted in their attentions for, she confessed, later she had commissioned Lyerd to kill William Byett's cattle, but the imp, evidently regarding cattle as small fry, had concentrated his attentions on Mistress Byett instead, and brought her to her grave. She confirmed that William Byett himself had called her an 'old trot' and an 'old whore' and 'other lewd speeches', hence, she sent Suckin to torment him.

It was Elizabeth Bennett's opinion that these two imps had been sent to her by Mother Turner in revenge for her having been denied milk on one occasion.

Next came Agnes, wife of John Glascocke, who was indicted as a spinster. She was accused of bewitching to death three people, Martha, daughter of Michael Stevens; Abraham Hedge, and Charity, daughter of William Page. She made no confession: on the contrary she pleaded not guilty but was convicted and condemned.

Alice, wife of William Hunt, was more forthcoming; 'She had, within six days before the examination, two spirits, like unto little colts, the one black the other white, called by the names of Jacke and Robbin.' These faithful creatures had warned her that she would be betrayed by Ursula Kemp. However, Alice did not scruple to betray her own sister, Margery Sammon, who, she asserted, maintained two familiars in the form of toads, Tom and Robbyn. Both the sisters had received these dangerous pets from their mother, now deceased, namely Mother Barnes. Alice Hunt's step-daughter, an infant of eight years named Phoebe, came into the witness-box and solemnly testified to her mother having 'two little things like horses, one white, the other black', which she had heard her mother order to visit 'Hayward of Frowick'. This was confirmed by Ursula Kempe who declared she had seen one of Mistress Hunt's spirits, like a ferret which, Tyffin told her, had destroyed six beasts belonging to the said 'Heywarde'. The charges against Alice Hunt were bewitching to death six cows, and also Rebecca, daughter of Henry Durrant.

Margery Sammon, Alice Hunt's sister, confessed that she had received from her mother two spirits. These she harboured in a wicker-basket, more than half-full of black and white wool. When Ursula Kempe was arrested, these creatures had received orders from their mistress to go (presumably for safe keeping) to Mother Peachy, 'whereupon they skipped over a barred stile, and went to Peachy's house'.

Joan Peachy, a widow of 'sixty and upwards' was Alice Hunt's next-door neighbour, and Alice's was the only evidence against her: she had heard Widow Peachy talking to her imps, but Joan stoutly denied possessing any imps. Just to be on the safe side Brian Darcy ordered her to be held in custody; but when none other came forward against her she was discharged.

Alice Manfield, a widow aged sixty-three, confessed that she received from Margaret Grevell four imps, Robin, Jack, William and Puppet, also called Mamet. There were two male and two female, all of them like black cats in appearance and they lived in a box lined with wool. Mother Grevell seems to have retained a controlling interest in her gift of livestock for it was she who sent Robin to plague a bullock of Cheston's, and Jack to afflict the man himself upon 'the great toe unto the death'. Robin informed Alice Manfield that her widowhood was attributable to his activities, for he had been sent by Margaret Grevell to vex Mr Manfield 'who accordingly suffered from strange sores till he died'. Alice herself had employed Puppet to stop John Sayer's cart, and had rewarded it with beer.

The four familiars made an excursion to Clapton: one gathers that it was a sort of day off for them. However, they could not keep out of mischief; they set fire to a barn full of corn, the property of Richard Ross and, what is more, with true delinquency, overstayed their leave of absence 'being away from home a sevennight' during which period they received their nourishment from Henry Celles and his wife, Cicely. The imps were employed on numerous minor mischiefs, such as turning people's beer sour during the brewing, and bringing disaster to batches of bread. Among the witnesses was John Sayer, who said he 'believed that Alice Manfield bewitched his cart in front of her door, so that he could not move it for an hour'. Alice Manfield was indicted, jointly with Henry and Cicely Celles, for burning Richard Ross's barn.

John Carter gave evidence against Margaret Grevell: after having caused her some slight annoyance he had difficulties with brewing. However, his son, 'a tall and lustie man' thirty-six years of age, had a way of defeating witches: he shot three arrows at the fat,* the first and second failed to hold, but the third time the shot was successful, after which the brewing went forward without mishap. The local butcher, Nicholas Strickland, also after a quarrel with the accused, had trouble with churning. Margaret Grevell was indicted for bewitching to death Robert Cheston, but she denied this, and all the other charges of witchcraft.

Elizabeth Ewstace, aged fifty-three, was accused by Robert Sanneuet of casting a spell upon him that had drawn his mouth awry, of killing his wife, of causing his cows to give blood instead of milk, and influencing his pigs to 'skippe and leape about the yarde in a straunge sort'. Felice Ovey came forward to tell how, after a quarrel with Elizabeth, she had trouble with her geese, and with a cow, and furthermore her husband, being stricken by a strange illness, believed himself bewitched by her. Elizabeth Ewstace was, like Widow Peachy, held in custody and ultimately discharged.

The next culprit on the list was Agnes Heard of Little Oakley: John Wade, after speaking to her, suffered many losses of sheep and cattle, and Thomas Cartwrite, who also lost some cows, attributed their death to Agnes Heard's witchery, for he had quarrelled with her just before.

William Lane's wife sold two pennyworth of milk to the accused after which transaction 'she would have fleet her milk-bowl, but it would not abide the fleeting, but would rop and roll as it were the white of an egg, also the milk being on the fire it did not so soon seath but it would quail, burn by and stink, which she said she thought might be long of the feeding of her beasts, or else that her vessels were not sweet, whereupon she scalded her vessels, and scoured them with salt, but it was never the better'. At length, in despair, she resorted to the expedient of dropping into the milk a red-hot horse-shoe, after which she was able to 'seath her milk, fleet her cream, and make her butter in

* Probably 'vat', a tub or barrel, but the word also means an accumulation of solids in or on a liquid.

good sort'. Andrew West and his wife testified jointly: it seems West had promised to make Agnes Heard the gift of a pig, and failing in his fulfilment one of his pigs went lame. He effected a cure by cutting the animal's ears off, and burning them. His wife was plagued by an inability to brew but she dropped red-hot iron in and broke the spell.

Another loving couple who came forward against Agnes were Edmund Osborne and his wife. The latter, having unsuccessfully endeavoured to obtain from the accused repayment of a debt of threepence, experienced difficulty with her brewing: 'her mesh fat wrought up as the fat doth when it was set a worke with good beer, and bore up a hand breadth above the fat, and as they thrust in a stick, it would blow up and then sinked again.' Dame Osborne resorted to red-hot iron after which treatment 'it rose up no more, and then she let go, and then she did seath the wort, and when it was sodden it stank in such sort that they were compelled to put same in the swill tub'.

The parson of Beaumont, Richard Harrison, said that 'he and his late wife did dwell in Little Oakley in a house of his said wife, and that he . . . had also the parsonage of Oakley in farm. And about Summer twelvemonth, he being at London, his wife had a duck sitting on certain eggs under a cherry-tree in a hedge. And when the said duck had hatched, his said wife did suspect one Agnes Heard, a light woman and a common harlot, to have stolen her ducklings'. The parson's wife went along to Agnes Heard and berated her soundly 'but she could get no knowledge of her ducklings, and so came home and was very angry against the said Agnes.

'And within a short time after [Richard Harrison] went into a chamber and there did read on his books for the space of two or three hours, bidding his wife go to bed with the children . . . and she so did. And being a while laid down in her bed his wife did cry out "Oh, Lord, Lord, help me and keep me", and he, running to her, asked her what she ailed. And she said, "Oh, Lord! I am sore afraid, and have been divers times, but that I would not tell you." [adding] "I am in doubt, husband, that yonder wicked harlot, Agnes Heard, doth bewitch me."'

The clergyman lived up to his cloth, replying, 'I pray you be content and think not so, but trust in God, and put your trust in Him only, and He will defend you from her, and from the devil himself also . . . what will the people say, that I, being a preacher, should have my wife so weak in faith.'

About two months later the parson's wife said, 'I pray you, as ever there was love between us (as I hope there hath been, for I have five pretty children by you, thank God), seek some remedy for me against yonder wicked beast (meaning the said Agnes Heard). And if you will not, I will complain to my father, and I think he will see some remedy for me, for if I have no remedy, she will utterly consume me.'

Harrison again called upon his wife to have faith in God, adding that if he could prove anything against Agnes Heard 'he would hang her'. Later, he went to the parsonage to gather plums when Agnes Heard, accompanied by 'Anwick's wife', came up to the hedge and asked for a few plums. The charitable, kindly clergyman gave none of the fruit, but addressed her, gently, thus: 'I am glad you are here, you vile strumpet! I do think you have bewitched my wife, and, as truly as God doth live, if I can perceive that she be troubled any more as she hath been, I will not leave a whole bone about thee, and besides, I will seek to have thee hanged!'

He told Agnes Heard that his wife would make her father privy to it . . . 'then I warrant thee he will have thee hanged, for he will make good friends, and is a stout man of himself.' For good measure Harrison threw in sundry comparatively minor accusations concerning her bewitchment of geese and hogs.

Just before Christmas 'his said wife was taken sore sick, and was many times afraid both sleeping and waking.' About two days before her death she said, 'Husband, God bless you and your children, for I am now utterly consumed with yonder wicked creature.' This speech was made in the presence of John Pollin and Mother Poppe. Mistress Harrison died 'in perfect faith': her last words were, 'Oh Agnes Heard! Agnes Heard! She hath consumed me!'

The accused had an illegitimate daughter, Agnes Dowsing, aged seven years, who informed the court that her mother had in a box 'six avices or blackbirds, white speckled and all black, and in another box, six spirits like cows, as big as rats, having little short horns, and they lie upon black and white wool.' The child said she had received a black and white cow called Crowe, and that her brother had a red and white one called Donne, but whether she meant that these two animals were also weird ones, or was merely indulging, childlike, in a boastful digression, does not appear. She continued her evidence on the subject of dietetics: the avices were fed on wheat, barley, oats, bread and cheese; the cows on straw and hay. Their beverages were water and beer. Agnes Heard denied that she was a witch, repudiated ownership of imps and avices, and declared that no kine named Crowe and Donne were among her livestock. The charges brought against her were bewitching a cow and sheep, the property of John Wade.

Alice Manfield's friends, Henry and Cicely Celles, came before the court in due course. The first witness was Richard Ross of Little Clapton, who said that after hard words with Henry Celles he suffered much trouble with his cattle and the sudden fire to his barn. The next to testify was Henry Celles Junior, aged nine, son of the accused. A spirit, which was like his sister but was all black, seized his brother John by the left leg and the little toe. John, quite naturally, cried out, 'Father! Father! Come, help me! There is a black thing hath me by the leg, as big as my sister!' The result was, asserted Celles the younger, his father said to his mother, 'Why, thou whore! cannot you keep your imps from my children?' Mistress Celles, being apparently a dutiful wife, immediately called the imp off. The following day little Henry told his mother that he was afraid of this imp; that he had sweat so much from fear that he could scarce get his shirt from his back. The good mother retorted, 'thou lyest, thou lyest, whoreson!'

The witness declared that he had seen his mother feeding her imps on milk out of a black dish, and carrying them to a heap of wood and broom under a crab-apple tree near the house. One of them, a male, was black and answered to the name of Hercules (Jack to intimate friends); the other, a female, was white with the name Mercury (and no friendly nickname). Both of them had eyes like geese. Henry said he had seen his mother remove four broom faggots to enable the imps to nestle beneath the crab-tree root, where a fleece was provided for their comfort. The night when Ross's maid was taken, the witness had heard his mother telling his father that she had sent Hercules on that mission, to which Henry Senior replied 'ye are a trim fool'. Henry's little brother, John, aged six and three-quarters, gave corroborative evidence: his father had called his mother 'a stinking whore', and asked why she could not keep her imps from her children, and the imps had been taken away in a basket.

Alice Baxter, an employee of Richard Ross, having trouble with her milking, 'felt a thing prick her under the right side, and later, as she was going home, there came a thing all white like a cat, and stroke her at the heart, in such sort as she could not stand, go, nor speak, and had to be carried home.' Robert Smith confirmed every word of it.

Thomas Death fell out with Cicely Celles after which 'his child, aged four, fell down dead, and after, by help being brought to life, was in a piteous case, and so died presently.' His pigs skipped and leaped about the yard and then died. His daughter Mary, who was taken ill suddenly, was advised 'by a cunning man' that within two nights she would perceive the cause of her seizure.

Mary herself, in the witness-box, explained how she had been stricken with 'numbness all over, and the next night heard a voice saying to her, "Look up", and raising her eyes she beheld Celles's wife and Barker's wife standing before her in the same apparel that they usually wore. They vanished, and next day she was mended.'

Both Henry and Cicely Celles denied all the charges, and Henry disappears from the scene. Perhaps the case against him was dropped, but Cicely was found to have several witch marks, and two charges were brought against her: bewitching to death John Death, and, jointly with Alice Manfield, burning Richard Ross's granary.

Of the twelve (out of a total of fourteen) St Osyth witches whose trial is summarized above, five, namely, Ursula Kempe, Alice Newman, Elizabeth Bennett, Agnes Glascocke and Cicely Celles, were found guilty and condemned to death, but two only (Ursula Kempe and Elizabeth Bennett) went to the scaffold: the other three were reprieved. Four, namely, Alice Hunt, Alice Manfield, Margaret Grevell and Agnes Heard were acquitted, and the remaining three (if we include Henry Celles) were discharged, as were the two we have omitted. This is a record of mercy shown in these affairs and the case stands an eternal credit to Brian Darcy, Esquire, J.P.

Another case in which evidence given by children is accepted, and familiars are described, is that of Joan of Stisted, a widow of eighty years of age who, on March 31st 1589, was brought before Anthony Hildemay. She confessed that she had obtained her knowledge of witchcraft from Mother Humfrye of Maplestead, who instructed her to kneel within a circle on the ground and pray to Satan, when the spirits would come to her. Twenty years since testing this system of invocation in the field of John Wiseman of Stisted, gentleman, two spirits in the similitude of black frogs appeared and offered to perform her wishes, in return for her soul. Agreeing to these terms she carried the frogs home, and fed them on bread and milk. The spirits, called Jack and Jill, would talk with her in her own language. She ordered them to milk Hurrell's beasts, to hurt the wife of John Sparrow of Stisted, and to overthrow the logs of John Glascocke of Stisted, and to hurt Barnaby Griffin, which they did, but they failed to injure William Unglee, miller, and Master Kitchen, minister, and George Coe, shoemaker, all of Stisted, because of their faith in God.

'Joan Cunny, "living very lewdly, had two lewd daughters, no better than naughty packs", each having a bastard son, the eldest being ten or twelve years of age. The two boys gave evidence: Joan Cunny, disappointed in being refused drink by Henry Finch's wife, the latter was taken ill, and within a week died. Mother Cunny confessed to having sent Jill to torment her. The same boy deposed that wanting wood, his grandam bade him go into the ground of Sir Edward Huddlestone, taking with him Jack the sprite, and carrying out instructions he came to a mighty oak-tree, which the imp "went about" and presently it blew up by the roots, there being no wind at the time.

'A marginal note states that she had nine spirits, two like a black-dog but faced like a toad, and they were sucked on her sore leg. The four principal spirits were Jack, who killed mankind; Jill, womankind; Nicholas, horses; and Ned, cattle.'

Black dogs seem to be the favourite form of a witch's familiar: Oliver Cromwell, who was considered by some of his contemporaries to be a warlock, had a black dog familiar named Grimoald.* Henry Cornelius Agrippa von Nettesheim had a black dog imp called 'Monsieur'. Cats, toads, birds, hares, ferrets, rats and mice are not far behind dogs in popularity, and bees, wasps, hornets and ordinary house flies are far from uncommon. That

* According to Montague Summers (*Witchcraft and Black Magic*), Grimoald was not a dog but 'a tall dark man with a sour frowning face'.

the quadrupeds were, in the main, simply domestic pets seems to be indicated: that the neighbours feared them, as appears between the lines of evidence against witches, is easily understandable. During the period of the witch mania the lower social orders, and particularly the rustic stratum, were themselves, despite their cunning and capability in acquiring property and accumulating currency, dull of understanding, extremely curtailed in outlook, and revoltingly selfish. To them it seemed that animals had been created by God solely for the service and profit of peasant farmers: one did not feed and pamper them in idleness. A diluted form of this debased idea of man's relationship to the other animals survives in rural communities to the present day. When a cow has delivered her last pint of milk she has also eaten her last mouthful of grass; her destination is the knacker's yard. Chained farm dogs are gaunt, their coats often matted with dried mud, and semi-starvation renders them snarling and savage. The cat, whose sole function on earth is to protect from the ravages of rats and mice the farmer's stock of grain, does not need feeding; it can fend for itself.

In modern times, in a rural community, the passionate lover of animals is regarded as queer, perhaps a little mentally deranged. In the witch mania period he or she was clearly one in league with the devil. Children giving evidence against their mothers seem to be particular vindictive towards the familiars, a reaction arising from jealousy of the attentions bestowed upon the pet. The witch's ultimate acknowledgement that the simple cat, dog or bird was indeed an evil spirit at her command who feasted on her blood was of the same value as all the rest of her 'confession'.

Shape-changing was a characteristic of a witch's familiar: cat today, dog tomorrow, toad in two days' time and back to cat by the week-end. The cat, Satan of Hatfield Peverel, Essex, was such a one. On 26 July, 1566, at Chelmsford, Elizabeth Frauncis confessed that she studied witchcraft from the age of twelve, under the tuition of her grandmother, and gave her blood to Satan, the white spotted cat who lived in a basket, and who spoke in 'a strange hollow voice' (he was evidently a tom cat). Apparently educated in medicine and pharmacy he prescribed for his mistress an abortive which was most effective, and later, in the form of a toad, he rid her of her husband.

Satan served faithfully and well in the Frauncis household for sixteen years, when he was transferred (with detailed instructions of how he must be treated) to Mother Waterhouse of Hatfield Peverel, a widow of sixty-three who, being tried on the same day as Mistress Frauncis, explained that on receiving Satan she kept him in wool in a pot. To test his obedience and gauge his potency as a killer she ordered him to slaughter one of her own hogs. This feat accomplished to her entire satisfaction, Satan was briefed to kill three of Father Kersye's hogs, drown widow Gooday's cow, and dispatch three geese. In addition, this versatile felid ruined a neighbour's brewing, caused another to lose the curds, killed another neighbour with a bloody flux and, ultimately, by request, made a widow of Agnes Waterhouse.

In reward of his signal services Satan was always given a chicken and a drop of Agnes's blood. At length, Agnes, requiring the wool upon which her faithful familiar was accustomed to repose, turned Satan into a toad.

Miss Joan Waterhouse, aged eighteen, who had seen 'the thing' in the shape of a toad in her mother's hand, had herself employed Satan 'in the likeness of a great dog', to frighten one Agnes Brown.

Agnes, aged twelve, upon examination, said there had come to her 'a thing like a black dog with a face like an ape, a short tail, a chain and a silver whistle about his neck, a pair of horns on his head and, in his mouth, the key of the milk-house door'.

Satan, the spotted cat, had, in the manner of an imp, overplayed his hand.

'In 1653 Anne Bodenham . . . was hanged at Salisbury upon an absurd and unsubstantiated charge of witchcraft. She was accused of nourishing familiars; and when she was searched in jail the women who performed this office swore that they had found two unnatural teats or witch-paps upon her body, the one on her shoulder, the other *in verendis*. She was said to have made a particular contract with the Devil, by whose help she could transform herself "into the shape of a Mastive Dog, a black Lyon, a white Bear, a Woolf, a Bull, and a Cat", although it does not appear how such metamorphoses would benefit her, and one might imagine that a black lion, a white bear, or even a wolf must attract considerable attention if met with in a Wiltshire lane. Such a tissue of absurdities was the evidence, and the whole trial is indeed a glaring example of judicial murder, which perhaps is hardly surprising when one considers that it took place under Cromwell's tyranny.'*

Such shape-changing by the witch herself is uncommon, and so is the familiar in the form of a large animal. As a rule they are small domestic animals. Evan Green of Stathorne, Leicester, had two familiars, one called Puss 'in the shape of a kitten', the other called Riff-hiff 'in the shape of a modiwarp'.†

Jane Holt of Faversham, Kent, had 'a thing like a hedgehog', and her neighbour, Elizabeth Morris, a large mouse. Joan Prentice of Hedingham, Essex, 'nourished a familiar "in the shape and proportion of a dunnish-coloured ferret, having fiery eyes". It answered to the name of Bidd. Joan Prentice sent Bidd to sour and ruin the beer (then in brewing) of William Adam's wife, causing her great loss and injury, and she also commanded him to torment young Sarah Glascocke. The child died in consequence of these devilments and sorceries. Two independent witnesses, Elizabeth Whale, a labourer's wife, and Elizabeth Mott, a cobbler's wife, gave testimony that they had often seen this mischievous ferret-imp, Bidd.'††

When Mary Hale, the blacksmith's daughter, of Little Gadsden, Herefordshire, began to mew like a cat, bark like a dog, and roar like a bear, she was assumed to be possessed by devils who, on being asked their identity replied, 'We are only two little imps, Goodwife Harod's and Young's, sometimes we are in the shape of serpents, sometimes of flies, sometimes of rats and mice.' §

Mary Bacon of Chattisham, Suffolk, 'discovered' by Hopkins, claimed three imps, a grasshopper, a mouse and a squirrel. Mary Bush of Bocton, Suffolk, confessed that the devil sent her three imps, one like a whelp, the other two like mice. These she had employed to kill three cows and twenty turkeys of Mr Pritiman, and two cows of Goodman Gornam. She had another imp like a toad and this she used to torment Elizabeth Heath.

Also among Hopkins's victims was John Bysack, of Woldingfield Magna, whose imps were in the likeness of snails of varying

---

* *Geography of Witchcraft*, Montague Summers, Kegan Paul, 1927.

† Old English, via Middle English, surviving in dialect, literally 'earth-thrower': the mole.

†† *Witchcraft and Black Magic*, Montague Summers.

§ *Daimonomogeia*, W. Drage, 1664.

colour and size. Their names were Sydrake, Jeffrey, Peter, Ayle-
ward, Sacar and Pyeman. The first killed fowls; the second, sheep;
the third, hogs; the fourth, cows; the fifth, horses; and the sixth,
Christians.

Another male witch, whose marks were revealed by Stearne,
Hopkins's assistant, was Henry Corse of Ratteesden; he had two
imps in the shape of mice.

Anne Cricke, of Mitcham, had three imps; a sparrow, Harrie;
and two mice, Jack and Will. Elizabeth Greene, of Wingfield, had
three imps like chickens; Giles, Alice and Bess. Faith Mills, of
Fressingfield, had three bird-imps, Tom, Robert and John. She
gave one to Thomas Aldus's child, who broke out in sores and
died, the others made a cow jump over a stile, a horse throw its
rider, and 'a cart stand fast on plain ground'. Anne Randall, of
Lovenham, had two imps, 'heavy and soft, which came in the
likeness of cats or kitlings of a blue colour, called Hangman and
Jacob. The former, sent to kill a horse of William Baldwin's, who
was slow in settling an account for firewood, exceeded his instructions and killed two horses. Margery Sparham, of Mendham,
had three imps, two like blackbirds named Will and Tom, and
one like a white 'moll', named Nan. This last she had had since
her girlhood, and she sent it to sea to earn its living; the two
blackbirds came to her after her father's death, and she sent them
off to protect her husband, who was a soldier. Alice Warner, of
Rushmere, used her imps to carry lice to other women, which
was but minor work for skilled imps. As a rule, causing such
infestation was a mere side issue, secondary to the main commission to kill a neighbour or some more or less valuable domestic
animal.

Montague Summers, learned to an extraordinary degree, whose
facts are always above suspicion, is, however, somewhat eccentric
in his conclusions. On familiars he says* 'the huge hosts of
demons, these foul but brilliantly alert intelligences, the rulers
of the darkness of this world, are divided into ranks and grades
and orders, into principalities and powers; there are lords and
menials, aristocracies and plebs, we may say. When the pact has
been struck it is not unusual that there should be assigned to
the witch a familiar, that is to say an attendant demon . . . Familiars are employed by the witch . . . for various hurtings and

* *Witchcraft and Black Magic*, Rider, 1946.

harms, for mischief generally, to destroy property, to afflict with illness, to

> "Raise jars,
> Jealousies, strifes, and heart-burning disagreements
> Like a thick scurf o'er life."

For several pages he gives examples of familiars in human form which have accompanied famous people: the second-selves were sometimes visible only to the psychic observer, many were tangible to all, but such attendants were not for the humble rural hag. 'In England the witch's familiar or Astral Spirit went under many names. He was called a bunn or bunting; a dandiprat— terms of endearment; imp; spirit; devil; fiend; fury; angel; little master; maumet; puckril; nigget; and (particularly in New En- land) spectre.

'The animal familiar, which in the British Isles was and is the commonest form as being the least likely to attract notice or arouse remark, . . . probably belongs to a lower order of evil intelligences. The old English country name under which he may conveniently be known is "puckril". . . .

'The animal form ordinarily assumed by a familiar was that of a dog or a cat, but he was able to appear in almost any shape; as a bird, a chicken, a ferret, a hare, a hedgehog, a rabbit, a rat, a toad, a wasp, a spider, a beetle or some other insect . . . It is true that in other countries save the British Isles the domestic familiar is not so often remarked, and no very great stress seems to have been laid upon this detail, which in English law was regarded of the first importance and most damningly significant.' *

After a survey of the familiars recorded in the famous witch trials, particularly the St Osyth witches' confessions, he says, 'to come down to our own days, a resident of Horseheath, a village about fourteen miles from Cambridge, gave the following details of the sorceries of Mother Redcap, a local witch, who died in 1926. "One day a black man called, produced a book and asked her to sign her name in it. The woman signed the book, and the mysterious stranger then told her she would be the mistress of five imps who would carry out her orders. Shortly after the woman was seen out accompanied by a rat, a cat, a toad, a ferret and a mouse. Everybody believed she was a witch and

* Summers, op. cit.

many people visited her to obtain cures" (the *Sunday Chronicle*, 9 September, 1928).'

Montague Summers does not confuse the familiar, the demon in animal form, with a normal domestic animal trained to do tricks and so impress those who consult a 'wise woman' in order to learn the future. He quotes Charles Godfrey Leyland, whose book, *Gypsy Sorcery and Fortune Telling*, was published in 1891: "the reader has often seen in London Italian women who have small birds, generally parrakeets or paraquitos, which will, for a penny, pick out for her or for him slips of paper on which is printed a 'fortune'. I can very well remember formerly to have noticed these amateur *Streghe*, so to speak, and their trained birds, paraquitos or yellow canaries, deftly picking out with their tiny beaks, little billets from a heap; but of recent years these women, in their gaily striped petticoats and bodices, all adorned with mosaic jewellery, the white linen *cuffs* on their heads, their ears weighed down with heavy silver rings . . . are no longer met with, and their picturesqueness seems completely to have disappeared." *

Brian Darcy, the merciful magistrate who heard the St Osyth case (whose little fable concerning the wiseacre who had come from beyond the seas to advise Queen Elizabeth I on the subject of witchcraft can be overlooked), very likely believed in the familiars described to him, nevertheless, his handling of the matter does not support the contention that the emotional climate was changing for the better with the growing establishment of Protestantism; that is a false reading of the signs of the times, for the most pious of Catholics and the most extreme of Puritans met in perfect accord on the territory of witch hunting.

This latter fact is heavily emphasized by the outbreak, as late as 1692, of witch-mania in Salem, Massachusetts. There, witchcraft was not only revolt against God, but was also political treason.

Montague Summers says,† 'There can be no doubt that the settlers in New England were not only firm believers in every

---

* In 1891 this final note of regret was premature. As recently as 1910 such a one had her pitch beneath the railway-bridge spanning Newington Causeway, London, S.E.

† *Geography of Witchcraft*, Kegan Paul, Trench, Trubner & Co. Ltd., 1927.

kind of Witchcraft, but well primed in every malevolence that could command itself to their verjuiced and tortured minds. They looked for the Devil round every corner and saw Satan's hand in every mishap, in every accident.* The Devil, in fact, played a larger part in their theology than God. They were obsessed with hell and damnation; their sky was clouded and overset; their horizon girded with predestination and the awful consciousness of Sin. It is almost impossible to conceive the effect a new land, a strange mysterious bourne beyond the waves of the illimitable Atlantic, must have had upon the muddled morbid minds and tortured souls of these stern and stoic pioneers.'

The trouble began in 1692 in the home of Rev. Samuel Parris, Pastor of Salem, whose slave-girl, Tituba, entertained parties of young women and girls with stories from her native folk-lore. Samuel Parris's daughter, Elizabeth, aged nine, and her cousin, Abigail Williams, aged eleven, the two youngest members of Tituba's audience, were affected strangely by the slave-girl's stories: they fell into fits of weeping accompanied by convulsions. Elizabeth was sent to stay with a certain Stephen Sewall, but the change failed to calm her.

These two pubescent girls now found themselves mistresses of a gratifying situation whereby they held the whole adult world of their environment at their mercy, and in that quality they were sadly lacking. Elizabeth Parris, brought up in the strict Puritan home where the Holy Bible was held to be little less than an incarnation, seized the book and flung it across the room. Abigail Williams, who lived with the Parris family, put up a notable act on 11 March when a solemn day of fasting and prayer for relief from bewitchment had been organized. She spent the time rushing wildly about, shrieking and generally disrupting the prayers and destroying the solemnity of the meeting.

From this beginning the hysteria affected other members of Tituba's audience: Ann Putnam, aged twelve; Mary Walcott, aged sixteen; Elizabeth Hubbard, aged seventeen; Susan Sheldon and Elizabeth Booth, both aged eighteen; Mercy Lewis, aged nineteen, and Elizabeth Proctor, aged twenty. The infection spread further afield: Phoebe Chandler, aged twelve; Martha

---

* Compare Dr River's description of the Melanesian mental orientation in such matters. Page 9.

Sprague, aged sixteen; Sarah Trask, aged nineteen; Margaret Reddington and Sarah Churchill, both aged twenty, began acting with physical contractions and the levelling of accusations against their neighbours. Dr Griggs, the local physician, diagnosed witchcraft in which opinion he was strongly supported by the pastors and judges. One unnamed citizen was not taken in: he said that if these girls were not soon restrained the entire population would be denounced as witches and devils, 'they should rather be had to the whipping-post'. In confirmation of this opinion John Proctor, who was Mary Warren's employer, reported that when she had first thrown fits he had kept her hard at work at the spinning-wheel, and threatened to thrash her. This treatment had kept the fits away. Next day, however, in his absence, she started her fits again.

Mary Walcott's aunt, Mary Sibley, who employed Tituba's husband, John Indian, ordered him to make a witch-cake, the recipe for which she had found in *The New England Almanac*: 'To cure ague. Take a cake of barley meal and mix it with children's water, bake it, and feed it to the dog. If the dog shakes you will be cured.' Exactly what relationship this well-meaning matron saw between ague and witchcraft does not appear, for even if the charmed cake was baked it was not administered. The Rev. Samuel Parris found out and fulminated.

Pubescent children and teen-agers who set their feet upon the path of such delinquency find at some point in the journey that there is no way back, hence they are compelled to progress from bad to worse, and they bring their victims to a felon's death with as little compunction as they had previously (for example) flung the Bible across the room. Tituba was the first to tell how spectres of certain neighbours appeared to them and tried to recruit them for the devil. The simple question 'Who is it that torments you?' when put to the children brought forth no inspiration, but, the questions becoming harder and more persistent (not to mention leading) names had to be supplied: first came poor slave-girl Tituba; following her, Sarah Good, a notorious beggar; then Sarah Osborne, a cripple who had been married three times, and last on the list, Martha Cory, the mother of an illegitimate son whose unknown father was unmistakably a Negro. Four more helpless wretches could not have been found in the entire colony.

On 1 March, 1692, a court of oyez and terminer,* at which John Hathorne and Jonathan Corwin, the most weighty magistrates of the district presided, was held at the Salem Meeting House : but they were simply magistrates, not lawyers.

Sarah Good was the first to be cross-examined : she was asked what evil spirit she had familiarity with, to which she answered shortly, 'None'.

'Have you made no contacts with the Devil?'

'No.'

'Why do you hurt these children?'

'I do not hurt them, I scorn it.'

'Who do you employ then to do it?'

'I employ nobody.'

'What creature do you employ then?'

'No creature, but I am falsely accused.'

'Why do you go away muttering from Mr Parris his house?'

'I did not mutter, but I thanked him for what he gave my child.'

'Have you made no contact with the Devil?'

'No.'

Hathorne, probably confounded by these simple, firm, direct answers to his questions, fell back on the expedient of ordering the children to look at the prisoner and see if she were not the person hurting them. The children, only too glad to wield the power thus conferred upon them did look, renewed their accusations, and were seized with fits.

Hathorne immediately followed up the advantage created by this visual demonstration :

'Sarah Good, do you not see now what you have done? Why do you not tell us the truth? Why do you thus torment these poor children?' The answer was again a firm negative, but the magistrate simply ignored all the prisoner's assertions of innocence, and condemned her to death.

Sarah Osborne's case was next dealt with : it was a replica of Sarah Good's, but she did not go to the scaffold. Her frail, crippled frame was unequal to the rigours of imprisonment, with heavy chains about her, and she died in jail.

Tituba, whose life as a slave had taught her how to avoid

* To hear and determine : a court of summary jurisdiction : a magistrate's court.

brutal beatings and general injustice, was shrewd enough to see that a simple declaration of innocence seemed to prove the way to the gallows, so she assumed the role of a penitent, 'confessed' and declared that she was herself a victim of the devil who would torment her if she failed to serve him.

Confession and penitence secured her acquittal, but she was held in jail pending her payment of the costs of her trial, and was ultimately sold to defray these expenses.

Hathorne's masterly cross-examination was repeated in the case of Martha Cory and she, too, was hanged.

Having now to their credit three judicial murders and a near miss these pious Puritan gentlemen should have been satisfied that their path to Paradise was sufficiently paved, but they were not. The persecutions progressed, the epidemic spread, and although Elizabeth Parris and Abigail Williams remained in the role of leading ladies in the drama, the impact of their hysteria upon affectible persons brought sundry other accusers to the fore who enjoyed themselves by throwing fits for the edification of Mr Justice Hathorne and his friends and supporters. No fewer than a hundred and fifty people were indicted and there is reason to suppose that details of a greater number exist but have not come to light having been misplaced in the court records.

That the local population was enjoying itself immensely is indicated by their behaviour when Rebecca Nurse, a woman of over seventy years of age and of blameless character, was found not guilty. 'The mob broke out into the wildest clamour, yelling with horrid threats that they would pull the house about the judge's ears and tear the jurors to pieces. Benches were smashed, and missiles began to be thrown, when the acquittal was hurriedly withdrawn and the sentence of death speedily pronounced.'*

Among the accused was Captain John Alden, friend of Miles Standish,† a man of credit and renown as an intrepid seaman, and an American hero on account of his achievements in killing Red Indians.

The children failed to identify him at the first attempt, and had to be prompted, but a little mistake of that kind was readily overlooked by Mr Justice Hathorne. At length they 'cried out

* Montague Summers, op. cit.
† The incident in Longfellow's poem is purely fictitious.

upon him, "There stands Alden! A bold fellow with his hat on before the judges. He sells powder and shot to the Indians and French, and lies with Indian squaws, and has Indian papooses!"' Having said their piece they performed the accompanying act of falling unconscious, and of promptly recovering when Alden touched them.

Alden was emphatically 'a bold fellow', and he probably kept his hat on before the judges to express his contempt of them. Nothing daunted by this demonstration he demanded, 'What's the reason *you* don't fall when I look at you? Can you give me one?' Mr Justice Hathorne evidently could not, for he did not, but committed Alden to jail pending a further hearing. Alden, however, did not wait for it: he broke jail, escaped over the border, and so lived to slaughter more Indians.

Another accused person of importance who, lacking John Alden's toughness did not escape, was the Rev. George Burroughs, a graduate of Harvard and a former pastor of Salem village, from which office he had retired a year or two earlier, after a quarrel with his congregation concerning their non-payment of his stipend. He was unpoplar in Salem because, due to the congregation's parsimony, he had been forced to contract debts that remained unpaid.

A warrant was made out against him, 'he being suspected of a confederacy with the Devil', and the court of oyez and terminer was strengthened by the addition to the bench of several weighty persons, including William Stoughton, the then deputy-governor of the colony. Cotton Mather gives an account of the proceedings.*

Burroughs's first accuser was Ann Putnam, aged twelve, ably assisted by Mercy Lewis, aged about nineteen, who lived with the Putnams, but who was a foundling and had been befriended and brought up by George Burroughs.

Ann Putnam said that she had been confronted by the apparition of a minister of religion who had choked her, and ordered her to write her name in a book. This she had refused to do, and had said, 'Oh, dreadful creature, tell me your name that I may know who you are.' The apparition most obligingly complied with the request, saying he was George Burroughs. 'He then

* *Wonders of the Invisible World*—an account of the suffering brought upon the country by witchcraft (1693).

told me that his first two wives would appear to me presently, and tell me a great many lies, but I should not believe them. There immediately appeared to me the forms of two women in winding-sheets, and napkins about their heads, [they] looked very red and angry and told [Burroughs] that he had been cruel to them, and that their blood did cry for vengeance against him . . . and immediately he vanished away. And as soon as he was gone, the two women . . . told me that they were Mr Burroughs's two first wives, and that he had murdered them . . . they both charged me that I should tell these things to the magistrates . . .

'This morning also Mrs Lawson and her daughter Ann appeared to me . . . and told me Mr Burroughs murdered them . . . also appeared another woman in a winding-sheet and told me she was Goodman Fuller's first wife, and Mr Burroughs killed her because there was some difference between her husband and him.'

Mercy Lewis identified the book Ann Putnam had been asked to sign as the devil's register of names that had been in Burroughs's study when she lived with them. Mercy added an artistic touch to her effort, '. . . Mr Burroughs carried me up to an exceedingly high mountain and showed me all the kingdoms of the earth, and told me he would give them all to me if I would write in his book, and if I would not he would throw me down and break my neck.'

Burroughs appeared to some of his accusers not merely as a spectre but in tangible form: Abigail Hobbs testified that when Burroughs brought her his book to sign she had felt his hand, and the fact of his having been eighty miles away at the time was not accepted as an alibi.

The girl's masterpiece in hysterical manifestation was their development of tooth marks when they accused Burroughs of biting them. His demeanour during the trial was calm and dignified. His statement in defence, 'there neither are nor even were witches that having made a compact with the Devil can send a devil to torment other people at a distance', though sound, reasonable and acceptable to the twentieth-century mind was, in the seventeenth century considered blasphemous and damning. On the scaffold, after maintaining his innocence, he recited the Lord's Prayer with perfect diction, a feat accepted as impossible for a witch, and this caused an outcry from the throng of spectators. They were pacified by Cotton Mather himself, who explained that the devil is never more dangerous than when filling the role of an angel.

The first sign of a weakening of the evil power behind the hysteria, with its hypnotic effect upon the authorities, came in October 1692 when the children 'cried out' against the wife of the Rev. John Hale, minister of the First Church of Beverly, 'but the acknowledged and distinguished virtues of this lady, her solid piety and a thousand charities, had made her so beloved by the people and had so idolized her in their hearts, that not at all could the crying out of the afflicted children sully or shake their confidence. . . . The whole community rose in defence of Mrs Hale and roundly declared that the children were perjurers and liars.'*

This set-back had the effect of shattering the whole occult complex of diabolical tension. Sir William Phips, Governor of the colony, forbade further trials: the children did their best by crying out against the Governor's lady whom they declared to be the supreme leader of all the witches. However, adult authority re-establishing itself quickly put a stop to such dangerous statements: no more of these amusing trials could be held, all prisoners, amounting to nearly two hundred, were released. The pastors and magistrates were, for a period, very worried men.

Robbins says,† 'there can be no mitigation of the crimes of the Salem girls. Never at any time, even during the hangings, was the slightest compunction or contrition shown. . . . They knew exactly what they were doing. Their acts during 1692 imply a state of utter delinquency, causing death without rhyme or reason, for sport. . . . The only document which proves the irrational viciousness of the accusations is Ann Putnam's confession, made fourteen years later.'

The servants of Satan, the accusers, were not punished, but their 'sport' caused twenty-nine persons to be condemned to death. Of this number nineteen were hanged; seven, whose execution had been delayed because they were pregnant, or for some other reason, were ultimately reprieved; eleven died in jail and one (other than John Alden) escaped. Among those whose constitution was unequal to the rigours of prison life was Dorothy

* Montague Summers, op. cit.   † op. cit.

Good, 'a child of four or five years old [who] being chained in the dungeon was so hardly used and terrified that she hath ever since been very chargeable, having little or no reason to govern herself.'

Among the hanged was Ann Pudeator: asked 'have you anything to say?' she answered, 'I am an old woman. I came to this strange land as a child. I stand accused now of matters I do not understand. I have worked hard, and striven hard to do good. I have little education, give me time to compose my thoughts. . . . I am condemned to die and knowing in my conscience as I shall shortly answer it before the great God in Heaven, who is the searcher and knower of all hearts, that the evidence of Jonathan Best and Samuel Pickworth which was given in against me were all of them false and untrue, besides which Jonathan Best hath been formerly whipped, and been recorded for a liar, I would humbly beg of your honours to take it into your judicious and pious consideration that my life may not be taken away by such false evidences and witnesses as these be. . . . I am altogether innocent and know nothing . . . concerning the crime of witchcraft for which I am condemned to die. . . .'

On 5 March, 1954, the representative from Salem, in the Massachusetts State Legislature, introduced a bill* which was carried unanimously for the reversal of the judgement.

Among the offences (to anti-Jacobites) committed by that much maligned monarch King James VI and I, is that he wrote a book entitled *Demonology*. That is was a good book and a successful book increases the offence, and that it was published at a period when the belief in the power of witches was on the decline is held to be the greatest offence of all.

King James believed in the reality of witchcraft first because he was a Scot, and Scotland, following the continental pattern of culture rather than the English, had always been vigilant against the witch cult, and secondarily, because of an overwhelmingly convincing personal experience.

Montague Summers says,† 'In no country did the witch-cult flourish more rankly, in no country did the prosecution of sorcery rage fiercer and the fires blaze brighter than in Scotland. The lonely hills and wild untrod moors, the echoing glens and remote

* House Bill No. 1392.   † op. cit.

glades, seemed the very places for the hauntings of mysterious powers, influences which were, however, in popular lore, always ranged on the side of evil, harbingers of death and destruction and hell.

'Even the realm of Faerie, whose denisons were thought of elsewhere as bright spirits friendly to humankind, lovely, gay, bounteous of goodly gifts, in Scotland becomes the Court of Elfame, a fearful country ruled over by the Devil, who is actually spoken of as a fairy-man, inhabited by malignant fiends, where the levels of elves and pretty pixies dancing their graceful rounds in the silvery moonlight, one a foul Sabbat of demons, hideous earlines, and their dark familiars. . . .

'The supremacy of the Devil seems an essential feature of Calvinistic teaching. How can anyone look for tranquillity and comfort, or ensure sweet communion with God, when his eyes are ever scorched and scarred by the red roar of the furnace of hell, his ears ever stunned by the ceaseless howling of the damned who are eternally agonizing in the pit of Tophet? . . . in its dour fanaticism the Kirk proved a sterner judge and a more cruel executioner than even Boguet or De Lancre, than Philip Adolph von Ehrenberg, the burning Bishop of Würzburg.'

King James was not easily deceived. He declared, having heard the 'confessions' of some of the North Berwick witches, which included their having gone to sea in sieves, that they were colossal liars, but one of them, Agnes Sampson, caused him to think again.

She 'declared unto him the very words which had passed between [him] and his Queen at [Oslo] in Norway, the first night of their marriage, with their answers to each other: whereat the King's Majesty wondered greatly. . . .' and well he might have done for the black liquor of occult manifestation had not yet been subjected to the fractional distillation that in these days yields so many self-contained subjects including 'telepathy' or 'thought transference', 'clairvoyance' and 'mediumship'.

Nevertheless, in 1604 the King exposed the fraud of Ann Gunther, a fourteen-year-old girl, living at North Horeton, Berkshire. Her father, who was a man of substance, called in the best doctors available, and their diagnosis was pretty sound: 'falling sickness' (epilepsy), and 'suffocation of the mother' (hysteria), but this did not please Miss Gunther, who had read reports of witchcraft cases.

She foamed at the mouth; she suffered attacks of blindness and deafness; she not only vomited pins but she exuded them from her breasts and fingers; and she accused three people of bewitching her: Agnes and Mary Pepwell, and Elizabeth Gregory.

On 27 August 1605 she was examined by the King in person and by him sent to Samuel Harsnett who, together with Dr Edward Jorden, extracted from her the confession that she had been encouraged to counterfeit symptoms by her father.

Brian Gunther and Ann, his daughter, were charged with conspiracy, but it seems, there being no records, that the case was never heard.

In 1616, King James, visiting Leicester, heard of the seizures of John Smith, a boy of thirteen, who had already brought nine persons to the gallows, and a tenth had died in prison. Perhaps the boy was overawed by being in the presence of the King, but he began to falter in his replies to the King's questions and was handed over to the ecclesiastical authorities for a thorough and close examination. They 'did in a few weeks discover the whole deceit'.

King James did not write *Demonology* for the sake of the income to be derived from it; the total sum would hardly have been sufficient for his purpose: he did not write it for the publicity arising out of authorship; the mere fact of his being King of the United Kingdom carried a far wider publicity: he did not write it to pass the time away for the Sovereign has not time; every second of his life is the property of his subjects. King James wrote the book in fulfilment of what he conceived to be his kingly duty: that of protecting his subjects from 'the fearefull aboundinge at this time ... of these detestable slaves of the Devill, the Witches.'

Chapter Three

ENGLISH law did not permit official torture, by means of instruments, to be employed as a means of extracting confession of guilt from the accused in witch-trials. We must not, however, be too smug about this because, as will appear, ill-treatment and brutality that did not fall within the definition of torture were very often applied, and there arose a number of specialists in whom cruelty was developed apparently to the exclusion of all emotion and human feeling. They became professional witch-finders and their services were in high demand.

On the Continent of Europe where torture was permitted, the frequency and the ferocity of its application varied from country to country according to both national temperament and the influence of the Inquisition: as might be expected the most savage torments, and those of the most frequent application, were the custom in Germany.

The Inquisition advocated torture, which might be inflicted not only on the accused, but also on witnesses. The function of the Inquisition was to enquire into deviations from the official teaching of the Church and thus to suppress heresy. A person brought before the Inquisition on suspicion, being unable to prove innocence, was handed over to the secular authorities to be sentenced.

Although the secular courts were free to hear the evidence and pronounce judgement (not bound by law to implement the judgements of the Inquisition), they were in fact, subservient; to oppose the Inquisition was to suffer excommunication. The earliest Inquisitions were local, under the jurisdiction of the Bishop, and their activities varied from area to area. This state of affairs, being considered unsatisfactory, caused Pope Innocent III to set up a universal Inquisition to be directed from the Vatican, and with power to supersede all local judgements. The Bull, dated 25 March, 1199, was implemented throughout Christendom by 1200.

Any offence, including murder, could be represented as heresy and the accused taken before the Inquisition. All evidence against the prisoner was accepted, and allowed to stand even if the witness withdrew it. The only result of such a retraction was that the witness was tried on a charge of perjury.

There were no witnesses for the defence, and the accused could not brief a lawyer, for to do so was to make him guilty of upholding heresy. Secular judges, and even laymen, were sometimes seconded to sit on the Inquisition, and even at that callous period it must sometimes have gone against the grain to be compelled to accept evidence from persons who would not have been admitted as witnesses in secular courts: such as children, convicted perjurers, persons without civil rights, and felons who had been punished on previous occasions.

Torture, which was supposed to be permitted by the Inquisition only as a last resort, was systematically and regularly applied, even though the accused had, in order to avoid it, already confessed to every accusation levelled against him. This point is heavily stressed in *The Amber Witch*. The book, a typical Gothic novel, making use of the technique introduced by Horace Walpole in *The Castle of Otranto*, namely, that of purporting to be the verbatim reproduction in print of 'an old and faded manuscript' is most convincing, and its author, the Rev. Dr Meinhold, most successfully typified proceedings for witchcraft against a wholly innocent person.*

It was not legal to subject a prisoner to torture more than once, hence, the second, third, and subsequent applications were not recorded as separate incidents but merely as 'continuation'. Ultimately the required confession of guilt, and a list of names of fellow-witches was obtained, after which, in the torture-chamber within sight of instruments, the victim was made to repeat his confession so that it could go on record as being a voluntary act without torture.

The confiscation of the property of the accused, the booty being shared by the civil authorities and the Inquisition, had a heavy impact on the frequency of witch-trials: it is significant

* Translated from the German by Lady Duff Gordon.

that in Juliers,* where confiscation was not permitted, there were no witch-trials.

By about 1500 the Inquisition's power was on the wane, and witch-trials were conducted exclusively by the secular authorities, but the Inquisitorial method was retained: torture was the means of securing confession, and the property of the victim went not only into the civic coffers, but into private pockets.

The medieval mind was enabled to tolerate torture and to justify injustice on the grounds that heresy, hence witchcraft, was a crime of conscience: the Church, and only the Church could reveal God's truth and goodness which was absolute and not subject to the individual's ideas of morality and ethics. God's opponent, Satan, who sought to gain ascendancy, employed every means of increasing the number of his adherents; heretics, being moved and motivated by Satan, were soldiers in his army fighting against God and His Holy Church. Heresy, hence witchcraft, was an exceptional crime and could not, therefore, be tried by normal standards of justice. No one was in a position to know the secret heart of the heretic, hence the only way in which service to Satan could be established was by the confession of the suspected person.

To be engaged in supporting Satan against God was an act of major treason for which the punishment was death. Since no one could be expected to admit guilt unless forced to do so, it was reasonable to use force to extract confession. The execution of the death sentence upon the accused was for the good of his soul by preventing his continuance in error, and for the general good of mankind in order that the forces of evil, and the enemies of God, might be reduced. The white witch, who claimed to effect cures, and to influence by spells for a beneficent end only, and who did not oppose God or support the Evil One, was, none the less, assisted in the work by the Devil and was therefore no less a heretic than was the malefic witch.

Persons taken on suspicion, and on anonymous accusation, were subjected to torture: torture induced confession; confession, condemnation. Acquittals, as in England, were unheard of on the Continent. There, to be suspected or accused was to be condemned. The Inquisition never gave a verdict of 'not guilty'. On such occasions as 'guilty' was withheld, 'not proven' was the best to be expected.

* An ancient Duchy, part of the Netherlands associated with Cleves.

Every witch brought to trial on the Continent of Europe went through the torture-chamber. Notwithstanding that there was sufficient evidence against the accused to burn her, to which she added her voluntary confession, torture was applied to ensure that the confession was genuine, and complete: the agony inflicted would invariably extract desired additions.

The methods employed were the same throughout Europe; only the savagery of the application of the methods varied. The gruesome performance began with the strappado: the victim's arms were drawn back and tied together at the wrists, the standing part of the line being riven through a pulley secured to the ceiling. The prisoner was hoisted and while suspended thus, the points of accusation on which confession was demanded were persistently repeated. Prisoners being prepared for torture were stripped naked in case they had concealed about them a magical cantrip composed by their master the Devil, that would make them insensible to pain. Female prisoners who were young and prepossessing, including nuns, were invariably raped by the executioner, or his assistant, or by both of them.

If this treatment was not sufficient, strappado was increased to squassation: weights were attached to the feet, the sufferer was drawn up and kept suspended for a while. The rope was then released but before the sufferer struck the ground it was checked, thus causing a violent jerk by which his limbs were disjointed.

Squassation,* an ugly word for an ugly form of wickedness, accomplished in a second the mutilation and agony inflicted over a prolonged period by the rack, a machine to be found in every torture-chamber, and one in frequent employment. What demons out of Hell, what devotees of Satan must they have been who could gleefully turn the crank, gloating, even laughing at the normally heart-breaking, blood-curdling cries of the victim?

Though 'far away and long ago' it is dangerous for the average person to feel secure in the reflection that this 'age of enlightenment' precludes the possibility of such horrors recurring. There are among us many who would preside, most efficiently, over a torture-chamber of the old type. It must not be forgotten that but a few years ago the German nation sanctioned the horror of Hitler's concentration camps, and, cap in hand after the war, pretended they had not been aware of the terror in their midst:

---

* From the same root as Italian *squassare*, to shake violently.

a terror that had shocked and revolted mankind in the remotest corners of the world.

That some of the medieval instruments of torture were employed by the Germans to extract information from prisoners suspected of espionage is not open to doubt. A great favourite with them was the thumb-screw, or pilliwinks, or thumbikins, or grésillous. This is not, as many people think, a means merely of twisting, and so dislocating the victim's thumb (which would be bad enough), but is a form of pressure-device, applied to the nerve-centre at the base of the thumb-nail. It was also used on the big toe. In its construction it was exactly the same as (but on a larger scale of course) the sockets into which the conducting wires are secured in an electrical fitting: that is, a short length of tube with a screw in the periphery that closes into the interior. The persecutors of the witches were often not content to inflict only the agony occasioned by the pressed and bruised sensitive nerve, but they continued to drive the screw inward until the bone was shattered and the marrow squeezed out with the blood.

Persons seized on suspicion only, or as the result of an anonymous accusation, were subjected to torture, and hence were condemned to death for every normal person will, under torture, 'confess' to anything put into his mind by the inquisitors, and will recite a list of names of accomplices: conscientious people would sometimes, upon recession of their agony, withdraw their forced accusations of others, but such heroism availed nothing: those whom they had named were seized, accused and tortured in their turn, and the accuser was again tortured in order to force a repetition of the former 'confession'.

Many of the torturers' victims were elderly women whose vitality was not equal to the ordeal. Death supervened and, according to the forensic argumentation of the time, proved their guilt. Death was not due to the official violence to which the victim had been subjected, but was brought about by the contrivance of the devil in order to prevent her revealing some especial secret to which she was privy.

The man who extracted a 'confession' from Alice Gooderidge at Burton,* by putting her into tight shoes and sitting her close to the fire, simply took a leaf from the Continental torturer's book, for there the boots, or Spanish boots, were in constant use.

* Page 37.

The territorial designation does not indicate that this particular aid to brutality had been invented by the Spanish Inquisition which in popular estimation represents the quintessence of cruelty. The truth is that the Spanish Inquisition, which was national and independent, was more merciful than the Papal Inquisition: admittedly, that is not saying very much in its favour.

The boots were not tight, as the shoes at Burton. On the contrary they were loose, knee-high, and made from very stout, tough leather, or else they were of metal. The victim was strapped into a chair (sometimes having sharp spikes at all pressure points) and into the boots of leather was poured boiling water, and into those of metal, molten lead.

When the boots were not employed, the prisoner was sometimes dropped bodily into a tub full of scalding water containing lime, and a substitute for the thumb-screw was to tear the finger- and toe-nails off with pincers;* sometimes red-hot tongs were used to seize, and twist off pieces of flesh. A person's repeated declaration of innocence was considered a sound reason for continuing, and increasing the severity of torture.

Robbins† gives a 'Verbatim Report of the first day's torture of a woman accused of witchcraft at Prossneck, Germany, in 1629. The hangman bound her hands, cut her hair, and placed her on the ladder. He threw alcohol over her head and set fire to it so as to burn her hair to the roots.

'He placed strips of sulphur under her arms and around her back and set fire to them.

'He tied her hands behind her back and pulled her up to the ceiling.

'He left her hanging there from three to four hours while he went to breakfast.

'On his return he threw alcohol over her back and set fire to it.

'He attached very heavy weights on her body and drew her up again to the ceiling. After that he put her back on the ladder and placed a very rough plank full of sharp points against her body. Having thus arranged her, he jerked her up again to the ceiling.

'Then he squeezed her thumbs and big toes in the vice,‡ and he trussed her arms with a stick, and in this position kept her

---

* This was a method used frequently by the Germans during the last war on prisoners of war suspected of espionage.

† op. cit.   ‡ Thumbscrew.

hanging about a quarter of an hour, until she fainted away several times.

'Then he squeezed the calves and the legs in a vice, always alternating the torture with questioning.

'Then he whipped her with a rawhide whip to cause the blood to flow out over her shift.

'Once again he placed her thumbs and big toes in the vice and left her in this agony on the torture stool from 10 a/m to 1 p/m while the hangman and the court officials went out to get a bite to eat.'

In the afternoon the poor creature was again whipped, and this routine was repeated the following day.

The major charge brought against the witches was the pact with the devil: no such charge was brought against their persecutors, and one feels that the reason for their immunity was that they were themselves incarnate demons, from the judges down to the hangman's junior assistant.

The idea of the witches' pact with the devil was developed from Isaiah XXVIII, 15, 'we have entered into a league with death; we have made a covenant with hell'.

Paulus Grillandus was Papal Judge in the Rome area, and author of an important work on witchcraft.* It was he who classified the pact into two categories; the private pact, and the public pact. The former enabled the witch to bind herself to the service of Satan by indirect means, as, for example, by proxy: the latter was the subject of either a 'public' ceremony performed with due solemnity before a gathering of witches, or was executed by a deed of agreement, duly signed, the 'ink' employed generally being the witch's own blood. Grillandus was in a position to establish as one of the facts of witchcraft this lawyer's scheme of how the allegiance to the devil was brought about, by the simple process of torturing prisoners until they confirmed his assertions. Fifty years later there were to be seen specimens of 'genuine' written pacts between the devil and his devotees, each of which was couched in the formal phrases that would, at the period, have been employed in the drafting of an agreement between two men of business.

With the conception of an agreement between man and demon

---

* *Tractus de Hereticis et Sortilegiis* (ca. 1525).

there developed the Faust legend. The result was that serious-minded natural philosophers, alchemists, mathematicians and others were suspected of having sold their souls to the devil in exchange for his granting to them superior knowledge and ability, to be at their command over a term of years.

The conception was not new: the early Church had condemned the desire for secular knowledge as part of the devil's dominion. To study natural science—or what passed for it—was to cast doubt upon Genesis, but mankind's urge towards secular enlightenment could not be suppressed, and in the Middle Ages astrology and alchemy were studies that attracted many men and lured them into the danger of being considered magicians.

This delusion died hard. Even Dr Dee, a man of vast intellectual ability, whose powers were appreciated by Queen Elizabeth I, and who lived at least two hundred years before his time, was accused of practising witchcraft and necromancy, and of causing the death of children by his magical conjurations. He escaped with his life, but he lost (hence, mankind lost) a large and valuable manuscript library when the mob broke into his house at Mortlake and burned it.

On completion of the pact the witch received the devil's mark: a kind of badge or symbol of affiliation. This, like so many other ideas relating to the organization of witchcraft, originated not with the witches themselves, but with their persecutors. Many victims of the witchcraft mania were illiterate peasant women with no ideas beyond the lore of kitchen, nursery, and the hen-coop, but their persecutors were men of intellect. Ludovico Maria Sinistrari was, in the seventeenth century, Professor of Theology at Pavia University, consultant to the Supreme Tribunal of the Inquisition of Rome, and author of (*inter alia*) *De Daemonialitate* which treats of matters relating to mankind's relationships with demons. In this work he says: 'The demon imprints some mark [which] is not always of the same shape . . . sometimes it is the likeness of a hare, sometimes like a toad's foot, sometimes a spider, a puppy, a dormouse. It is imprinted on the most secret parts of the body; with men, under the eyelids, or perhaps under the armpits, or on the lips or shoulders, the anus or elsewhere; with women, it is generally on the breasts or private parts.'

These devil's marks, in reality merely scars, or skin blemishes such as might be discovered on any human body, were supposed to be anaesthetic, hence, pricking was a universally accepted test for witchcraft. If the prisoner apparently felt no pain when a needle was driven into the devil's mark, it was proof of guilt.

There might have been a number of different reasons for the anaesthesia, and high on the list must be placed the psychological reaction to the shock of exposure and the rough handling. Further, tactile sensibility varies in different parts of the body: two points pressed as much as an inch apart on the back of any normal person will be cognized as one point only.

The witch's mark was something altogether different from the devil's mark, although the two tend to become confused. The devil, on the occasion of concluding the pact, and making his mark, presented the witch with an imp, or a familiar spirit, who would work all kinds of evil, including the killing of human beings at the witch's command. The two gifts were related. As a reward for their faithful services these imps were allowed to suck a little of the witch's blood, and the witch mark was the 'little teat or pop' that made this possible.

The witch's mark was sought for—and found—in the same localities as devil's marks, but they differed from the latter, which were, as a rule, mere flat discolorations, by being in the nature of cutaneous excrescences; warts and the like, which also had the characteristic of being anaesthetic to pricking.

In a few cases (but in very few), polymastia or polythelia was discovered, but the vast majority of these 'little teats or pops' were simply warts, moles, or other common blemishes of a like nature. Elizabeth Wright, one of the accused in the case of Thomas Darling's imposture,* was 'found to have behind her right shoulder a thing much like the udder of a ewe that giveth suck, with two teats, like unto two great warts,† the one behind under her armhole, the other a handfull off towards the top of her shoulder. Being demanded how long she had those teats, she answered she was born so.'

Alice Samuels, aged eighty, sent to her death by the Throckmorton girls, was found, by the jailer who removed the clothes from the body, to have 'a little lump of flesh, in manner sticking out as if it had been a teat, to the length of half an inch, . . . not willing to conceal so strange a matter, and decently covering

* See page 36.
† Which is doubtless what they were.

that privy place a little above where it grew, they* made open show thereof unto divers that stood by.'

The dark, devil-directed period of English history that incited the people against their true King—martyred Charles—gave rise also to Master Matthew Hopkins, 'Witch Finder Generall'. Hopkins, 'a lawyer of little note', failing to obtain a living in Ipswich, moved to Manningtree and soon seized the opportunity of turning Roundhead bigotry, brutality and ignorance to good personal account.

Of him, Montague Summers says,† 'he had neither the training nor the knowledge to deal with the hideous anarchy of witchcraft; his motive was vilest lust for gains and this swept both innocent and guilty alike into his net. He desired not the glory of God but the fullness of Mammon. He did not fight against the armies of the devil but shed blood to fat his purse. He was no true man but a charlatan and a deceiver, "a monster of impudence and iniquity", one who plunged into deep and dangerous waters from no sense of duty but from an itch for notoriety, a greed for self—it was not so much his crusade as his insincerity which made his name stink in men's nostrils, which causes him to be written down even today as the foulest of foul parasites, an obscene bird of prey of the tribe of Judas and of Cain'.

Hopkins was a fiendish torturer fundamentally as diabolical as any who applied the apparatus legal on the Continent of Europe. His methods were to keep his victims without either food or sleep, sitting cross-legged on a high stool, or upon a table. Forty-eight, or seventy-two hours of such cramped sitting, starvation and sleeplessness, reduced the prisoner to a state in which it is likely that she was barely aware of the fact that she was speaking and totally oblivious to what she might have been saying.

Hopkins's 'head assistant' was John Stearne, and he had another, a female, one Mary Phillipps, evidently a prototype of the females who, protected by huge, savage alsatian dogs, inflicted torture in Hitler's concentration camps.

The three of them, together with junior assistants, would keep a prisoner walking up and down a room, night and day, without respite, until, dazed with fatigue, he confessed his guilt.

* The jailer and his wife.
† *The Discovery of Witches* ... Cayrne Press, 1928.

Hopkins's first victim was a helpless hag named Elizabeth Clarke, who after sufficient brutality confessed, and accused five others. Having thus set latent evil in motion, neighbours rallied round, informing him of suspect witches, and thirty-two accused persons were brought before the local justices and sent for trial at Chelmsford.

The Witch-Finder General made a speciality of searching for, and of course finding, the witch's mark, 'the little teat or pop' by which she suckled her familiars, and the unfortunate Elizabeth Clarke went to the gallows having been found guilty of 'entertaining evil spirits'. The Witch-Finder General's information, given on oath, and confirmed by John Stearne, included the statement that 'the said Elizabeth forthwith told this informant and, one Master Sterne . . . [that] if they would stay and do the said Elizabeth no hurt, she would call one of her white imps and play with it on her lap. But this informant told her they would not allow of it. And that staying there a while longer, the said Elizabeth confessed she had carnal copulation with the devil six or seven years, and he would appear to her three or four times a week at her bedside, and go to bed with her and lie with her half a night together, in the shape of a proper gentleman, with a laced band, having the whole proportion of a man and say to her "Bessie, I must lie with you." And she never did deny him.'

The investigators stayed another quarter of an hour when four imps entered the room : a white dog, a greyhound, a polecat and a black imp. The female assistant swore to having seen the imps and so did two lesser associates, Edward Porsley and Frances Mills.

Hopkins was the author, in 1647, of a pamphlet entitled *The Discovery of Witches: in answer to several queries, lately delivered to the Judges of Assize for the county of Norfolk*. The proud author declared his work to be for 'the benefit of the whole kingdom'. In it he claimed that his unique abilities of detection were the outcome of experience 'which though it be meanly esteemed of, yet [is] the surest and safest way to judge by'. He explains that 'the Discoverer never travelled far for it, but in March, 1644, he had some seven or eight of that horrible sect of Witches living in the Towne where he lived, a Towne in *Essex*, called *Maningtree*, with divers other adjacent Witches of other Towns, who every six weeks in the night (being always on the

Friday night) had their meetings close by his house, and had their severall solemne sacrifices there offered to the Devill, one of which this discoverer heard speaking to her *Imps* one night, and bid them goe to another Witch, who was thereupon apprehended, and searched by women who had for many yeares knowne the Devill's marks, and found to have three teats about her, which honest women have not: so upon command from the *Justice* they were to keep her from sleep two or three nights, expecting in that time to see her *familiars*, which the fourth night she called in by their several names, and told them what shapes, a quarter of an houre before they came in, there being ten of us in the roome; the first she called was,

1. *Holt*, who came in like a white kitling.

2. *Jarmara*, who came in like a fat Spaniel without any legs at all, she said she kept him fat, for she clapt her hand on her belly, and said he suckt good blood from her body.

3. *Vinegar Tom*, who was like a long-legg'd greyhound, with an head like an Oxe, with a long taile and broad eyes, who when this discoverer spoke to, and bade him goe to the place provided for him and his Angels, immediately transformed himselfe into the shape of a child of foure yeeres old without a head, and gave halfe a dozen turnes about the house, and vanished at the doore.

4. *Sack and Sugar*, like a black Rabbet.

5. *Newes*, like a Polcat. All these vanished away in a little time. Immediately after this Witch confessed severall other Witches, from whom she had her *Imps*, and named to divers women where their marks were, the number of their *Marks*, and *Imps*, and *Imps* names, as *Elemanzer*, *Pyewacket*, *Peckin the Crown*, *Grizzel*, *Greedigut*, etc., which no mortall could invent; and upon their searches the same Markes were found, the same number, and in the same place, and the like confessions from them of the same Imps, (though they knew not that we were told before) and so preached one another thereabouts that joyned together in the like damnable practise, that in one Hundred in *Essex*, 29 were condemned at once, 4 brought 25 miles to be hanged, where this Discoverer lives, for sending the Devill like a Beare to kill him in his garden, so by seeing diverse of the mens Papps, and trying wayes with hundreds of them, he gained this experience, and for ought he knowes any man else may find them

as well as he and his company, if they had the same skill and experience.'

This literary masterpiece was written and published by Hopkins as a defence against criticism that ultimately came to be levelled. His troubles began in April, 1646, when a clergyman named John Goule preached against him, and published a pamphlet entitled, *Select Cases of Conscience*, wherein Hopkins's brutality was exposed. After this, which, coming from the hand of a clergyman could not be ignored by the judges, the Witch-Finder General's accusations were not so readily accepted as they hitherto had been. Torture was contrary to English law, and Master Matthew Hopkins employed methods of extracting confession that ranked as torture without instruments.

In *The Discovery of Witches*, which is in the form of questions and answers, he displays sufficient cunning to give the appearance of impartiality: for example, on the matter of 'the little teat or pop' he gives the other side of the subject in '*Querie 5*. Many poore people are condemned for having a Pap, or Teat about them, whereas many People (especially ancient People) are, and have been a long time, troubled with natural wretts on severall parts of their bodies, and other natural excrescencies as Hemerodes, Piles, Child-bearing, etc. And these shall be judged only by one man alone, and a woman, and so accused or acquitted.'

His reply is that 'the parties so judging can justify their skill to any, and shew good reasons why such markes are not meerly naturall . . . and for further answer for their private judgements alone, it is most false and untrue, for never was any man tryed by search of his body, but commonly a dozen of the ablest men in the parish, or else where, were present, and most commonly as many skilfull matrons and midwives . . .'

'He judgeth by the unusualnes of the place where he findeth the teats . . . if a witch plead the markes found are Emerods, and I finde them on the bottome of the back-bone, shall I assent with him. Knowing they are not neere that veine, and so others by child-bearing, when it may be they are in the contrary part.

'They are most commonly insensible, and feele neither pin, needle, aule, etc., thrust through them.'

Trial by ordeal was used as a means of determining the guilt or innocence of an accused person in the archaic civilizational period, at least three thousand years B.C. It survived in Anglo-

Saxon times, and under Edward the Confessor the water ordeal became a general method of detecting guilt. It was not abolished until 1219, but it survived as an unofficial folk test of witchcraft for several centuries after its official abolition, and took on a new lease of life after the publication of James VI and I's *Demonology*, which, being Scottish, was influenced in its views by Continental, not by English attitudes of mind.

The King's book added a mystical sanction to the ordeal by suggesting that God had given to water the power to reject a witch as a sign that she had wilfully rejected the water of baptism, hence, guilt was proven by the victim floating, and innocence by her sinking.

The person to be thus tested was 'cross-bound'. The left thumb was securely lashed to the right big toe, the left big-toe to the right thumb, and thus trussed the suspect was lowered into an expanse of water, either static or flowing. Horse-ponds and mill-ponds were generally the scenes of such trials, but streams also served.

'Swimming a witch' was a brand of entertainment supplied by the Witch-Finder General, and it is reasonably certain that there was a crowded audience on each occasion. However, despite its popularity, no one knew better than ex-lawyer Hopkins that it was illegal, and in his *Discovery* . . . he cunningly catered for official disapproval:

'*Querie* 10. But there has been an abominable, inhumane, and unmerciful tryall of these poore creatures, by tying them, and heaving them into the water; a tryall not allowed by Law or concience, and I would fain know the reason for that.

'*Answer*. It is not denied but many were so served as had Papps, and floated, others that had none were tryed with them and sunk, but marke the reasons.

'For first the Divel's policie is great, in perswading to come of their owne accord to be tryed, perswading them their marks are so close they shall not be found out, so as diverse have come 10 or 12 Miles to be searched of their own accord, and hanged for their labour (as one *Meggs*, a Baker, did, who lived within 7 miles of *Norwich* and was hanged at Norwich Assizes for witchcraft), then when they find that the Devil tells them false they reflect on him, and he, (as 40 have confessed) adviseth them to be sworne, and tels them they shall sinke and be cleared that way, then when they be tryed that way and floate, they see the Devill deceives them again, and have so laid open his treacheries.

'2. It was never brought in against any of them at their tryals as any evidence.*

'3. King *James* in his *Demonology* saith . . . [there follows a paraphrase of what King James had written on the subject].

'4. Observe these generations of Witches, if they be at any time abused by being called Whore, Theefe etc. by any where they live, they are the readiest to cry and wring their hands, and shed tears in abundance and run with full and sorrowfull acclamations to some Justice of the Peace, and with many yeares make their complaints: but now behold their stupidity; nature or the elements reflection from them, when they are accused for this horrible and damnable sin of Witchcraft, they never alter or change their countenances, nor let one Teare fall. . . .'

In self-defence 'he utterly denies the confession of a witch' [that is, rejects it] when it is forced from her by each and all of the methods he customarily employed, and he declares 'what confession of a Witch is of validity and force in his judgement, to hang a Witch: when a Witch is first found with teats, then sequested from her house, which is onely to keep her old associates from her, and so by good counsell brought into a sad condition, by understanding of the horribleness of her sin, and the judgement threatened against her; and knowing the Devill's malice and subtile circumventions, is brought to remorse and sorrow for complying with Satan so long, and disobeying God's sacred Commands, doth then desire to unfold her mind with much bitterness, and then without any of the before-mentioned hard usages or questions put to her, doth of her owne accord declare what was the occasion of the Devil's appearing to her, whether ignorance, pride, anger, malice, etc. was predominant over her, she doth then declare what speech they had, what familiars he sent her, what number of spirits, what names they had, what shape they were in, what imployment she set them about to severall persons in severall places, (unknowne to the hearers), all which mischiefs being proved to be done, at the same time she confessed to the same parties for the same cause, and all effected, is testimony enough against her for all her denyalls.'

* Of course not. Even at that period the most biased judge could not accept illegal evidence.

Hopkins may have been a bad and unsuccessful lawyer, but as a lawyer he would have known how to write clear and convincing English. His *Discovery* . . . from first to last is confused and confusing, and a just conclusion is that it was deliberately so. The literary effort did not save him: his services were no longer in high demand, and the heavy sums he pocketed—despite his denial of this in the *Discovery* . . .—were no longer to be his.

He retired to Manningtree with sufficient ill-gotten wealth to live in comfort till his death, 'after a long sickness of a Consumption' in 1647. This happy event is recorded in the parish Register of Mistley-cum-Manningtree, 'August 12, Matthew Hopkins, son of Mr James Hopkins, Minister at Wenham, was buried at Mistley.'

Popular imagination could not allow so vile, so brutal, so feared a character to sink into a simple grave from natural causes.

Legend grew that he had himself been a wizard and had stolen from the devil the private register of all witches in England. It was believed that he was himself eventually put to the water ordeal, and he floated like a cork.

Samuel Butler, the 'Ingoldsby' of his period, whose *Hudibras* was such a constant source of amusement to King Charles II, wrote of Hopkins: *

Has not this present *Parliament*
A Leger to the *Devil* sent,
Fully empower'd to treat about
Finding revolted *Witches* out:
And has not he, within a year,
Hang'd three score of them in one *shire*?
Some only for not being *drown'd*,
And some for sitting above ground,
Whole *days* and *nights* upon their breeches,
And feeling pain, were hang'd for *Witches*.
And some for putting *Knavish* tricks
Upon *green-geese* and *turkey chicks*,
Or *Pigs*, that suddenly deceast.
Of griefs unnat'ral as be guest;
Who after prov'd himself a *Witch*,
And made a Rod for his own *breech*.

* Part II, Canto iii.

One does not go so far as to deny the existence of demons. Were not a host of them exorcized from the possessed man, and cast upon the Gadarene swine? But one can hardly accept the suggestion that all the dogs and cats and hares that trotted along beside the hags who came before the 'justices' on charges of witchcraft were indeed demons incarnate, or that the prisoners untutored and superstitious, distraught, and confused by fear if nothing worse who 'confessed' recounting scenes of wholesale slaughter of numerous head of cattle by, say, their attendant mouse, were indeed possessed of such devastating powers.

Phantasy is a form of day-dreaming to which all human beings are subject, but neurotic and hysterical persons excessively so. This psychological cinematograph, projected from the unconscious, usually depicts the fulfilment of a tabooed desire, and most frequently is of a sexual character.

Many of the persons accused of practising witchcraft were neurotic or hysterical or epileptic, and all were abnormal even if they differed from their neighbours only by being of a superior spiritual and intellectual quality, hence, what is known in modern times as highly-strung, and therefore no less susceptible to intense phantasy than were the hysterics and the neurotics.

Even in normal people phantasy may be externalized: may be translated from the scene of the mind, lifted out of the subjective and placed in the objective mental life so that it seems as though the phantasmagorical experience has an existence in fact. The day-dream has become a memory.

Since there is no better guinea-pig than oneself, the present writer will, in support of the foregoing, place on record that he recently wasted a considerable amount of valuable time by scouring a maze of small streets in search of a certain shop whose window-display had attracted his attention when, hurrying to keep an appointment, he had passed through the area. In all, three visits were paid to the district, and the search for the shop became more avid on each occasion. At last, very angry at failure, and when he was on the point of enquiring from a police constable who had come into view, it was suddenly revealed, like a light being switched on in a dark room, that the shop had no objective existence, but was simply an externalized phantasy (or perhaps night-dream).

The sudden emergence from this second state, and the return to normal rational mental processes made the experience both startling and amusing. Such a shop, a kind of ironmonger's and engineer's supply store, could not possibly exist in the district, which is a market for exotic fabrics; and the very modern, attractive window consisted of a 'contemporary' arrangement of items of the past: drop-feed sight-lubricators, steam-engine governors, rolls of leather belting and split wood pulleys for power transmission, hurricane-lamps, and glass chimneys for table-lamps.

The visual impression is, after nearly two years, as intense, vivid and realistic as it was at the time of the experience, but there is no longer a trace of delusion: the address of that fascinating shop is High Street, Fairy Land.

Such a psychological process may have been productive of the witches' claims to have had a sexual relationship with the devil. However, Inquisitors and justices took the matter very seriously and demanded the fullest and most intimate details.

Theologians and demonologists, men of superior intellectual powers and great learning, discussed the matter with conscientious attention in order to explain how the devil, a spirit, could copulate with a woman of flesh and blood, and having decided that the devil could assume any form he wished in order to perform the act, they found themselves confronted with an even graver problem in its logical sequence, namely, could the devil beget offspring?

Some witches claimed that the devil entered their bed in the form of a man, although he might rise from it in some other shape: a bull, a stag, or a dog. All agreed that intercourse was painful and unpleasant, many stated that his penis was part horn (or iron) and part flesh, but after that their experiences differed very considerably.

De Lancre (1553–1631) was a French lawyer and, as a judge, he proudly boasted of having condemned to the stake six hundred witches (burning was a Continental custom: English witches were hanged). He wrote, *inter alia*, a book entitled *Tableau de l'inconstance des mauvais anges** known by the short title of *Tableau*. It is a detailed description of his investigations of witchcraft in the Pays de Labourd, a Basque territory in south-west

* *Description of the Inconstancy of Evil Angels*, 1612.

Guienne. He declared that the entire population numbering 30,000 were infected but, much to his disappointment, he was unable to burn them all.

One of his victims, Marguerite de Sare, aged seventeen, declared that the devil 'had a member like a mule's, having chosen to imitate that animal as being the best endowed by nature; that it was as long and as thick as an arm.'

Henri Boguet (1550–1619), another lawyer and witch-judge, active in the St Claude region, was author of a book very similar to De Lancre's, in which he said that the witches reported the devil's member to be no longer than a finger, and correspondingly thin. De Lancre comments, 'all that can be said is that Satan serves the witches of Labourd better than he does those of Franche-Comté.'

The devil's ability—or lack of it—was a matter productive of much theorizing. The confessions of the witches were not helpful; some claimed that their intercourse with the devil had resulted in pregnacy and that they had ultimately given birth to a monster, or a composite being. In 1275 Angela de Lebasthe, on trial at Toulouse, declared she had given birth to a creature having a wolf's head and a serpent's tail; another boasted of having been the mother of a two-footed serpent, and a Scottish woman produced 'so misshapen a thing as the like before had not been seen'.

However, not all of the devil's progeny were monsters: the idea of his being capable of begetting offspring appealed to the popular mind and such a parentage was attributed to all persons whom they either feared or hated and the legend of the diabolic descent lingers in relation to certain historical characters: Robert Duke of Normandy was a reputed son of Satan, and his own illegitimate son, William, even more wicked than his father, was he who usurped the Saxon Crown. Merlin was the devil's descendant; so were Martin Luther, Plato, and Alexander. The whole race of Huns were reputed to be devil-begotten.

The contemporaneous theologians and jurists who entertained doubts concerning the devil's ability to become the father of either monster or man contended that the devil, being a spirit, was asexual and notwithstanding his incontestable ability to materialize himself in any shape and of either sex, the physical attributes were matters of appearance only, that the body he used was merely a condensation of air and moisture and for that reason, as many witches declared, he was freezing cold and his ejaculation was like icicles, hence it must be sterile.

This point of view was unpopular and suffered defeat by the supporters of the devil's offspring idea pointing out that although all witches stated that the devil's body was cold and that intercourse with him was painful, not a few of them said that his semen was abnormally hot. In these cases the ejaculation was not generated in the devil's diaphanous body, but was collected by him from normal human night emissions and, in spite of his own subnormal temperature, kept warm by him for the purpose of begetting monsters and evil men to persecute mankind.

Numerous witches asserted that the devil's member was bifurcated and that he effected intromission of the vagina and the rectum simultaneously, and not a few improved on that by declaring it to be tripartite; the third appendage, which was of great length, he presented for penilingus.

It seems that the devil, notwithstanding his abnormal, in fact, miraculous potency, was unable to fulfil all his obligations, and was compelled to delegate a certain class of imp to represent him and act for him: namely, the incubus, who performs the sexual act with women, and the succubus, who pays similar attentions to men. The theologians, on the grounds that demons were spirits, and spirits were sexless, argued that there was but one class of imp involved who assumed the sex suitable to the occasion.

Montague Summers says, in *Witchcraft and Black Magic*, '. . . Witches perform the carnal act with incubus devils, an abomination deeply deplored by Pope Innocent VIII in the Great Bull of 1484. "It has come to our knowledge and stricken are we to the heart to learn it, that many persons of both sexes utterly jeopardizing their souls' salvation are wont to have connection in horrid venery with evil spirits, both incubi and succubae." The incubus (*one who lies upon** anything, and hence in common phrase, a burden, a heavy task, or trouble) is an evil spirit who assumes a male form; a succuba (in late Latin, a harlot) is the evil spirit assuming a female form, and since spirits in their own nature have no sex, the famous Dominican, Charles René Billuart, in his *Treatise upon Angels*, points out that "the same evil spirit may serve as a succuba to a man, and as an incubus to a woman."

* Montague Summers's italic.

'St Albertus Magnus relates how: "the accounts of entities, both incubi and succubae, are most exactly true and beyond all dispute. We ourselves know persons who have had actual experience of this. . . ."

'At Bologna, in 1468, a sorcerer was condemned for keeping a common brothel with succubas. John Nider, O.P., Prior of the Strict Dominican house at Basle, in his *Formicarius*, a treatise on Visions and Revelations, written during the Council of Basle, 1435–1437, records (Book V, Chapter ix), how at the time of the Council of Constance (1414–1417) a succubus residing in that city accumulated immense wealth by her harlotries.'

The question of whether or not offspring could result from a woman's intercourse with an incubus was discussed, and followed the same lines as that concerning Satan himself. Thomas Aquinas, in *Summa Theologica* said, 'Nevertheless, if sometimes children result from intercourse with demons, it is not because of the semen emitted by them, or from the bodies they have assumed, but through the semen taken from some man for this purpose, seeing that the same demon who acts as a succubus for a man becomes an incubus for a woman.'

Ludovico Maria Sinistrari (1622–1701), a Franciscan, who was professor of theology at Pavia, consultant to the Supreme Tribunal of the Inquisition, and Vicar-General to the Archbishop of Avignon, said, in his *De Daemonialitate*, 'What incubi introduce into the womb is not ordinary human semen in normal quantity, but abundant, very thick, very warm, rich in spirits and free from serosity. This, moreover, is an easy thing for them since they merely have to choose ardent, robust men, whose semen is naturally very copious, and with whom the succubus has relations; and then the incubus copulates with a woman of a like constitution, taking care that both shall enjoy a more than normal orgasm for the greater the venerial excitement the more abundant is the semen.'

Sinistrari supports the unorthodox point of view that incubi were not ordinary imps of hell, but were in a class apart, being spirits intermediate between men and angels who degraded themselves by falling to the sin of lust, but by so doing honoured mankind.

On this theme Montague Summers is enlightening: *'In ante-

* *Witchcraft and Black Magic.*

diluvian times it is recorded "that the sons of God saw the daughters of men that they were fair; and they took them wives of all which they chose. There were giants in the earth in those days; and also after that, when the sons of God came in unto the daughters of men, and they bore children to them, the same became mighty men which were of old, men of renown. . . ." (Genesis VI, 2, 4 [A.V.]). Philo in his Platonic treatise *On the Giants*, for all his view of transcendental allegory, warns us: "Let no one suppose that what is here said is a myth".

'. . . Dr Driver, in his excursuses on the *Book of Genesis*, fifth edition, 1906, pp. 82–3, a commentary which has as its aim "to interpret the meaning of each book of the Bible in the light of modern knowledge to English readers", explicitly states: "the 'sons of God' (or 'of the gods') denotes elsewhere semi-divine supra-mundane beings, such as, when regarded, as is more usually the case, as agents executing a Divine commission, are called Angels (i.e. 'messengers'). And this, which is the oldest interpretation of Genesis VI, 2, is the only sense in which the expression can be legitimately understood here." If we read "Sons of God", it is figurative, and signifies spiritual beings created by God. If we take it as "sons of gods", it implies members of that class of Divine beings to which Yahweh himself in one sense belongs, although immeasurably inferior to Him. This is hardly admissible, and we are far safer if we prefer "sons of God".

'Dr N. P. Williams, in his Bampton Lectures, *The Ideas of the Fall and of Original Sin*, 1927, writes of the first eight verses of the sixth chapter of Genesis: "As these verses stand, the only construction to be put upon them appears to be as follows: The 'sons of God' are Divine beings, of an order inferior to Yahweh— or, to employ a later and more familiar term, 'angels'—who gave way to lusts, and committed sin by deserting their heavenly abode and mingling the divine essence with the seed of man. This unnatural action introduces the principle of evil into humanity." . . . It is very plain that these "sons of God" became upon their apostasy Incubi demons . . . [which] is maintained by a very large number of learned men.'

Montague Summers gives among the supporting extracts from the works of weighty commentators, the following from 'Dom Dominic Schram, a famous Benedictine writer, in his *Institutes of Mystical Theology*, published in Paris in 1848. . . . "It is positively certain and proven that—whatever the incredulous may say—there actually exist such demons, incubi or succubi. The men and women who suffer these impudicities are either so abandoned that they invite and allure demons, or else they freely consent to the promptings of demons tempting them to indulge in so dark abominations. That these and other filthy wretches may be assaulted and overcome by the demon we cannot doubt, and I myself have known several persons who, although they were greatly troubled on account of their crimes and utterly loathed this foul intercourse with the demon, were nevertheless compelled by violence, and sorely against their will to endure these horrible assaults of Satan." I remember Monsieur Aubolt de la Haulte Chambre relating how once, when he was accidentally benighted, he was given hospitality and slept in a very ancient bedroom, where he passed a most unhappy and disturbed night. There appeared in the darkness strange lascivious shapes which seemed absolutely corporeal and human. He was in misery until the dawn. The result, after he had reached home, was an indisposition of several days due to fatigue and excessive nervous strain. This caused him to miss an engagement with J.-K. Huysmans, to whom, when they next met, he disclosed the reason of his recent illness. "My poor boy!" exclaimed the great man. "Did you not know that, explain it as we may, the house you were staying at, at least the room you actually occupied, is infested by these fleshmongering spirits, these bawdy incubi?"'

Nuns and female saints were most particularly subject to the attentions of incubi. St Margaret of Cortona was troubled by a demon who persisted in singing lewd songs while the saint was engaged in prayer. Sinistrari informs us of the case of a nun who always retired to her cell after dinner and locked the door. Her next-door neighbour, ear pressed to the thin partition, heard most suspicious sounds and, in the way that was common enough in convents, fetched the Superior. This lady, in her authority, demanded that the door should be opened immediately, which was done without delay, and the suspected nun proved to be alone. The inquisitive next-door neighbour, however, contrived to bore a hole in the partition and on the next occasion, peeping through, saw the nun performing the sexual act with a handsome youth. All the other inmates were given the opportunity of having a peep through the hole, and at length the suspected nun, under threat of torture, confessed to her intimacy with an incubus.

Another nun who confessed to carnal trafficking with a demon declared that he always appeared to her in the likeness of Bishop Sylvanus who, when interrogated on the matter, declared that an incubus must be assuming his likeness. This explanation was, at the time, accepted without hesitation.

Priests observed that numerous girls and young women, although seeking spiritual aid, were by no means anxious to be rid of their demon lovers, and relationship with incubi was classified in three distinct groups: voluntary intercourse, as practised by witches; involuntary intercourse, brought about by a witch's spells, and totally involuntary intercourse, wherein the demon assaulted his victim.

The entertaining of an incubus was condemned as a sin far greater than normal adultery, or fornication, because the demon lover, being other than human, made intercourse with him a form of bestiality. This point of view was adopted by theologians and jurists all over Europe until the end of the witch persecution mania, and had, in fact, grown up with it. Incubi were believed in at an early date, but their attacks were thought invariably to be against the wills of their victims: there was, in fact, before the witch-trials started, a glimmering of enlightenment. Gervasius of Tilbury records the approved medical opinion in 1214, namely, that nocturnal pollutions were physical phenomena: a point of view not again maintained until Doctor De Saint-André, physician to Louis XV, wrote, in 1725, 'the incubus is most frequently a chimera, which has no more basis than a dream, a perverted imagination, and is very often the invention of a woman. . . . To conceal her sin . . . a nun in name only, a debauchee, who affects the appearance of virtue, will palm off her lover for an incubus. . . .'

Ernest Jones, M.D.,* says, 'Women seem to have been troubled by these nightly visitors more than men, and widows and virgins, more particularly nuns, more than married women. Cloisters were especially infected by incubi, and many instances have been recorded of epidemics of such visitations. The theological teaching about the reality of incubi evidently permitted mani-

* op. cit.

festations that otherwise would have had to find some other means of expression ...

'In the reports of the actual examples of visits by incubi there appears in the most ambiguous way a feature which has special significance. . . . It is that every possible gradation is to be observed between the pleasurable excitement of voluptuousness on the one hand and extreme terror and repulsion on the other. This variation, and the impossibility of demarking it at any point, shows again the intimate connection between libido and morbid dread. It forcibly reminds one of exactly the same gradation that can be observed between erotic dreams and nightmares.'

After several pages of quotation from foreign authors, and examples from their experiences, Ernest Jones returns to the theme: 'We may make an interesting contrast between these pleasant and unpleasant experiences, with all their intermediate types, from several points of view. Psychologically the matter is, thanks to Freud's investigation, very simple. His doctrine of intrapsychic repression gives us the full explanation . . . wishes culminating in unpleasant experiences differ from those of the opposite kind merely in being subject to internal repression or condemnation, so that they are unconscious. Another way of putting this is to say that the erotic wishes in question may be compatible with the standards of the subject's ego, and therefore accepted by it, or not. (In more recent terminology one may say that such wishes may be either ego-syntonic or ego-dystonic.) The gradual evolution of insight into this state of affairs provides a curious study in human nature, to which we shall now turn.

'It has been necessary to lay stress on the gradualness of the distinction between these two types of wishes, or of the experiences they gave rise to respectively, and, although we have said that certain of these wishes are acceptable to the ego, this is, strictly speaking, never completely true. That is to say, all erotic wishes without exception that disturb sleep, have to overcome a certain amount of internal opposition, some being, of course, more heavily censured than others. Even at the present day it is customary for nocturnal emissions to be ascribed rather to some 'natural' physical activity on the part of the sexual apparatus rather than to any actual wishes that set this apparatus in operation. The tendency has thus always been to avoid any personal responsibility for nocturnal erotic wishes, even those most lightly censured, and to ascribe them to some other agency. In the history of mankind we can clearly distinguish two stages in this respect. To begin with, the dream experiences were ascribed to the action of external personal agents, such as lewd demons; the wishes were, as a psychiatrist would say, projected outward on to other beings. The second stage consisted in projecting the wishes on to various bodily processes, non-mental and non-sexual. We are even yet only beginning to emancipate ourselves from this form of projection, and the medical world in particular shows the greatest timidity in making this step. It will further become plain that this evolution proceeded earlier in the case of those dream wishes that are relatively acceptable to the ego than in the case of strongly repressed ones; in consequence, superstitious causes— demons or indigestion, according to the epoch—continued to be evoked in explanation of the unpleasant experiences later than for the pleasurable and evidently sexual experiences.'

W. Sampson, the dramatist, whose play, *The Vow-Breaker, or the Fair Maid of Clifton* (1636), puts the following in the mouth of Ursula, 'I have heard you say that dreams and visions were fabulous; and yet one time I dreamt fowle water ran through the floor, and the next day the house was on fire. You us'd to say hobgoblins, fairies and the like were nothing but our own affrightments, and yet o' my troth, cuz, I once dream'd of a young batchelour, and was ridd with the night-mare. But come, so my concience be cleere, I never care how fowle my dreames are.'*

It ought perhaps to be mentioned that the 'true' incubus was a demon who had assumed basic human shape, the differences, such as cloven hooves in place of feet, or bifurcation of the penis, were but minor. Transubstantiation might occur after the event. In many of the witches' confessions it may be observed, the demonesque sexual partner appeared in the form of a beast, or that of a composite creature, part human and part animal. Canine, bovine, equine and monstrous sexual partners were not strictly incubi.

In the Middle Ages incubi were accepted by both canon and civil law, and the distinction between sexual relationship with incubi and incubation was more clearly observed and more widely known than it is at the present day. Incubation was the practice of sleeping in a sacred place; in a grave, or by a holy-well, or in

* Quoted by Dr Ernest Jones.

the temple, for oracular purposes: poets to receive inspiration; the sick, and particularly the sterile and the impotent, to receive from the gods the blessing of a cure. The temple of Aesculapius was an incubation centre that receives much attention in ancient Greek literature, hence our immediate ancestors—either educated in the classics or not at all—thought that incubation was Greek in origin. It was (one might safely say 'is'), however, far older than Greece and Rome, neither is its practice confined to the Mediterranean basin. It is as old as Egypt and as wide as the world. In incubation, union is achieved not with an evil demon, but with a member of the local pantheon, or with a divine being dispatched by the gods and authorized by them to bestow the gift, or effect the cure desired by the suppliant.

In the temple of Aesculapius the serpent, symbolizing the phallus, hence related to ancestor worship, represented the god, and in classical antiquity many famous men were said to be sons of the serpent. The early Christian Church degraded the serpent and equated him to Satan, but the pagan rite lived on and the Archangel Michael, and both St Damien and St Hubert were competent to cure sterility.

In the first decade of this century incubation was used in remote rural areas as a fecundity rite, the sleeper wrapping himself in a sheepskin in the old, primitive way. The present writer is not aware of any reports of the continuation of the superstition since the First World War, but holds the opinion that it is still practised in spite of television carrying the ways of a sophisticated world into the humble habitations of the most insular and isolated of folk.

Chapter Four

IN 1933, Dr Margaret Murray published a book entitled *The God of the Witches*.* All who admired her as an Egyptologist, anthropologist and folk-lorist of outstanding merit were saddened by this publication because in it Miss Murray had bent the facts to fit the theory.

The European witches, according to Miss Murray, were merely devotees of a secretly surviving pre-Christian cult, and in order to bolster up this theory she asserted that the covens, or confraternities in which they were supposed to be organized consisted in thirteen members. She adduced eighteen examples; nine from Scotland, five from England, and the remaining four from places as wide asunder as North America, France, Germany and Ireland. Apart from the manifest absurdity of suggesting that eighteen out of several thousand trials conducted in the areas mentioned during the period under review (namely, from 1567 to 1673) are representative, even this meagre few reveal, when examined by other scholars, that the number thirteen is not correct.

L'Estrange Ewen says,† 'Examining the five English examples cited by Miss Murray, viz. St Osyth, 1582; Lancashire, 1613; St Albans, 1649; Somerset, 1664; and Northumberland, 1673, it does not appear that they in any way support her argument. With regard to the St Osyth case . . . the gaol calendar notices twelve witches arraigned. . . . Turning to the famous Lancashire trial, 1613, . . . thirty-five witches can be traced, but although twenty-six of these comprised the first two groups they cannot with any reason be divided equally. In the St Albans affair John

---

* She had previously (1921) published *The Witchcult in Western Europe. A Study in Anthropology*. Her last book, *My First Hundred Years*, was published in 1963 on her hundredth birthday.

† *Witchcraft and Demonism.*

Palmer named Elizabeth Knott and thirteen others as being witches in Hitchin, Norton and Weston. . . . The Somersetshire witches of 1665, as noticed in Hunt's depositions, were twenty-five in number, forming two groups, between which no connection is traceable. . . . The Northumberland servant maid, Anne Armstrong (1673), being an hysteric, is not worthy of credence. Presumably she had absorbed some Scottish beliefs, and tells of thirteen women besides the black man, she herself making a fifteenth; and again she declares that every "coven" of thirteen had a devil, i.e. fourteen in all. Neither in these cases nor elsewhere can anything be found supporting the view that the witches worked in parties of a fixed size, and the Coven may be ruled out of English witchcraft.'

Indeed, it is presumable that all the grouping of witches that took place was fortuitous, because any kind of constitution would demand organization, and it is manifest from the general ignorance revealed during the trial that the witches, with but few exceptions, lacked the ability and the temperament, the knowledge of procedure and the executive ability to conduct a coven.

The respectable orderliness of witches' organization in covens might have emerged from the minds of their persecutors, either laymen or ecclesiastics, and have been acknowledged by the witches themselves since under Continental torture or British browbeating they would ultimately give tongue to any statements that the judge desired them to make. After formation in groups had become established, by the justices, as normal and necessary to the practice of witchcraft, the number thirteen was selected for them by the demonologists.

The god of the witches was Satan (not a pagan deity selected by Margaret Murray) and the activities of the witches was mainly murder and mischief in defiance of the Church's teaching, hence, the witch cult denied Christianity, ridiculed and parodied it. Christ and the Apostles constituted a group of thirteen, therefore the same number of profane Satanists conferred to celebrate their obscene, unholy rites, and plan their future abominations. The suggestion that a coven of witches numbered thirteen because at their meetings they danced naked within the confines of a magic circle nine feet in diameter, and thirteen is the maximum number that can be so accommodated is a comparatively modern assertion.

Notwithstanding the improbability of the witches' having been subject to organizational discipline, Montague Summers accepts the coven idea, but rejects the standardization of numbers. He says: * 'They pledge themselves to frequent the midnight assemblies. These conventicles or covens (from *conventus*) were bands or companies of witches composed of men and women, apparently under the discipline of an officer, all of whom for convenience' sake belonged to the same district.' In another part of the same work, commenting on Dr Murray's book he says, 'The other arguments brought forward by Miss Murray to support her thesis of the continuity of a primitive religion are mainly "the persistence of the number thirteen in the Covens, the narrow geographical range of the domestic familiars, the avoidance of certain forms in the animal transformations, the limited number of personal names among the women-witches, and the survival of the names of some of the early Gods. . . ." Miss Murray does not explain why the number thirteen should form any link with an earlier ritual and worship. . . . "The avoidance of certain forms in the animal transformation" is upon a general view of witchcraft found to be nothing other than the non-occurrence of the lamb and the dove, and these two were abhorred by sorcerers, seeing that Christ is the Lamb of God, *Agnus Dei*, whilst the dove is the manifestation of the Holy Ghost.'

In *Witchcraft and Black Magic* he says, 'The number of members which constitutes a witch-coven is a point that has been much discussed. . . . Many examples of the coven of thirteen persons could be cited; on the other hand, an equal number of examples show differing numbers of members in the coven. Ten witches formed the coven of Great Waltham, Stisted, Dagenham, and Sible Hedingham in 1589, of whom four were hanged. The witches of Worboys who killed Lady Cromwell were three in number—Mother Samuels, her husband and their daughter—they were executed at Huntingdon in 1593. At least thirty-five witches can be traced in connection with the famous Pendle Forest trials (1613), the first Lancashire witches. Seven witches were concerned in the Fairfax case (1622), and six of these stood their trial at the August Assizes, York. . . . Today some of the London covens of Satanists are composed of as many as thirty or

* *History of Witchcraft.*

more members, men and women; some circles again are quite small and consist of half-a-dozen or ten initiates.'

The witches often asserted that the devil himself was present at their meetings. This 'devil' was assumed to be some local person of a higher educational and social status than the rest of the group. He acted as their master and leader. This, too, is taken seriously by Montague Summers. He say,* 'In 1579, at Windstor, the master of a coven of witches who used to meet "in the pits" towards the back of Master Dodges' house was old Rosimond, the wise man of Farnham. They had wrought great trouble, and were responsible for the deaths of Master Gallis, mayor of Windsor, of several farmers and servant wenches who had offended them in some way. Farnham Common, Bucks, is five and a half miles from Windsor.

'The Rev. George Burroughs was the Grand Master of the Salem witches. He used to brag that he was "above the ordinary Rank of Witches", and openly boasted that he had the promise of being a "King in Satan's Kingdom." †

'A very striking example of a Grand Master of the Witches, a notorious revolutionary who employed the Satanists to further his political ends and who was a menace to the Kingdom, is found in Francis Bothwell, . . . other Grand Masters who organized subversive societies, burrowing in secret like moles, were the diabolist Cagliostro; Jacob Falk, "the biggest rogue and villain in all the world", "the Ba'al Shem of London"—a Ba'al Shem, says Margoliouth, being "an operative Cabbalist; in other words, thaumaturgist and prophet";—Adam Weishaupt, "the Illuminatus", who was inspired by a "fanatical enmity inimical to all authority on earth"; the vile Anarchasis Clootz; and, in the nineteenth century, Albert Pike, "the Viceregent of Lucifer", as he has been called, and his successor Adriano Lemmi. There are today‡ several grand masters who, although they themselves may not suspect it, are known as Satanists, and ardent missionaries of their hideous cult.'

Although witches were Satanists who, at their gatherings which undeniably took place from time to time, performed some

---

* op. cit.

† Perhaps an example of dangerous derision uttered when the odds were against the speaker, and in the hearing of people dull of understanding.

‡ Date of publication, 1946, but as true to-day, 1969, as then.

obscene travesty of Christian observance, there is not a traceable organization similar in form to the organization of the Church. The devil had no Pope, no Cardinals, no priests, no world-wide discipline.

Cotton Mather, writing in New England,* said 'the witches form themselves after the manner of Congregational Churches', and according to Margaret Murray, 'the cult was organized in as careful a manner as any other religious community'. However, L'Estrange Ewen† says, 'Organization and propaganda in the furtherance of projects emanating from any synod of devils in England were entirely wanting, the work being left to local agents. These vassals of the Evil One usually laboured quite independently, planning overlapping schemes of wickedness, and claiming credit for each other's dirty work. Any collaboration, except on the smallest scale, is unnoticed in English records, but occasionally, when the agents or witches worked in company, they appointed a leader, and sometimes the officer was an outsider, usually a man, who posed as a devil. . . . To become an accredited representative of the Foul Fiend was a simple process, one had but to utter a curse, and a naughty angel appeared as rapidly as the genie upon the rubbing of Aladdin's lamp.'

The devil worshippers were invariably anarchists. In our own day many criminals profess extreme 'Left' political opinions, the reason being that thereby they justify their anti-social acts: if property is not property, stealing is not stealing. There is no doubt that from time to time mass meetings were convened by Satanists who, perhaps, held office, and who were plotting the downfall of a rival, or the deviation of the Crown. A meeting of such a nature appears to have been held in Scotland in 1590 when two hundred witches, warlocks, and other Satanists gathered in the haunted church of North Berwick where they invoked the Evil One to supplicate his guidance and assistance in compassing, by magic, the removal of King James and the enthronement of the Earl of Bothwell. In how far the 'business' of the meeting was taken seriously, and conducted along conventional lines it would be hard to guess, but no very vivid imagination is required to picture the eating and drinking, the rowdyism, the debauchery

---

* *Wonders of the Invisible World,* 1693.
† op. cit.

and sexual licentiousness that both preceded and followed the invocation.

Such a gathering of criminals would be classed as a witches' sabbat, the annual, or more frequent congregations of witches in some remote, and often normally awe-inspiring place for various assumed purposes: to plot against throne and state; to plan the death, by either magic or poison, of some person in authority; to celebrate the Black Mass, but above all, to feast and to frolic, to perform lewd dances, and to indulge in promiscuous sexual relationships including homosexuality and bestiality.

In modern times the idea of the witches' sabbat, cleansed and romanticized, has been the theme of much fiction, and the witch of the fairy-tale invariably travelled to her rendezvous on a broomstick. Such transvection certainly appears in the confessions, but it was not the only means of travel, nor yet the most frequent. Many witches walked to the meeting place; a number went on horseback, or were conveyed by some other beast of burden; not a few declared that the devil supplied transport, and many claimed to have ridden a goat.

Apart from the subversive political meetings, the convening of, and attendance at which there is no reason to doubt, the sabbat, like the coven, was conceived in the minds of the Inquisitors and justices, and, by suggestion, taken over by the witches themselves. In the early trials there is no mention of attendance at these obscene meetings: the idea seems to emerge about the year 1400 and to become established in the course of the following century. By 1600 every important writer on witchcraft and demonism gave credence to the objective reality of the sabbat. Some detailed descriptions of the common procedure at these orgies were written. The first item on the agenda was a 'service' in worship of Satan (the Black Mass was a later amplification); new witches were then enrolled, entered into the pact, received the devil's mark and, on some occasions, were issued with their familiars. After this 'serious' business came the banquet, followed by lewd dancing leading to sexual excesses of every kind.

The usual hour of commencing activities was ten o'clock at night and the revels sometimes ended at midnight but more often continued till cock-crow. English sabbats were comparatively tame affairs compared with those celebrated on the Continent where the mockery of the Christian faith seems to have been given a more prominent place, and the numbers in attendance to have been far greater. Robbins* mentions 'a famous physician of Ferrara told Spina of 6,000 people dancing and feasting near bonfires at night. One unusual confession in 1440 mentioned 10,000 women riding on sticks to an assembly at Volpute (Burgundy). De Lancre, using the confessions he extorted from his victims, let his fancy run wild: "The Sabbat resembles a fair of merchants, mingling together, angry and half crazed, arriving from all quarters, a surging crowd of some one hundred-thousand devotees of Satan."'

'With reference to the nocturnal meetings and orgies', says Montagu Summers in *The Geography of Witchcraft*, 'there is a decree of a General Council of Ancyra, which passed into the *De ecclesiasticus disciplinis* ascribed to Regino of Priim (906) and thence to the canonists S. Ivo of Chartres and Johannes Gratian. Section 364 of the Benedictine Abbot's work relates that "certain abandoned women turning aside to follow Satan, being seduced by the illusions and phantasms of demons, believe and openly profess that in the dead of night they ride upon certain beasts with the pagan goddess Diana and a countless horde of women, and that in these silent hours they fly over vast tracts of country and obey her as their mistress, while on other nights they are summoned to pay her homage". John of Salisbury, who died in 1180, in his *Policraticus* speaks of the popular belief in a witch-queen named Herodias, who called together the sorcerers to meetings by night when they had feasting, sacrificed babies to ghouls and ghosts, and gave themselves up to blasphemies and debauchery, in a word the Sabbat.'

There was no special day of the week dedicated to the sabbat assembly. Although the word itself is related to 'sabbath', the fact is that Saturday is seldom mentioned as a day of meeting, the reason for which boycott is given by some commentators that Saturday was sacred to the Virgin. Mondays, Wednesdays and Fridays seem to be the most favoured days. The numbers attending a sabbat and the place of meeting varied greatly. Some were held indoors, others in the open air. The indoor gatherings might take place in the hovel of one of the witches or, on the other extreme, the mansion of some wealthy local devil-worshipper.

* op. cit.

Outdoor meetings are generally assumed to have been larger, and of greater importance. It is on these alfresco orgies that romantic fiction is based. The most famous gathering ground was the Brocken, or Brockenburg in the Hartz mountains, where a major sabbat was conducted on Walpurgis night; other important assemblies in the witches' calendar were said to be held on Candlemas (2 February); the Eve of St John Baptist (23 June); Lammas day (1 August); and the festival of St Thomas (21 December). Grand Sabbats were also held, according to popular belief, on any of these festivals on the Venusberg, and the Heuberg (Black Forest). In France the classic site was Puy-de-Dôme, Auvergne. In Guernsey the witches gathered on the beach of Rocquaine Bay. The witches of Brewham, Somerset, assembled on the local common, and also in a coppice known as Husseys-Knap. The Salem witches were supposed to celebrate their midnight orgies either at a house in the village where they partook of the devil's sacrament, red bread, and red drink, or else on 'a plain grassy place, by which was a cart path, in which were the tracks of horses' feet.'

The formalities of the sabbat varied in different countries, and even in different parts of the same country, but 'blazing blasphemy and the most crapulous obscenity' as Montague Summers puts it in *Witchcraft and Black Magic* was common to all of them. In the same work he describes the proceedings at a sabbat thus: 'as a preliminary, the President, who may be the Grand Master of the locality or else the materialization of some evil entity, is adored and worshipped by all present. They pay him homage in the most infamous and beastly manner with prostrations, genuflexions, obeisances, lewd gestures and the reverential kiss of obscenity, *osculum infame*. Sometimes the coven present black candles to their Master. This piece of ritual is found in North Italy, France, Scotland, and the west of England. Guazzo says that the witches carried "pitch black candles, and these burned smokily with a blue flame," as was also observed at North Berwick. This would proceed from the sulphurous matter kneaded with the wax. The candles were, so to speak, mock votive tapers, and further served the practical purpose of giving a dim half-light among those mysterious shades.

'The witches then deliver a report of their ill-deeds committed since the last synagogue.* Bodin tells us that each sorcerer must render an account of all the evil he has wrought, the mischiefs and murders, the destruction of crops, cattle, barns, byres, and the like, the persons overlooked, lamed, and injured in purse and person. When the Northumberland coven met in 1673, "All of them who had done harm gave an account thereof to their protector, who made most of them who did most harm, and beat those who had done no harm."

'Next, instructions are given to the congregation. Thomas Cooper, sometime Vicar of Holy Trinity, Coventry, an Oxford Divine highly reputed for his great learning and one who has much experience in cases of witchcraft, in his *The Mystery of Witchcraft*, published in 1617, writes that at these meetings the Devil-President "delivers unto his Proselyte, and so to the rest, *the Rules of his Art*, instructing them in the manner of *hurting* and *helping*, and acquainting them with such *medicines* and *poisons* as are usual hereunto." Spells were taught orally and had to be conned with great care and exactly recited with the correct intonation: the Somersetshire witches of 1665 were instructed in the art of moulding wax images, and they learned where and how and with what words these figurines must be pierced with long thorns or pins: the qualities of drugs and the action of poisons were explained; especially did the witch midwives learn how to procure abortion and what emmenagogues were most potent and most pernicious.† One witch-midwife of Strasbourg confessed that she had procured more miscarriages and killed more children than she could count. The witches were adepts at the horrid art of poisoning, and when charms seemed to be too slow, a tempered draught would often do the trick. Old Simon Forman—"sweet Father Forman", as the Countess of Somerset called him—not only supplied the lady with puppets and talismans, but also brewed strange potions in which he mingled phosphorus, subacetate of copper, arsenic, and corrosive sublimate for her enemies to drink. Dr Lambe, the warlock of Westminster,

---

* *Synagogue*: literally—an assembly: used as an alternative to sabbat, and perhaps influenced by Rev. II, 9 '. . . and I know the blasphemy of them which say they are Jews, and are not, but are the synagogue of Satan'.

† The sabbat becomes quite an educational establishment: a 'summer school', a late evening class.

was famous for his knowledge "of that noble and deepe science of Physicke", but he "fell to other mysteries"....

'Frequently, and especially was this the case with the larger and more important covens, high politics were and are the principal subject of question and debate at these Sabbats, and the powerful gangs of witches strove to decide the destiny of countries and the fate of kings. In 1786 a very secret Sabbat or circle was convened at Frankfurt, a meeting of Satanists among whom were present Cagliostro; the Cabbalist, Duchanteau; the "Philallèthes" Savalette de Langes, a traitor "versed in all dark mysteries, complotter in all vile plots"; pseudo-Rosicrucian, magician Martiniste; the Illuminatus Christian Bode, alias Amelius. It was here that the deaths of Louis XVI of France and Gustavus III of Sweden were decreed. Very similar meetings are held today; very similar murderous resolutions are determined and have been passed into effect. The revolutions that have troubled the vexed peaceful nations, the broils and unrest culminating in the world chaos of an almost universal misery, tyranny, and anarchy, are all fomented, deliberately organized, and energetically assisted by the Black International, the Satanists, who go under a dozen trifling occult names, who mockingly dub themselves political parties. Only too true and of profoundest significance were the words spoken of the holy prophet full three thousand years ago: "Rebellion is as the sin of witchcraft".

'When the business of the Sabbat had been dispatched it was usual for the whole crew to turn to revelry and feasting of their kind. There were often dances, and these, as it may be supposed, were no graceful and elegant movements, a pleasing and agreeable recreation, an exquisite art, but the choreography of hell, awkward jiggertings and lewd leapings, the muckibus caperings and bouncings, the loutings and mowings of idiots. Boguet, De Lancre, and several writers have been particular in the descriptions of the witches' dances, as learned from the confessions of these wretches, and the Capuchin Jacques D'Autun speaks of sorcerers who gyrate hand in hand, and twist and twine their limbs as driven by maniac fury.'

Commenting on the music that accompanied the frenzied dancing at the sabbat, Montague Summers reveals the 'violins, flutes, tambourines, rebecks, fifes and drums, hautboys, the basshorn, a hurdy-gurdy, citterns, the Jew's-harp and (especially in Scotland), the pipes.' He compares the dancing of the witches with that of certain savage peoples, in both cases it being merely a preliminary to sexual excesses.

The words 'jazz' and also the 'juke' of juke-box are descended from an African root meaning both music and coitus. A German writer, Emil Ludwig, in a psychological study of the nation, entitled *The Germans*, refers to Wagner as 'the most dangerous of Germans'. This composer's music (notwithstanding its greatness), is condemned as being obsessed by sex, inflated by lust for power, and shaped by treachery: while it bolsters the German cultural myth, and 'transports the listener into a state of mystical ecstasy' it hardens the natural brutality of the Hun race, brings greater boldness to their innate insolence, and nourishes their appetite for world conquest.

The demonologists of the past sometimes give details of the form and order of the proceedings at a sabbat. These descriptions vary in detail but are unanimous in asserting that black candles were burned, infants murdered and their blood used for the devil's sacrament (their flesh often being eaten), and that all present were compelled to perform the *osculum infame*, the devil being represented by, or being himself 'in the chair', in the form of a black goat.

At the gathering in North Berwick (1590) Agnes Sampson 'which was the elder Witch was taken and brought to Haliciud house before the King's Maiestie* and sundry other of the nobility of Scotland, where she was straitly examined, but all the perswasions which the Kings maiestie vsed to her with ye^e rest of his counsell, might not prouoke or induce her to confess ...' however, after the 'perswasions' had been removed from the verbal to the instrumental sphere she did confess 'that vpon the night of Allhollon Even last' two hundred witches went to sea, 'each one in a Riddle or Cive, and went in the same very substantially with Flaggons of wine making merry and drinking by the waye in the same Riddles or Cives, to the Kerke of North Barrick in Lowthian, and that after they had landed, tooke handes on the land and daunced this reill or short dance, singing all with one voice:

*James VI and I.

Commer, goe ye before,
commer, goe ye.
Gif ye will not goe
before, commer let me.

Agnes Sampson said the devil, in the likeness of a man, was in attendance, and putting his bare buttocks over the pulpit, all present kissed it 'in sign of duetye to him'. In another version 'the devil caused all the company to come and kiss his arse'. The business of this meeting was to formulate a plot to bewitch the King to death, and it was agreed that if his demise could not be effected by enchantment they would have recourse to poison.

In romance witches dance round a cauldron wherein simmers an unsavoury brew from which medicines and love-potions were decocted, but the pot aboil at a sabbat or a coven, or in the secrecy of an individual witches' hovel produced no such harmless if nauseating stew. The witches, in spite of their general ignorance were versed in herbalism, and they produced most potent poisons, either to destroy their own personal enemies or, perhaps more often, to sell to a rich patron who came to them with this end in view.

Death by poison was so common down at least to the end of the sixteenth (perhaps well into the seventeenth) century, that it was assumed, by common consent, to account for the demise of anyone in public affairs who contracted a sudden, fatal malady. Agnes Strickland* comments that at the period, death from natural causes seems to have been regarded as fictitious.

Shakespeare knew his witches well:

First Witch: Thrice the brinded cat hath mewed.
Second Witch: Thrice and once the hedge-pig whined.
Third Witch: Harpier cries, 'tis time, 'tis time.
First Witch: Round about the cauldron go;
                        In the poison'd entrails throw.
                        Toad, that under cold stone
                        Days and nights has thirty-one
                        Swelter'd venom sleeping got,
                        Boil thou first i' the charmed pot.
All: Double, double toil and trouble;
                        Fire burn, and cauldron bubble.

* *Lives of the Tudor Princesses.*

Second Witch: Fillet of a fenny snake,
In the cauldron boil and bake;
Eye of newt, and toe of frog,
Wool of bat, and tongue of dog,
Adder's fork, and blind worm's sting,
Lizard's leg, and howlet's wing—
For a charm of powerful trouble,
Like a hell-broth boil and bubble.

All: Double, double toil and trouble;
Fire, burn, and cauldron bubble.

Third Witch: Scale of dragon; tooth of wolf;
Witches' mummy; maw and gulf
Of the ravined salt-sea shark,
Root of hemlock digg'd i' the dark,
Liver of blaspheming Jew;
Gall of goat; and slips of yew
Sliver'd in the Moon's eclipse;
Nose of Turk, and Tartar's lips;
Finger of birth-strangled babe
Ditch-deliver'd by a drab—
Make the gruel thick and slab;
Add thereto a tiger's chaudron,
For th' ingredients of our cauldron.

All: Double, double toil and trouble;
Fire burn and cauldron bubble.

Second Witch: Cool it with a baboon's blood,
Then the Charm is firm and good.

. . .

Enter Macbeth.

Macbeth: How now, you secret, black, and midnight Hags!
What is't you do?

All: A deed without a name.

Wallace Notestein, later Professor of English History at Yale University, wrote *A History of Witchcraft in England from 1558 to 1718*, which work he submitted, in 1905, as a thesis to gain a Doctorate in Philosophy from Yale University. In 1909 it was published by the American Historical Association who conferred on the author their prize, and a British edition, bearing the imprint of Oxford University Press, made its appearance in 1911.

Notestein has but little on the subject of witches' assemblies, but he touches on the subject in dealing with the intellectual reaction that followed upon the publicity given to the criminal activities of Matthew Hopkins and his helper, John Stearne. Four names stand out: Henry More, Meric Casaubon, Robert Filmer and Thomas Ady.

'More was a young Cambridge scholar and divine who was to take rank among the English philosophers of the seventeenth century. Grounded in Plato and impregnated with Descartes, he became a little later thoroughly infected with the Cabalistic philosophy that had entered Europe from the East. It was the point of view that he acquired in the study of this mystic Oriental System that gave the peculiar turn to his witchcraft notion ... it was in 1653 that More issued *An Antidote to Atheisme*. The phenomena of witchcraft he received as part of the evidence for the reality of the spirit world ... More had made investigations for himself, probably at Maidstone. In his own town of Cambridge there was a story—doubtless a college joke, but he referred to it in all seriousness—of "old Strangride" who "was carried over Shelford Steeple upon a black Hogge and tore his breeches on the weathercock." He believed that he had absolute proof of the "nocturnal conventicles" of witches. . . . His effort to account for the instantaneous transportation of witches is one of the bright spots in the prosy reasoning of the demonologists. More was a thoroughgoing dualist. Mind and matter were two separate entities. Now, the problem that arose at once was this: How can the souls of witches leave their bodies? "I conceive" he says, "the Divell gets into their body and by his subtile substance more operative and searching than any fire or putrifying liquor, melts the yielding Campages of the body to such a consistency ... and makes it plyable to his imagination; and then it is as easy for him to work it into what shape he pleaseth." If he could do that, much more could he enable men to leave their bodies. . . .'

Casaubon, (who later wrote a most important work on Dr John Dee's experience in occultism), 'was skeptical of the aerial journeys of witches ... it was a matter, he wrote in his *Treatise concerning Enthusiasme* (1655) of much dispute among learned men. The confessions made were hard to account for, but he would feel it very wrong to condemn the accused on first evidence.'

Sir Robert Filmer* published in 1653 *Advertisement to the Jurymen of England* for the purpose of alerting the minds of such persons as were called for jury service, to the danger of their giving a false verdict because, he felt, the bulk of the evidence adduced in witch-trials was worthless.

In 1656 Thomas Ady published his *Candle in the Dark*, a work in which he fearlessly contended with all English writers (whose works he had evidently read and not simply accepted by hearsay) who accepted witchcraft as a social fact. He protested that King James's book was not the King's own work: he endeavoured to instil common sense and reason into the minds of his fellow countrymen, but it appears from his work that he was himself not certain that no part of the evidence against witches was factual.

L'Estrange Ewen says,† 'It is incredible that people, however devil-ridden, would turn out of bed, winter and summer, regardless of weather, and proceed naked in the dead of night to some desolate rendezvous, and it is perhaps unnecessary to add that the whole conception was largely hallucination induced by drugs and amplified in the torture chamber under the persuasion of the Holy Inquisitors. In one of the rare cases where a sensible examination was made by those zealous enquirers, a woman, who confessed to nightly attending the Sabbat, having been carefully watched by officials, was found to throw herself into a trance, in which state she remained even with a lighted candle held to her foot. In the morning she gave a detailed account of her attendance at an assembly of witches.'

Francis Bacon wrote, in *Sylva Sylvarum*, 'the witches themselves are imaginative and believe oft times they do that which they do not; and people are credulous in that point, and ready to impute accidents and natural operations to witchcraft ... the great wonders which they tell of carrying in the air, transporting themselves into other bodies etc., are still reported to be wrought, not by incantations, or ceremonies, but by ointments, and anointing themselves all over.'

He further said, but himself is unlikely to have taken it

---

* A commemorative brass, to several members of the Filmer family, illustrated in *Brasses*, by Julian Franklyn, (2nd edition 1969) published first in 1964 by MacGibbon & Kee, is to be seen in East Sutton Church, Kent.

† op. cit.

seriously, that the flying ointment was made from the fat of disinterred children, mixed with oatmeal, the juice of smallage, wolfbane and cinquefoil, adding that soporiferous decoctions were the most likely to be employed to this end.

The French demonologist, Nicholas Remy, in his oft reprinted work, *Demonolatreial*, (1595), writes: 'Witches do often and in fact Travel to their Nocturnal Synagogues; ... but it must be known before they go to the sabbat they annoint themselves upon some part of their bodies with an unguent made from various foul and filthy ingredients, but chiefly from murdered children, and so annointed they are carried away on a cowl-staff, or a broom, or a reed, or, a cleft stick or a distaff.'

Montague Summers,* commenting on this passage, says, 'the ointment itself has no power or value, but is a mere empty jape of Satan to add ceremony and circumstance to the proceedings. The same may be said of the staff or broom, which is actually an empty symbol. It is, none the less, very certain that witches can be and are levitated and so transported to the sabbat.'

The temptation, which is very great, to join the ranks of the materialists and reject, utterly, the idea of mystical flight through the air must be sternly resisted, notwithstanding that such transportation was, in the vast majority of cases, only hallucination.

Transvection and levitation were not the same in essence although both had the same appearance and effect: without the employment of concealed mechanical apparatus the physical body rises from the ground, even to a considerable height, and remains thus unsupported for a comparatively long time. It is recorded of numerous saints that they levitated on various occasions. Among those who did so is St Francis of Assisi. Several times, he rose in to the air 'to a height of three, and often to a height of four cubits.' †

This mysterious release from the power of gravitation is not exclusive to saints, nor confined to the past. It is a strange, inexplicable phenomenon that has been accurately observed and reliably reported in both the nineteenth and the twentieth centuries.

Daniel Douglas Home (1833–1886), the famous medium, who,

* *Witchcraft and Black Magic.*

† This archaic lineal measure was not rigidly standardized: it varied in its length from time to time, and from place to place, but, it seems, was never less than eighteen or more than twenty-two English inches.

while on a visit to Florence narrowly escaped assassination due to a rumour that he was a necromancer who used the sacraments of the church as a means to raise the dead, most impressively levitated on more than one occasion. Sir William Crookes, writing in the *Quarterly Journal of Science* (1874) says, 'The most striking case of levitation which I have witnessed has been with Mr Home. On three separate occasions have I seen him raised completely from the floor of the room ... On each occasion I had full opportunity of watching the occurrence as it was taking place.'

There are about one hundred recorded incidents of Home's rising in the air, but the most impressive demonstration took place in December, 1868. There is some doubt whether on the thirteenth or on the sixteenth of the month, and there is some confusion concerning the address at which it took place, both Ashley House, Victoria Street, and No 5 Buckingham Gate being given.

The confusion seems to be caused by Lord Dunraven giving the place and date of his writing the report,* instead of the address of the scene of the occurrence and its date.

No 41.–*Séance at 5, Buckingham Gate,*
Wednesday, December 16th.

'... Home then got up and walked about the room. He was both elongated and raised in the air. He spoke in a whisper, as though the spirits were arranging something. He then said to us, "Do not be afraid, and on no account leave your places"; and he went out into the passage. Lindsay suddenly said, "Oh good heavens! I know what he is going to do; it is too fearful" .... "he is going out of the window in the other room, and coming in at this window." We heard Home go into the other room, heard the window thrown up, and presently Home appeared standing upright outside our window; he opened the window and walked in quite coolly. "Ah!" he said, "you were good this time", referring to our having sat still and not wished to prevent him. He sat down and laughed. ... I got up, shut the window [in the next room] and in coming back remarked that the window was not raised a foot, and that I could not think how he had managed to squeeze through. He arose and said, "Come and see." I went with him; he told me to open the window as it was before, I did so: he told

*Psychical Research Society.

me to stand a little distance off; he then went through the open space, head first, quite rapidly, his body being nearly horizontal and apparently rigid. He came in again, feet foremost, and we returned to the other room. It was so dark I could not see clearly how he was supported outside. He did not appear to grasp, or rest upon, the balustrade, but rather to be swung out and in. Outside each window is a small balcony or ledge, 19 inches deep, bounded by stone balustrades, 18 inches high. The balustrades of the two windows are 7 feet 4 inches apart, measuring from the nearest points. A string-course, 4 inches wide, runs between the windows at the level of the bottom of the balustrade; and another 3 inches wide at the level of the top. Between the windows at which Home went out, and that at which he came in, the wall recedes six inches. The rooms are on the third floor.'

As is usual with 'classic' manifestations of the witch-cult, the jurists and the theologians seemed to know a great deal more about the flying ointment and its use than did the witches themselves. At one of the few English witch trials where the use of an infant to manufacture ointment was mentioned, it was also revealed that the witness, Grace Sowerbutts, (aged fourteen), had been primed by 'one Master Thompson, which she taketh to be Master Christopher Southwood, to whom she was sent to learn her prayers, did persuade, council and advise her, to deal as formerly hath been said against her said grandmother, aunt, and Southworth's wife.'

The witness had declared that she 'saw them enter the chamber ... and bring forth a little child and sitting down, thrust a nail into its navel, and afterwards insert a pen* and they did suck there a good space.' The effect of this extraction was that the child died soon afterwards and no sooner was it buried than the accused disinterred it. After making a stew, of which they invited the witness to partake, they 'seethed the bones in a pot to obtain ointment to annoint themselves.'

In Continental reports the magic ointment is of frequent occurrence, and it may indeed have been made and used; for certain drugs, in ointment form, can be absorbed by the system and they will produce hallucination: nightshade, hemlock, mandrake and poppy are well known. In addition to the toxic effect of the drug was the psychic accompaniment of the ritual and the rubbing

* A hollow quill.

which could produce a kind of self-hypnosis, and under that spell anything is possible.

If a person in the normal course of life sustains a minor burn a blister may be raised but no permanent scar is likely to be left; if, however, a person under hypnosis is touched with some object that is not hot, say a black-lead pencil, and is at the same time informed that he is burned at that spot, not only will a blister be raised, but a permanent scar will be left. There seems to be little doubt, if any, that criminals act in a state of hypnosis of which they themselves are generally unaware, and which seems to surround them like an aura. The apparently amazing skill of the common pickpocket is often a matter of comment while the fact is that the average pickpocket performs his work comparatively clumsily, and is protected by the hypnoidal condition in which he lives and which he unconsciously transmits to his victim and to adjacent people who might be witnesses. When the time comes for the hypnotic tension to recede, or to burn out, he is easily apprehended. Some criminals, being aware of this, ensure the hynoid condition by intoxicating themselves with ether before venturing on a criminal enterprise. One of the explanations of the famous Indian rope trick is that it never really takes place but that the entire audience is placed under hypnosis and thus each member sees what the conjurer informs him he is seeing.

The witches who anointed themselves (or were anointed by their companions) with the narcotic ointment lapsed into a second-state and, so entranced, subjectively mounted their broomsticks, whirled off up the chimney and travelled through the air to the sabbat, which experience they subsequently externalized.

In the English witch-trials but little reference is made to journeying through the air on a broomstick, nor is there anything that can rank as a full-scale sabbat.

The first trial of the Lancashire witches introduces the theme, but the meeting to which reference is made is more in the nature of a normal, than of a magical conventicle with the (or a) devil acting as president.

Montague Summers, always picturesque in his phrasing, opens his account* of the case thus: 'In the lonely forest of Pendle, among the wild hills of Eastern Lancashire, there eked out her wretched sustenance a blind beggar of some four score years, a

* *The Geography of Witchcraft*, Routledge & Kegan Paul, 1927.

"wicked fire-brand of mischief", generally acknowledged to be "a generall agent for the Devill in all these partes", Elizabeth Southerns or Demdike. This ancient crone had been a witch longer than memory could serve, and she had dedicated her children and grandchildren to the service of Satan. Her bitter rival, in age, influence and evil was a hag named Ann Whittle, or rather Chattox, "a very old, withered, spent, and decreped creature, her sight almost gone; a dangerous witch of very long continuance; always opposite to old Demdike; for whom the one favoured the other hated deadly : and how they curse and accuse one another in their examinations may appear. In her witchcraft always more ready to doe mischief to men's goods than themselves; her lippes ever chattering and talking; but no man knew what. She lived in the forest of Pendle amongst the wicked company of dangerous witches ... from these two sprung all the rest in order; and, even the children and friends of these two notorious witches."

'There was in fact a deadly feud between the two families, and both having been long exercised in supernatural practices and devoted body and soul to the Demon, fearful was the mischief they wrought in their angry struggles for supremacy in wickedness.'

Where Montague Summers is himself quoting in the foregoing passage it is from *The Wonderful Discoverie of Witches in the County of Lancaster*, printed in 1613 by Master Thomas Potts, Clerk of the Court where the trial was held in 1612.

Chattox, it appeared, had been a disciple of Demdike from whom she had learned all she knew of the black arts, but as so frequently happens, the disciple broke away from her mentor for whom she conceived a bitter hatred, and the two became keen rivals to corner the entire local business in charms and potions. The publicity campaign pursued by each of them was similar to modern political propaganda : every misfortune, death and disaster that occurred for miles round was boasted by each as all her own work.

Ultimately their advertising proved only too successful. Roger Nowell, J.P., who was both religious and gullible, heard of the enormities they claimed as their work, and he, shocked and horrified, had Demdike and her granddaughter Alizon Device, with Chattox and her daughter, Ann Redfern, brought before him and he committed the four of them to gaol in Lancaster Castle to await trial.

Thomas Potts, notwithstanding his prosaic calling, had much of the artist in him. Having given so vivid a thumbnail sketch of old Demdike he could not resist a portrait of her granddaughter: Alizon Device, he said was 'branded with a preposterous mark in nature, even from her birth, which was her left eye standing lower than the other, the one looking down, the other looking up, so strangely deformed as the best that were present in that honourable assembly and great audience did affirm, they had not often seen the like.'

The incarceration of this quartet was bad news for the Pendle witches and Elizabeth Device, old Demdike's daughter, displaying admirable loyalty, skill and organizing ability, called a meeting to discuss the disaster and so find ways and means of rescuing the prisoners. This meeting was held at old Demdike's home, known as Malking Tower, which gives the impression from its name alone of being one of the stately homes of England, but which was most certainly nothing of the kind.

On Good Friday, 10 April, 1612, there were present the convener, Elizabeth Device, and her two children, James and Jennet (this girl was nine years of age); Alice Nutter alias 'Dick Mile's wife', (described as a gentlewoman); Katherine Hewit, John Bulcock and his mother, Jane Bulcock, Alice Gray (of Colne), Jennet and Christopher Hargreaves (the latter 'otherwise known as Jackes'*), Elizabeth Hargreaves (wife of Jackes), Christopher Howgate and his wife Elizabeth, Grace Hay (of Padiham), Ann Crunkshaw (of Marsden), Jennet Preston and a number of others. Some of those present, it appears, had simply come along for the ride. Notwithstanding the purpose of the meeting, and the serious danger now surrounding the whole community of witches 'there was great cheer and merry company.' A very substantial, solid and unwitchlike meal was served consisting of 'Beefe, Bacon, and Roasted Mutton: which Mutton ... was of a Wether of Christopher Swyers of Barley: which Wether was brought in the night before.' However, it was not all feasting and good cheer: the business of the meeting was transacted. This, they declared sub-

---

* 'Jackes' was a slang term used at the period for a privy, or close-stool. There is nothing to suggest that in this nickname it carried that connotation, but it may well have done.

sequently, had simply been that of naming a spirit, but James Device volunteered information far more acceptable to the justices.

According to him the meeting had devised a plan to blow up Lancaster Castle, murder Master Cowel the jailer and so effect the release of their friends. James is far too ambitious for modern taste. He had probably heard about Guy Fawkes and the Gunpowder Plot and in his ignorance probably thought the demolition of such a building could be achieved by throwing a thimblefull of gunpowder in at a window. This heroic information was given before Mr Roger Nowell who, having heard of the party, had ordered Elizabeth Device and James to be brought before him.

Elizabeth Device, cornered by the cross-examination, confessed to having bewitched to death three persons. She admitted holding the meeting at Malking Tower but stoutly denied having plotted to rescue the prisoners. She had revenge on her traitorous son, James, by accusing him of himself being a witch and under examination he admitted having bewitched to death two persons. He also gave information against both the matriarchs, Demdike and Chattox, against his mother, and against his sister, Alizon. This last entertained no scruples in informing against both octogenarians. Jennet Device displayed a phenomenal memory, hardly to be expected in a child of nine years: she gave the names of numerous people who had attended the meeting, and fullest details of damning conversations every word of which she had heard and now remembered. This sweet child did not waver by one word in giving information against her mother.

Roger Nowell entertained no doubts concerning such flimsy evidence and sent twenty-one people to await trial. Old Demdike, not being disposed to be obliging, died in gaol. They were 'put on their trial before Sir Edward and Sir James Altham, the Justices of the Northern circuit, who reached Lancaster on the sixteenth of August. Mother Demdike ['s] ... depositions, especially as regards her familiar, who "appeared unto her in the likenes of a broune Dogg, forcing himselfe to her knee, to get blood under her left Arme" had been taken down before the magistrates and covered her memory with execration. Five members of the two Pendle broods made ample confession. Mother Chattox, Elizabeth Device, Alizon and Jennet, a child aged nine, her daughters; and their brother James. They involved one another in the most hate-

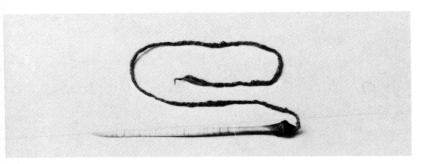

DEATH BY ENCHANTMENT: a 'pointing bone' with a thong of human hair attached. When a sorcerer points this bone at a man, and chants a death-spell, the victim, who both hears and sees the operation, will surely die: all the knowledge and skill of modern European medicine cannot save him.

(Crown copyright. By courtesy of the Trustees of the British Museum.)

NECROMANCY: magic shoe called *Kurdaitcha*. After being enchanted by the medicine man they set out on the trail of a dead soul. When overtaken, the soul is unable to resist the temptation of slipping the shoes on, whereupon they turn about and so bring the soul back to earth.

Also, after enchantment, they conceal the footprints of a man setting out upon a mission of vengeance.

They are woven of emu feathers and fibre.

(Crown copyright. By courtesy of the Trustees of the British Museum.)

FAMILIAR: a double-headed figure carved in wood representing spirits or demons believed to have been the familiars of past sorcerers. The modern practitioner, when about to work magic, calls the ancient demon into the figures in order to secure its aid.

GRIMOIRE: a book of spells and astrology used by the shaman in invoking spirits and working magic. The volume is made from a folded strip of bark, and is bound in wood.

PUPPET: African version of the European puppet used to kill a person by pushing pins or nails into the figure. Note the nails driven into this figure.

HEALING MAGIC: on the North West coast when a man falls sick it is believed that his soul has abandoned his body. The medicine man, when called, arrives with his carved wooden soul-trap, chases the undutiful soul, and if he catches it forces it to return, whereupon the patient recovers.

(Crown copyright. By courtesy of the Trustees of the British Museum.)

WHITE WITCHCRAFT: a witch-bottle and its contents, namely, a heart-shaped piece of fabric pierced with pins, a mass of human hair and some nail-parings. A number of such bottles have been excavated from London building sites but they are as a rule empty. In this example the cork was intact, hence the preservation of the contents.

In the seventeenth century they were prepared by white witches as a form of counter-magic, to inhibit malefic witchcraft from their clients, but it is interesting to observe so little difference between the methods employed.

(Photo by courtesy of the Pitt Rivers Museum, University of Oxford)

BLACK WITCHCRAFT: desecration of a grave at Tottenham Park Cemetery, 31 October 1968. The coffin was found up-ended with an iron cross thrust through the woodwork. There was other destruction, suspected to have resulted from black magic Hallowe'en rites.

(Photo: Press Association)

ful sorceries, and in spite of many grotesque, but not necessarily untrue, details the tale they told was foul and horrible to a degree. All the bestial malice, crass stupidity, empty revenge, and besotted superstition of the remote countryside are there compounded. Especially remarkable is the testimony of James Device ... "that upon Sheare Thursday was two years, his grand-mother, Elizabeth Southerns, alias Demdike, did bid him this Examinate goe to the Church to receive the Communion (the next day after being Good Friday) and ther not to eat the Bread the Minister gave him, but to bring it and deliver it to such a thing as should meet him on the way homeward; notwithstanding her perswasions this Examinate did eat the Bread: and so in his coming homeward some fortie roodes off the said Church, there met him a thing in the shape of a Hare, who spoke unto this Examinate, and asked him whether he had brought the Bread." It is not surprising that he was condemned for "as dangerous and malicious a witch as ever lived in these parts of Lancashire, of his time, and spotted with as much innocent blood as ever any witch of his yeares." ' *

L'Estrange Ewen † says old Demdike's 'young grandson was a physical wreck and unable to stand at the trial, having strength only to deny his two confessions, and to plead not guilty.'

Others repudiated their confessions, but Alizon Device did not. She seemed quite proud of having stricken a peddler: 'by this devilish art of witchcraft his head is drawn awry, his eyes and face deformed, his speech not well to be understood, his thighs and legs stark lame, his arms lame, especially the left side, his hands lamed and turned out of their course; his body able to endure no travail.' This is accepted by numerous authorities as a reasonably good description of the effect of a paralytic stroke.

With the exception of three minor charges, in all cases the prisoners were indicted for bewitching a person to death. Both the old women and the young Alizon Device confessed to nourishing dogs, supposed to be spirits, who delighted in being despatched on evil errands, and Ann Redfern was accused of, and several of the Devices admitted making, clay images with the hope of working evil to their enemies.‡

* Montague Summers, op. cit.
† *Witchcraft and Demonism.*
‡ L'Estrange Ewen, op. cit.

Ten of the prisoners were hanged: Dame Chattox, Ann Redfern, Alice Nutter, Elizabeth, Alizon and James Device; Katherine Hewit, alias Mouldheels; John Bulcock and Jane his mother; and Jennet Preston.

The meeting at Malking Tower is as near as witchcraft in England ever got to a sabbat, and clearly it does not qualify; it was held at mid-day not at midnight; those in attendance did not travel through the air on broomsticks, but took advantage of such normal transport as they could make available; the menu, remarkably lacking in boiled baby, frog, toad and serpent's venom was very prosaic and typical of a hearty English mid-day dinner; the business of the gathering was for the practical purpose of discussing the arrests, not to pay homage to the devil; no pacts were signed with blood; no new recruits were enrolled.

Notestein* goes so far as to discredit the holding of a meeting at Demdike's home. He says, 'Those who believed in the "Sabbath" of witches must have felt their opinions confirmed by the testimony of the witnesses at Lancaster. Even the modern reader, with his skepticism, is somewhat daunted by the cumulative force of what purports to be the evidence and would fain rationalize it by supposing that some sort of meeting actually did take place at Malking Tower and that some Pendle men and women who had delved in magic arts till they believed in them did formulate plans for revenge. But this is not a probable supposition. The concurring evidence in the Malking Tower story is of no more compelling character than that to be found in a multitude of Continental stories of witch gatherings which have been shown to be the outcome of physical or mental pressure and of leading questions. It seems unnecessary to accept even a substratum of fact. Probably one of the accused women invented the story of the witch feast after the model of others of which she had heard, or developed it under the stimulus of suggestive questions from a Justice. Such a narrative, once started, would spread like wildfire and the witnesses and the accused who were persuaded to confess might tell approximately the same story. A careful re-reading of all this evidence suggests that the various testimonies may indeed have been echoes of the first narrative. They seem to lack those characteristic differences which would stamp them as independent accounts. Moreover, when the story was once

* op. cit.

started, it is not improbable that the justices and the judges would assist the witnesses by framing questions based upon the narrative already given. It cannot be said that the evidence exists upon which to establish this hypothesis. There is little to show that the witnesses were adroitly led into their narratives. But we know from other trials that the method was so often adopted that it is not a far cry to suspect that it was used at Lancaster.'

One must congratulate Professor Notestein on his rational, clear thinking, his resistance to acceptance of what is accepted only because it is accepted; nevertheless, this attempt to 'debunk' the Malking Tower meeting has inherent in it the faculty of 'auto-debunking'. One of the accused women most certainly did not invent the story of the witch feast after the model of others of which she had heard, because the stodgy mid-day 'ordinary' at old Demdike's stronghold was nothing like any witch-feast that anyone, man, woman or child, before or since had, or has ever heard, or is ever likely to hear of. If the meal served at Malking Tower was like a witch-feast, then every workman's cook-shop in the country is continually serving witch-feasts. Further, there is no reason to suppose that people of the meagre intellectual development manifest among the Pendle witches would have known anything at all about Continental witchcraft, and very little more of the Continent than is now known about Atlantis or Lemuria: in other words, if they'd heard of the Continent they did not necessarily believe in such a place. Hell would have had more geographical certainty in their minds.

Transvection, or levitation, in English witch practice is almost as rare as is the sabbat: Julia Cox, aged seventy, tried at Taunton by John Archer, Justice of the Common Pleas, in 1663, was seen by one witnesss only to come flying in at the window 'in her full proportion'. The accused, in her confession, declared that one evening 'there came riding towards her three persons on three broomstaves, borne up about a yard and a half from the ground'. Two of the mysterious trio she recognized as a witch and a wizard who were subsequently hanged, but the third member of the party was 'a black man' who asked her to sign a pact with her own blood. Mother Cox declared that she had refused the offer and that she was innocent. However, being unable to repeat The Lord's Prayer she was found guilty and hanged.

Elizabeth Style, of Bayford, confessed at Taunton Sessions, 1664, that 'before going to the meetings, the witches anoint their foreheads and hand-wrists with an oil provided by the spirit, which smells raw, and then they are carried in a very short time, using these words as they pass, "Thout, Cout, a tout, tout, throughout and about". And when they depart they say, "Rentum tormentum". At their first meeting, the man in black bids them welcome, and they all make low obeisance to him, and he then distributes some wax candles like little torches, which they give back at parting. When they anoint themselves they "use a long form of words", and when sticking in thorns into the puppets they say, "a pox on thee, I'll spite thee". At every meeting, before the spirit vanishes, he appoints the place and time of the next meeting, and at his departure there is a foul smell. When they meet in their bodies, they eat, drink, and dance to music. . . . They are carried [to the sabbat] sometimes in their bodies and their clothes, at other times without, and Examinate thinks their bodies are sometimes left behind. Even when their spirits only are present, yet they know one another.

'They bewitch man, woman or child, sometimes by a picture made in wax. . . . Examinate had been at several general meetings in the night at High Common, and a common near Matcomb, at a place near Marnhull, and at other spots. . . . Upon the Devil vanishing all were carried to their several homes in a short space, and at their parting they said, "A Boy! merry meet, merry part".*

Elizabeth Style does not reveal the means of transport, but 'in the popular imagination the witch is always associated with the broomstick, employed by her to fly in wild career through mid-air. This belief seems almost universal and the broomstick is, of course, closely connected with the magic wand or staff which was considered equally serviceable for purposes of equitation. The wood whence it was fashioned was often from the hazel-tree, witch-hazel, although in De Lancre's day the sorcerers of Southern France favoured the "Souhandourra"—*cornus sanguinea,*—dog-wood. Mid hurricane and tempest, in the very heart of the dark storm, the convoy of witches, straddling their broomsticks, sped swiftly along to the Sabbat, their yells and hideous laughter

* Ewen, quoting Glanvil.

sounding louder than the crash of elements, and mingling in fearful discord with the frantic pipe of the gale.'*

Notwithstanding the universality and popularity of the belief, it is certain that witches did not ride broomsticks, nor sows, nor cows, nor goats, nor horses through the air to the sabbat; it is equally certain that they were themselves convinced of their having so ridden as a result of intoxication with narcotic ointment, or due to trance, or as a result of the externalization of the very common flying dream. What does emerge as an undeniable fact is that witches compounded ointments.

These unguents were of two kinds: those that induced in themselves the sensation of flying, and those that they administered to their enemies as poison. In these latter they also traded, supplying deadly concoctions to persons who plotted the death of someone of whom they wished to be rid.

Witchcraft activities are, on the whole, open to grave doubt since neither the evidence of accusers and witnesses, nor the confessions of the prisoners are acceptable. Hence when murder, or multiple murders are alleged, and agreed to as one of the items of guilt in what was primarily a trial for witchcraft, it is reasonable to assume that the death or deaths, although desired by the witch, would not today bear sufficient weight to bring about an arrest, far less a trial, and most certainly not a conviction.

The compounding and vending of poisons is, however, in a far different category. In spite of all the gibberish and incantation, the addition of ingredients under the control of phases of the moon and such like posing and posturing which the operator fancied to be essential magic without which the resultant brew would lack potency, the fact remains that the preparation of the poison required no such magic nor many of the ingredients that the witch included. The toxic effect of a strong solution of poppy-head and nightshade was all too coldly practical. Those witches who traded in poison were competent pharmacologists as far as vegetable simples would carry them.

Acceptable proof of this is to be sought not in the reports of trials primarily for witchcraft when murder came out, but in the far more realistic trials for murder when witchcraft came out.

* Montague Summers, *History of Witchcraft*.

An example, indisputably authentic, was the case of the murder of Sir Thomas Overbury. He was the son of Nicholas Overbury of Bourton-on-the-Hill, Gloucestershire, Esquire, and having graduated in law and employed his charm of manner wisely, was given employment in the office of the Secretary of State.

His friend, Robert Carr, a few years younger than himself, was one of the favourites of James VI and I, but lacked the wit to remain so, and put himself under the guidance of Overbury. He met Frances Howard when she was sixteen years of age and had already been married for three years to the young Earl of Essex. 'Frances was already ungovernable, self-willed and completely feather-headed and unlikely to grow up into a suitable companion for the rather solid and solemn young man to whom she had been married. In London with her mother, she was allowed almost immediately to take part in all the gaiety that was going at Court. She never really had a chance. Almost every influence to which she was exposed was likely to bring out the worst in her. She saw far too much of her wicked old uncle, Northampton, who petted and spoiled her and imparted to her some of his own cynical outlook, but nothing of his cynical wisdom. One of her mother's intimates, of whom she saw a great deal, was a Mrs Thornborough, wife of the Bishop of Bristol, who encouraged in her an interest in palmistry and fortune-telling and a great deal of silly superstition. Mrs Thornborough's other hobby was equally unfortunate. She was something of an amateur chemist and "given to making extracts and powders".'*

She became the mistress of Henry, Prince of Wales, and later, of Carr. In 1609 Essex, his education completed, returned from abroad. He was eighteen years of age and eager to claim his bride.

Overbury, whose hold upon Carr was resented by many powerful people, did not realize what danger he was putting himself in when he wrote love-letters and poems for Carr.

Essex 'was shy and awkward and he did not belong at all to the more polished, courtly world in which his wife had grown up at Whitehall. . . . Inevitably he was unskilful and tactless and equally inevitably she refused to allow a clumsy young fool,

* *The Murder of Sir Thomas Overbury*, Wm. McElwee. Faber & Faber, 1952.

whose very existence blocked her happiness and whom she had only once before seen in her life, suddenly to assert rights which she found intolerable.'*

Lady Essex consulted a certain Mrs Turner with whom she was acquainted. Officially, Mrs Turner was Court Dressmaker: unofficially, she was a vendor of love philtres and abortives which she obtained from Dr Forman, who lived in Lambeth. He was a dangerous character who, having escaped the gallows on a charge of necromancy, made a living by astrology and quack-medicine.

Mrs Turner took the Countess of Essex across the river to consult Forman, who, probably having been notified of the impending visit, had the stage most impressively set: in a locked room, decorated with cabbalistic symbols, magic-circles, pentagrams, and the like, with an array of moumets ready-made in both wax and metal, he initiated his client as a practitioner of the black arts and a disciple of Satan.

After several visits Lady Essex was provided with potions of two kinds, one to cool the ardour of her husband, and the other to stimulate that of Carr. Overbury persisted in encouraging the relationship and continued to write Carr's love-letters for him.

Lady Essex, in need of further supplies, wrote to both Mrs Turner and Dr Forman, addressing the former as 'Sweet Turner' and signing herself 'your sister, Frances Essex', and the latter as 'Sweet Father', ending with 'your affectionate loving daughter, Frances Essex'. Sweet Father had, however, fallen down dead suddenly and his wife had called upon Mrs Turner to come and clear up all incriminating evidence. Mrs Turner undertook the task in which she was accompanied by 'trusty, toothless Margaret'.

Although the relationship between Carr (created Lord Rochester) and Frances of Essex progressed favourably, the Countess began to think of a divorce and marriage to his newly created lordship. However, Overbury did not approve: 'Once Rochester was married into the Howards, with Lord Treasurer Suffolk for a Father-in-law, and Northampton to direct his affairs, he would have no more need for Sir Thomas Overbury',* who promptly began a campaign of blackmail against Lord Rochester in order

* McElwee, op. cit.

to prevent the divorce. 'Rochester decided that he must somehow free himself from ... dependence on Overbury; Lady Essex that Overbury must be put out of the way altogether.'*

Mrs Turner had, on the death of Forman, found another warlock known as Dr Savory, but he was one who did not give extended credit, and had threatened Mrs Turner that he would charge her with witchcraft if she did not promptly settle an outstanding account, hence, Lady Essex was reduced to consulting 'cunning Mary Woods' who practised as a fortune-teller and sold love-potions, although 'cunning Mary' secured herself by giving her clients to understand that she would, in the event of their denouncing her, inform the court that they had come to her for poison to dispose of their husbands. When Lady Essex sent for cunning Mary, in late 1612, the latter stole money and a diamond ring, and Lady Essex had her arrested when, true to the threat by which she normally secured herself, she declared the money and the ring had been given to her as a reward for her providing poison to dispatch Essex, and steps were taken to hush the matter up.

Overbury, carried away with self-conceit, felt sure that Lord Rochester could not manage without him, hence, when the Countess's powerful friends arranged for Overbury to be offered official employment overseas he insolently refused to obey the King's command. None was more dumbfounded than himself when under a strong guard he descended the river to become a close prisoner in the Tower.

Sudden incarceration of this kind at that period was not of great significance. It was reasonable to assume that Rochester would, when the Essex divorce was completed, prevail upon the King to release the prisoner, but Lady Essex, motivated by both her hatred and fear, remembered her determination to encompass the prisoner's death. To help in the scheme she arranged for one Richard Weston to be appointed as servant to Sir Thomas.

This Weston, who was a sorry scamp, had been an apothecary's assistant, which calling endowed him with useful knowledge; he had been a coiner, for which he had served a term of imprisonment, and was now Mrs Turner's servant. Since Savory had proved difficult, Mrs Turner had sought and found another prac-

* McElwee, op. cit.

titioner in the black arts, one Franklin,* who supplied a phial of red arsenic, which Weston was to administer to Overbury. However, assuming that the Lieutenant of the Tower was privy to the plot he took no pains to conceal it, with the result that the phial was smashed in the gutter. But it might have been dangerous to interfere, so the story that the dose had been administered was carried by Weston to Mrs Turner. After a lapse of time he again visited Mrs Turner for the purpose of collecting his promised reward, but was simply ordered to complete the dirty work.

Overbury was receiving tarts and other delicacies, and it was decided by Lady Essex and Mrs Turner to join in making him such gifts. Franklin supplied at least one of the ingredients. When Overbury fell alarmingly ill it was made the excuse for sending him more delicacies; 'there was a brace of partridges in which lapis costitus had been mixed with the pepper seasoning and there was arsenic and mercury sublimate in many of the tarts and jellies. All these were carried round in the most casual way by anyone who happened to be going with messages.'†

Rochester, perhaps a little frightened, arranged medical aid for Sir Thomas, and the Lieutenant of the Tower saw to it that only the persons approved should have access to the prisoner, but the Countess offered a bribe of £20 to get a dose of mercurial sublimate, to be supplied by Franklin, introduced into the next enema administered to the prisoner. This proved to be the last straw. The abnormal resistance to poison demonstrated by Sir Thomas Overbury was at an end. After a night of agony he expired at seven o'clock the following morning.

Franklin boasted of his hand in the affair. Weston was worried lest he himself be poisoned to silence him, and both were irritated by the Countess's shortage of ready cash with which to reward them according to her promises. The young man who had administered the final enema was hurried off to the Continent by his friends; nevertheless, Lady Essex herself, feeling sure of her own safety, turned not a hair. She took it for granted that the

* Not an ancestor, nor yet a collateral relation of the present writer who aspires to nothing worse than a pirate over whose corpse, chained at Execution Dock, three tides flowed and ebbed.

† McElwee, op. cit.

entire world was subject to her whims and that she could even commit murder with impunity.

The divorce proceedings were difficult, tortuous and long drawn-out, but ultimately her marriage to Essex was annulled and she contracted a new marriage with Carr, who had been created Earl of Somerset. There was, however, one matter that was most displeasing: her new husband was no longer the King's favourite.

Meanwhile the wheels of God were grinding slowly, steadily and surely. The young man who had administered the fatal enema to Overbury felt sick, and, in fear of death, made a secular confession. This was carried to the King, and since there is no privacy for the head that wears the crown, common knowledge soon set tongues wagging.

The lesser lights involved in the plot had ample cause to apprehend the result of the ever-flourishing rumour. Mrs Turner and Weston had a meeting to compare notes and synchronize their story lest the worst came to the worst, but neither knew all that the other knew, nor how the *canard* had been set afoot.

King James VI and I is frequently described as 'the wisest fool in Christendom', but he was very far from being a fool. In this matter he perceived two things very clearly: first, that Overbury, whom it was known he disliked, had died while held a prisoner of the King and that malicious tongues would not fail to lay these two facts side by side and, secondly, that the entire story might be a fabrication to damage Carr and his bride. To keep his own feet on safe ground, and to show that justice must be done, King James ordered Lord Chief Justice Coke to make careful enquiries into the matter. The first person taken into custody was Weston, whereupon the remaining conspirators, in a panic, made frantic haste to protect themselves.

Notwithstanding that Forman's papers had already been searched, toothless Margaret was sent to make a further investigation. Mrs Forman, informed that the authorities might descend upon her at any moment, handed a few documents to Margaret, but cunningly concealed a quantity of incriminating evidence which, ultimately, she delivered to Coke's men in order to protect herself. In addition to this, numerous other damning letters came to light, as well as a number of Forman's figurines.

The arrest of Weston, frightening in the extreme, brought Franklin to a meeting with Frances Howard and Mrs Turner.

The warlock was warned that in the event of his being offered pardon in exchange for information he had better not fall into the trap for, having extracted the confession, they would certainly go back on their word and hang him. The conspirators were unaware of what, and how much, Weston had revealed, but he, in his first examination, declared Overbury's death to be due to natural causes. In the course of six further examinations Weston implicated Mrs Turner, Franklin and the Countess of Essex. Mrs Turner was next to be seized.

Frances Howard knew that sooner or later she would, herself, fall into Coke's net, and she sought avidly for information on what the prisoners had revealed. She sent, every day, a messenger to Mrs Turner in custody, and learnt only that in both of two examinations she had revealed nothing. These visits, which were effected to the accompaniment of bribery, had the effect of causing the King to set up a Commission. Lord Ellesmere was at its head; its members were, in addition to Coke, Lord Zouch, and the Duke of Lennox, both of whom Carr had good reason to reckon among his enemies. Carr, in his panic, abused his authority by having a box of Weston's broken open and letters extracted. The result of this blunder was that both he and Lady Essex were made prisoners under house arrest: he at his 'Chamber near the Cockpit at Whitehall', she at her house in Blackfriars. They were foolish enough to communicate with each other, and to send another messenger to Mrs Turner, and so made their closer arrest inevitable.

Weston, brought up for trial, heard the accusations against him, but refused to plead and so held up the proceedings. Coke, beside himself with rage at being thus thwarted, proceeded with the trial. Such behaviour was illlegal and Coke wrote asking the King for special permission, which he received. However, it occurred to him 'that any interference with the course of the law would bring scandal on His Majesty's Justice', so he sought other means. Not having found a way out of the dilemma he reluctantly decided to pronounce sentence on the King's command, but, at the resumed hearing, he was spared; for Weston pleaded 'Not guilty' and the trial recommenced: '. . . Richard Weston, being about the age of sixty years, not having the fear of God before his eyes, but instigated and induced by the devil . . .' Hyde, who was conducting the prosecution, was at a serious disadvantage because he was unable to prove that any particular dose of poison had been administered on the day stated in the indictment, or that it had caused the death of the victim: that was precisely Weston's defence.

In spite of this difficulty the jury returned a verdict of guilty and Coke sentenced the prisoner to death. The next on the list was Mrs Turner. Coke had secured the puppets she had obtained from Forman, and these exhibits he sent to the King who, upon sight of them, could not fail to detect witchcraft at work. Mrs Turner, cocksure and full of confidence, knowing nothing of what had taken place, began to waver as Hyde read the indictment against Weston, adding that the prisoner had been an accessory. On learning of Weston's execution she collapsed. The prosecution harped on the witchcraft theme: letters from the Countess of Essex to both the prisoner and Forman were read; exhibits, consisting largely of figurines, were produced, some naked, others expensively dressed, and the defence claimed that they were not puppets for killings by enchantment, but Court Dressmaker's samples. Mrs Forman had supplied other exhibits: some obscene puppets in both lead and wax which, by no stretch of imagination could be accepted as fashion models, parchments written with cantrips and embellished with cabbalistic symbols. One of these had a piece of human skin attached. There were charms in which names appeared, to be used to invoke the devil's aid in tormenting the intended victim. Suddenly a loud crack was heard and all present assumed that the devil was for once protecting one of his servitors. So great was the panic that it took a quarter of an hour to restore order. After this had been accomplished Mrs Forman was called to give evidence. In addition to confirming the relationship between the prisoner and her late husband, she revealed how Mrs Turner and toothless Margaret had invaded her home to destroy papers.

Coke told the prisoner that she was 'a whore, a bawd, a sorcerer, a witch, a papist, a felon and a murderer: the daughter of the devil Forman', and, on obtaining the inevitable verdict sentenced her to death.

Franklin, who must have been living in terror of the long arm of the law reaching out for him, in the spirit of the best form of defence being attack, sent an unsolicited statement to Coke who, armed with it, brought to trial the Lieutenant of the Tower. That worthy, notwithstanding his righteous indignation at the first attempt on Overbury's life, had been unquestionably aware of, and complacent to, the subsequent attempts.

The Lieutenant behaved with dignity and defended himself with eloquence. He clearly made a favourable impression on the jury. At this point Coke produced Franklin's confession which, although not evidence, had a most depressing effect on the prisoner whose murmur of 'Lord have mercy upon me' was overheard by the jury and undid all the good of the Lieutenant's spirited defence. Their verdict was 'guilty'. The Lieutenant was given the privilege of being hanged on Tower Hill instead of at Tyburn, and after his demise his accuser, Franklin, stood in the dock.

Weston's indictment was again used and Franklin was cited as an accessory. His weak defence was that he had supplied the poisons to the Countess and Mrs Turner but had not been aware of the use to which they were to be put. The death sentence was passed but its execution was postponed in the hope of obtaining from this sorry rogue some more information.

Meanwhile, Carr and his wife were both kept close prisoners. She, being pregnant, planned to commit suicide by the simple expedient of applying a cold water pack to her abdomen after delivery, but in this she was frustrated.

The trial of Lady Essex and her husband was not a matter Coke handled: it took place before the House of Lords where the Attorney-General took charge of the prosecution. There was no direct evidence of Carr's connection with the poisoning of Sir Thomas Overbury. The Attorney-General, in a letter to the King, said the evidence against the prisoner was 'of a good strong thread, considering impoisoning is the darkest of offences, but that the thread must be well-spun and woven together, for your Majesty knoweth it is one thing to deal with a jury of Middlesex and Londoners and another to deal with the Peers.'

The King wished for an excuse to pardon both of the prisoners, but did not wish to offend public opinion by doing so.

The Countess of Essex was at length taken to the Tower where she screamed and wept when she found she was to be confined in the chambers that had been the last home of her victim. Out of mercy she was given another apartment. Every step was taken to persuade her husband to plead guilty and depend on the King's clemency. The prosecution feared the danger of his refusing to plead for it was not conceivable that James would then permit his former favourite to be pressed to death. They also feared that the prisoner, if pleading not guilty, would, in his fight for life, make accusations against the King himself and against the present favourite and so increase the by no means negligible danger of stirring up public opinion to denounce the proceedings as mere Court intrigue. There were many complications to be overcome but at length the trials were staged in Westminster Hall. Twenty-two peers, under the chairmanship of Lord Ellesmere, took their seats and a panel of judges were present to help and advise them: Lord Chief Justice Coke; Lord Chief Justice of Common Pleas, Sir Henry Hubbard; Lord Chief Baron of the Exchequer, Sir Laurence Tanfield; Judges Dodderidge, Altham, Nicholls, Crook and Houghton. The Great Seal rested impressively on the table.

Her ladyship, preceded by an official carrying the headman's axe, the cutting edge facing forward, came slowly into the Hall, where she stood pale and weeping. After lengthy and legal preliminaries, the Clerk of the Arraigns, addressing her as Countess of Somerset, ordered her to hold up her hand. The indictment was read and again the Clerk of Arraigns called to her, 'Frances, Countess of Somerset, what sayest thou? Art thou guilty of this felony and murder or not guilty?'

In a low, but audible voice she pleaded guilty.

The Attorney-General then made a long and impressive speech on English justice, and summarized the entire nauseating business from beginning to end. The King's instructions for the matter to be investigated were then read. Ultimately the Clerk of Arraigns asked whether the prisoner had any reason to put forward why the death sentence should not be passed. Her reply, uttered in a voice scarcely audible was, 'I can much aggravate, but nothing extenuate my fault. I desire mercy, and that the Lords will intercede for me with the King.'

The Lord High Sheriff accepted the white staff and pronounced sentence: 'Frances, Countess of Somerset, whereas thou hast been indicted, arraigned, pleaded guilty and thou hast nothing to say for thyself, it is now my part to pronounce judgement. Only this much before; since my Lords have heard with what humility and grief you have confessed the fact, I do not doubt they will signify so much to the King and mediate for his grace towards you. But in the meantime, according to law, the sentence must be this: Thou shalt be carried from hence to the Tower of London, and thence to the place of execution, where you are to be hanged by the neck until you are dead, and the Lord have mercy on your soul.'* She passed from the Hall, again preceded by the axe, but this time the cutting edge was towards her.

Her husband, at the Tower, on being informed that his trial would take place the following morning received so great a shock that he went into an hysterical fit, raved and roared and refused to go to Westminster Hall, declaring they would be compelled to carry him by force. The King, he asseverated, would not dare bring him to trial. His theme was not new, but his violence was so far in excess of previous demonstrations that the Tower officials thought it necessary to send a message to the King in case they were late in arriving at Westminster Hall next morning. James replied, '. . . I expect the Lord Hay and Sir Robert Carr have been with you before this time . . . they may first hear him, before you say anything unto him, and when that is done, if he shall still refuse to go, you must do your office† except he be either apparently sick or distracted in his wits, in any of which cases, you may acquaint the Chancellor with it, that he may adjourn the day . . .'

In the morning the prisoner had enough sense to make no resistance and he stood in the Hall with, on each side, a man having over his arm a cloak so that in the event of his uttering slander against the King he could be silenced and carried from the Hall and the trial proceed, quite illegally, in his absence.

The prisoner, however, made no scene. While the Clerk read the indictment he looked around and saw, facing him, the Earl of Essex, taking the opportunity to gloat. Lord Ellesmere opened by saying, 'Robert, Earl of Somerset, you have been arraigned and pleaded "not guilty". Now I must tell you, whatever you have to say in your own defence, say it boldly, without fear; and though it be not the ordinary custom, you shall have pen and ink to help your memory. But remember that God is the God of truth. A fault defended is a double crime. Hide not the verity, nor affirm an untruth, for to deny that which is true increases the offence. . . .' The subject of the trial was whether or not the

* Quoted in full by McElwee, op. cit.   † Use

prisoner had procured Weston to administer the poison to Sir Thomas Overbury.

The Attorney-General opened with a long and most eloquent speech on the crime of poisoning in general, but he was unable to adduce any evidence against the prisoner. He made a case of hearsay and corruption, and continued so long that it was dusk before the prisoner was allowed his defence. Candles were sent for and the hearing continued. The case against him had been full of detail, quotations from letters, and matters that had emerged during the trials of the small fry. Considering the lateness of the hour, the prisoner's fatigue, and the Attorney-General's ocean of verbiage the defence was admirable; nevertheless, it was weak and confused, hence unconvincing, and Carr was found guilty.

Notwithstanding that he was condemned on hearsay and circumstantial evidence, it seemed that Carr was in less hope of a Royal Pardon than was his fundamentally wicked wife. She was a witch, a patron of poisoners, who consorted with witches, warlocks and sorcerers; a murderer in spirit and in fact, whose meek and apparently repentant demeanour, backed by her humble confession of guilt, was merely a cunning pose because she was aware that confession and apparent penitence were held in high esteem and half-way to a reprieve.

While Carr remained a close prisoner, his wife was allowed a great deal of freedom and the grounds on which her pardon was based included the statement that she was not the agent of the devil and prime mover in the murder, but was herself the victim of base persons who influenced her against her will.

The evil woman lived in the Tower in luxury: her suite of rooms were handsomely furnished and she had the services of three maids. She was visited by her friends, and felt gay enough to engage in intrigues and to influence marriages. Ultimately her husband's rigorous confinement was relaxed and he occupied a suite of rooms intercommunicating with those of his wife who, when not engaged in some wicked malefic plot, amused herself by quarrelling violently with him.

They were released, under restraint, from the Tower in 1621, and went to live at Grays, where they were not allowed to travel more than three miles from their house. The marriage, for which Carr had sacrificed his best friend, and his wife had abandoned Essex and committed foul murder, proved no blessing. Their hatred of each other, pent up at Grays, caused each to wish that no pardon had been granted. Just over a decade after her release, Frances Howard died in a state of dementia. Her husband lingered on for many years in misery and in debt.

This apparently lengthy summary of the Overbury murder is, in fact, highly condensed: no reference is made to the intricate web of intrigue, rival families' interferences in order to implicate and so ruin their rivals; malodorous domestic politics and unscrupulous foreign policy; Court plots and counter-plots, and the creeping and crawling of place-seekers. Although the matter may seem more suited to general history than to an examination of occult practices and therefore digressive, it is in fact nothing of the kind, but is closely related to our theme. It will, perhaps, be wise to repeat and underline its utility as a bolster and prop and a proof of the acceptability of some of the allegations made against witches.

It was no mere inquisition, but was a trial, and a highly important one, of persons guilty of a dastardly outrage that was not without wide social significance in casting reflections on the good name and character of members of noble families and did not spare even the King himself.

The judgement seat was occupied by no local magistrate ignorant of law, and often as credulous, gullible and superstitious as were the humble rustic miscreants over whom he held, by dint of his superior social status, the right of summary jurisdiction: it was the Lord Chief Justice and no lesser man who conducted the trials. It is said of Coke, and it may be true, that he was a harsh, biased, bullying judge, who browbeat and badgered a jury in order to force them to arrive at his own preconceived verdict. If it were true then Coke differed only in degree from today's judges who, in their summing-up, make it abundantly clear to the twelve just men and fools what verdict they are to return. If Coke carried this system to intolerable extremes, it did not diminish or alter facts that emerged under cross-examination, even if he interpreted those facts to fit his own ideas concerning the prisoner's guilt or innocence.

In each case which Coke heard, the prisoner was not an insignificant, elderly, irrascible, semi-destitute village hag, hated and feared by her neighbours because she cursed them soundly when they refused to give her (say) an apple, or when they insulted her, and now brought to book on a charge of witchcraft on an information laid by one of them that she, having glanced at the brewing, caused the beer to turn sour; but was an unscrupulous poisoner, or a more or less prosperous compounder and vendor of poisons, and they were on trial on the capital charge of murder, or of being accessories before or after the fact of murder. That all of them proved to be witches, or warlocks, or Satanic sorcerers, emerged during the hearing, and was not used in evidence against them.

This defeats, most effectively, the prevalent, modern sophisticated assertion that none of the witches executed for their crimes was guilty in the slightest degree; that each one of them was a poor, pitiable old woman who fell an unfortunate victim of the European cultural psychopathogenic sickness of the period. It does more than this: it establishes with certainty that at least some of the witches were indeed guilty of one item of the indictment, namely, that of poisoning, or of procuring or producing poisons for the use of others. It further establishes that witches accused of, or who confessed to, the making and vending of puppets to enable their patrons to commit murder by magic, were not the victims of mere superstition and fantasy.

It is easily understandable that a wicked person wishing to be rid of one considered an enemy, or of a relation who stood between him and the ultimate inheritance of a fortune, would resort to the administration of poison; but it is not so easily understandable that such a one would purchase a puppet to secure the same end by magical means, and without the revelation that there was indeed a traffic in these objects, it would be reasonable to reject accusations and confessions that such transactions were entered into. The Overbury murder trials qualify for a place in the literature of witchcraft on account of the two foregoing points alone but, as will be seen, there is also a significance to be noted in the aftermath of the trials.

To return, however, to the subject of figurines or puppets, sometimes termed 'pictures', in the witch trials. The medium in which they were modelled was, in most cases, wax, but following this a close second was clay. The method of employing such an effigy to bring disease and death to the person whom the doll was declared to represent was to thrust into the figure either pins or thorns, muttering meanwhile an incantation calling upon an evil spirit to afflict so-and-so with torments in the place where the spike was thrust. Another method of bringing the victim to an end by a high fever was to roast the puppet before a slow fire. Because of the apparent need for imprecations it seems most strange that 'laymen' procured them to use in silence or, at most, to the accompaniment of a self-composed curse or string of curses.

The principle involved in accomplishing murder by the use of such figurines, or puppets, or pictures, or moumets, or mummets, or child-babies, was the universal and very ancient belief in sympathetic magic: that by maltreating and finally destroying an image the person represented would suffer pain, severe illness and ultimately waste away to death.

Sympathetic magic was sometimes strengthened by a tincture of homoeopathic magic, namely, building into the effigy a hair, or a nail-paring of the intended victim.

'Mention of these wax or clay puppets occurs again and again in English witch trials,' says Montague Summers in *Witchcraft and Black Magic*, and he quotes Mother Demdike* as having declared 'that the speediest way to take a man's life away by witchcraft is to make a picture of clay, like unto the shape of the person whom they mean to kill, and dry it thoroughly: and when they would have them to be ill in any one place more than another, then take a thorn or pin, and prick it in that part of the picture you would so have to be ill: and when you would have any part of the body to consume away, then take that part of the picture, and burn it. And when they would have the whole body to consume away, then take the remnant of the said picture and burn it; and so thereupon by that means, the body shall die.'

Again to quote the same authority, 'In Italy—and in other countries—the charm is sometimes a little differently worked, the variants being known as "The Spell of the Black Hen". The figure of a hen painted black, and stuffed with hair, if possible the hair of the intended victim, or parings of his nails mingled with the hair, is thrown into water to rot away. The black hen may even be knitted of black wool or cut out of black cloth. Black pins are stuck into the stuff, which is buried, or somewhere concealed to perish.'

Within the present writer's own experience, and as recently as 1963, an old-fashioned woman's hat-pin, the prong about eight

* See p. 116.

inches long, having a white porcelain head which had been painted in black to represent a face, had been pushed down behind the wallpaper where the lath and plaster joined a newel-post, so that only the painted head protruded and this, being tucked tight into the angle formed by the post and the wall was visible only with difficulty. It was a clumsy attempt by a rather unskilled witch to bring about the death of her husband, but he, totally unaware of the *maleficia* being directed against him, not only did not die, but persisted in enjoying robust health. Having discovered the puppet, and upon enquiry been enlightened concerning its meaning and purpose, he had (somewhat superstitiously) insisted on disposing of it by putting it in the fire, which was a great pity.

Turning again to Elizabeth Style, tried at Taunton,* she informs us that 'About a month since, Examinate, Alice Duke, Ann Bishop and Mary Penny, about nine o'clock at night on the common near Trister Gate, met a man in black clothes. . . . Alice Duke having brought a picture in wax, to represent Elizabeth Hill, the man took it in his arms, anointed its forehead and said, "I baptize these with this oil", and further words. He officiated as godfather, and Examinate and Ann Bishop as godmothers, the puppet being called Elizabeth or Bess. The man in black, this Examinate, Ann Bishop and Alice Duke then stuck thorns into several places of the neck, hand-wrists, fingers and other parts of the picture.' Afterwards they consumed wine, cakes, and roast meat (all brought by the man in black), and they danced and made merry, being bodily present, and in their clothes. On a second occasion the same persons met, and baptized a picture brought by Ann Bishop, representing John, son of Robert Newman, of Wincanton, and also pricked it with thorns, and at a third meeting, near Marnhull, a picture representing Ann or Rachel Hatcher, brought by Dunsford's wife, was baptized and treated as before. . . .

'Ann Bishop, about five years past, brought a picture in wax to their meeting, which represented Robert Newman's child, and was baptized in the name of Peter.' †‡

---

*p. 122.   †Ewen quoting Glanvil.
‡ Were two children of Robert Newman's victimized, both John and Peter? or was 'this Examinate' becoming fatigued and confused?

John Walsh, of Netherbury, Dorset (1566), revealed that 'pictures of clay are compounded of earth from a "new made grave, rib bone of man or woman burned to ashes", a black spider, with an inner pith of elder, tempered all in water in which toads have been washed.'

In February 1579, Elizabeth Stile, alias Rockynham, of Windsor,* confessed that 'Father Rosimond of Farnham, widower, and his daughter are witches, the former being able by devilish means, to transform himself into the shape and likeness of any beast.' Dame Stile also accused Mother Dutten, Mother Devell and Mother Margaret.

These half-dozen boon companions were in the habit of meeting 'within the backside of Master Dodges in the Pittes' for the purpose of enchanting to death any person against whom any one of them had a grudge. They disposed of 'Lanckforde, a farmer of Windsor, Master Gallis, mayor of Windsor, one of Lanckforde's maids, a butcher named Switcher, and another butcher named Masclyn.'

These deaths were engineered by fashioning 'pictures of red wax about a span long and three or four fingers broad' into which was thrust 'an hawthorne pricke'. On another occasion Mother Stile, Mother Dutten and Mother Devell made a picture for George Whittyng, servant to Matthew Glover of Eton, to harm one Foster ...'

Another record of such a transaction is to be found among the Domestic State Papers where, under the date January 1589, it is stated that Mrs Dewse employed Robert Birche, described as a 'conjuror', to 'make pictures of wax of her enemies'. Among those whom Mrs Dewse prepared to torment to death was 'that thief, Justice Younge, who lives by robbing papists; and another Sir Rowland Howard, and to stick them with pins, and prick them to the heart.'

The word 'conjuror' was, at the time of Elizabeth I, frequently used as a description of male witches: in the same Calendar of State Papers is to be found 'information touching certain men taken up in the parish of Edmonton for practising witchcraft and conjuring': there were found in their possession 'mystic articles, powders, and rats bane'.

* Not to be confused with Elizabeth Style of Bayford, tried at Taunton, 1664.

In the late sixteenth century the induction of disease and death by the use of puppets was a cause of special anxiety. There is an entry in the Privy Council Register at the time of the trial of Elizabeth Stile, recording that Sir Henry Nevell and the Dean of Windsor were to enquire into the making of puppets by the witches taken at Windsor because 'there has lately been discovered a practice of that device very likely to be intended to the destruction of Her Majesty's person'.

The discovery referred to was a puppet in the likeness of the Queen with a spike driven through it, left to rot away in Lincoln's Inn Fields. The Queen, who had laughed the matter off, nevertheless took the dual precaution of moving her Court to Greenwich, and of sending Dr Dee to deal with the matter. Dee who was normally as simple and trusting as a child, displayed on this occasion shrewdness, foresight and wisdom by asking for 'Mr Secretary Wilson' to accompany him on the enterprise 'to witness that I do it only by godley means'. It is observed in an article by the present author on Dr Dee, published in *Tomorrow* * that to handle the thing demanded the same kind of cool, cautious courage as was displayed in our own time by the men who undertook unexploded-bomb disposal.

In 1801 there was published by Lackington, proprietor of the 'Temple of the Muses' in Finsbury Square, a curious and extraordinarily verbose work entitled *The Magnus, or Celestial Intelligencer* . . . by Francis Barrett, who also conducted classes in occultism. He begins 'Book II part I' by informing the reader that 'in our following Treatise of Magnetism we have collected and arranged in order some valuable and secret things out of the writings of that most learned chemist and philosopher Paracelus . . . [and] . . . we have extracted the very marrow of the science of Magnetism out of the copious and elaborate works of that most celebrated philosopher (by fire) Van Helmont.'

In 'Chapter VI, of Witchcraft', he says, 'let a witch therefore be granted, who can strongly torment an absent man by an image of wax, by imprecation or cursing, by enchantment, or also by a foregoing touch alone, (for here we speak nothing of Sorceries, because they are those which kill only by poison, inasmuch as

* Vol. 9, No. 1. American title, 'The Amazing Dr Dee': original title, 'A Brief Note on Dr Dee'.

every common apothecary can imitate those things) that this act is diabolical, no man doubts: however, it is profitable to discern how much Satan and how much the witch can contribute hereunto.

'First of all, thou shalt take notice, that Satan is the sworn and irreconcileable enemy of man, and to be so accounted by all, unless any one had rather have him to be his friend; and therefore he most readily procures whatsoever mischief he is able to cause or wish unto us, and that without doubt and neglect.

'And then although he be an enemy to witches themselves, forasmuch as he is a most malicious enemy to all mankind in general; yet, in regard they are his bond-slaves, and those of his kingdom, he never, unless against his will betrays them, or discovers them to Judges.

'From the former supposition I conclude, that if Satan were able of himself to kill a man who is guilty of deadly sin, he would never delay it; but he doth not kill him, therefore he cannot.

'Notwithstanding, the witch doth oftimes kill; hence also she can kill the same man, no otherwise than as a privy murderer at the liberty of his own will slap any one with a sword.'

In 1645, a witch tried at Great Yarmouth buried a wax image to cause a child to languish: another puppet burial was revealed in the Lancashire Witches trial, old Demdike made a picture of Ann, daughter of Anthony Nutter and this she interred accompanied by some human teeth previously obtained by Chattox from Pendle Churchyard.

Since sculpture, portraiture in the round, is a fine art, one is justified in questioning the witches' ability to make the figurines, but this dubiety is misplaced. It is not necessary to produce a likeness, not even a figure approximating to accurate human morphology; a model as lumpy as a child's rag-doll would do. It became an effigy of the person represented by being declared so: the effect could be increased by dressing the puppet in somewhat the style as customarily adopted by the intended victim. Compare the modern annual obstruction of the entrances and exits of London's tube-railway stations by bundles of rag and rubbish which wanton, importunate children refer to as 'The Guy' while they pester the public for money to buy fireworks. The witches were doubtless aware of numerous methods of manufacture, one of which was the casting of the wax in a mould, in the way toy soldiers were made. In 1586 'Stephen Kylden, late of Southwark, and Jane, his wife' were indicted for 'engraving my Lord Treasurer's picture in wood and therewith to make his picture in wax to the intent to destroy him in his body and feloniously to bring him to death by art magic and enchantment.'

Chapter Five

WITCHES were sometimes accused of having 'overlooked' people or their children, or their livestock and so caused disease and death. The belief in 'the evil eye', ancient and universal, is not exclusive to the uneducated urban and rural peasant population; it is accepted at high social and cultural levels and occasionally even by people of superior mental attainment and critical ability.

The eye is acknowledged to be an organ of emotional expression: love, malice, hatred, pain and pleasure. Materialists deny this, contending that the eye is simply involved in the general facial expression; that any seeming change in the eye is illusory, arising from changes in the musculature of the surrounding tissues. They hammer their contention home by referring to the mongoloid epicanthic fold which gives to the orb itself the appearance of being set at an oblique angle. The final fact is, however, not proof of the former fallacy: the most stolidly stupid materialist is unable to assert that the iris does not expand and contract under stimulus of light. It can do more than that: under stimulus of the onset of a burst of hysterical frenzy it can change in both lustre and colour: the surface of the entire orb assumes a hard, cold glitter, the iris fades till it is barely distinguishable from the white. The former condition seems to be caused by suspension, or reduction, of the functions of the lachrymal gland, and the latter may indicate a curtailment of blood-supply.

What the eye cannot do is emit a beam, or ray, or wave, or force that upon striking the victim penetrates his body and causes the sickness that will destroy him. Nevertheless, Barrett* says: 'We have so far spoken concerning the great virtues, and wonderful efficacy of natural things; it remains now that we speak of a wonderful power and faculty of fascination; or, more properly, a magical and occult binding of men into love or hatred,

* Francis Barrett, op. cit.

sickness or health; also, the binding of thieves, that they cannot steal in any place; or to bind them that they cannot remove, from whence they may be detected; the binding of merchants, that they cannot buy nor sell; the binding of an army, that they cannot pass over any bounds; the binding of ships, so that no wind, though ever so strong, shall be able to carry them out of that harbour; the binding of a mill, that it cannot, by any means whatsoever, be turned to work; the binding of a cistern, or fountain, so that the water cannot be drawn up out of them; the binding of the ground, so that nothing will bring forth fruit, or flourish in it; also, that nothing can be built upon it; the binding of fire, that, though it be ever so strong, it shall burn no combustible thing that is put to it; also the binding of lightnings and tempests, that they shall do no hurt; the binding of dogs, that they cannot bark; also the binding of birds and wild beasts, that they shall not be able to run or fly away. . . . We call fascination a binding, because it is effected by a look, glance, or observation, in which we take possession of the spirit, and overpower the same, of those we mean to fascinate or suspend; for it comes through the eyes . . . rays or beams . . . into the eye of him or her that is opposite . . . wounds their hearts, infects their spirits, and overpowers them.

'Know likewise, that in witches, those are most bewitched, who, with overlooking, direct the edge of their sight to the edge of the sight of those who bewitch or fascinate them; whence arose the saying of "Evil eyes, etc".'

The idea of the eye's power to project mysterious force as a lantern projects a beam of light is precisely what is accepted, even today, by those who believe in the evil eye and they will, in discussion, rationalize by pointing out that nothing is seen to pass between a camera and the person, or object, being photographed but that obviously something does pass. Comparison is also made with X-rays and with the transmission of wireless telegraphy, which latter has, in recent years, been bolstered up by the introduction of television.

It was on the foundation of evil-eye fears that anxiety was expressed of a rumour, spread during the 1914–18 war, that the Germans had, among their secret weapons, a 'death-ray' apparatus. Due to the phenomenal advance in wireless transmission there was, at the commencement of the Second World War, a far wider, deeper, and socially dangerous belief in the successful development of a death-ray by the enemy, and—'just in case'—scientific investigation was made to ascertain the possibilities. This research did not succeed in either revealing or disproving the likelihood of there being so formidable a power, but the time, talent and treasure expended on the work was not wasted: what the research team did discover was 'radar'.

Although the evil eye is believed to be the wilful and wicked acquisition of the possessor, it is also acknowledged, particularly in Italy, that *mal'occhio* may be an affliction. For example, Pope Pius IX (1792–1878), well loved and respected, was also pitied because none doubted the disastrous effect of a side-glance from him. King Alfonso XIII, who was dethroned in 1931 discovered, in exile, that his reputation of being evil-eyed, could, when he was no longer fenced about by the sanctity of regal status, be a cause of embarrassment and distress: in addition to his being constantly subjected, while living in Italy, to the annoyance of seeing protective gestures made against him by all who, passing in the street, recognized him, he suffered on one occasion the humiliation of finding himself the sole person present at a party organized in his honour. The twenty Italian noblemen who had been invited failed to put in an appearance: behaviour rather less than 'noble', less, even, than manly.

The superiority goal of the coward, or the weakling, is to possess a terrible, potent killing force enabling him to be revenged without risk: by *post hoc* argumentation he gleefully persuades himself that having darted his fierce, malefic glance at the object of his dislike, every minor and major mishap that subsequently befalls the person is the result of the 'overlooking'. Such glory gained by self-deception would be a harmless hobby if humankind was not affectible and suggestible, but because the normal man is both he will—must—whether he believes in the evil-eye or not—begin to attribute all reverses to his being brought under 'fascination', and anxiety (if not actual fear) will cause him to court disaster by trying to avoid it when there is, in fact, nothing to avoid. It is not necessary to have objectively given offence to attract the evil-eye: the mere possession of something that arouses covetousness can bring the curse upon one, hence, it is wise to take precautions. At all social levels in Europe, certainly up to 1914 and possibly even later, it was customary for male children to be dressed, during their first half-decade, as females: one might envy a man his sons, but daughters are a disaster. With the same object in view, particularly at peasant level in Eastern Europe, children, especially boys, were disparaged and insulted by their parents. If a man bemoans his misfortune in being the father of a sickly, petulant, stupid child, who will, supposing he survives, prove nothing but a source of sorrow and expense no one will envy him: 'the eye' will not be turned in his direction.

In Sir Richard Burton's translation of *The Book of the Thousand Nights and a Night*, the story of 'Ala Al-Din Abu Al-Shamat' [Aladdin Abush-Shámát] there occurs, at the end of the Two Hundred and Fifty-first night's recitation* the following: 'Thereupon the Consul cried out to him, saying, "Silence, Allah curse thee, genus and species! This is my son." Rejoined the Deputy, "Never in our born days have we seen thee with a son", and Shams al-Din answered, "... I reared him in a souterrain† for fear of the evil-eye, nor was it my purpose that he should come forth, till he could take his beard in his hand. ..."'

At this point Burton interpolates a note: 'i.e., when the evil eye has less effect than upon children. Strangers in Cairo often wonder to see a woman richly dressed, leading by the hand a filthy little boy (rarely a girl) in rags, which at home would be changed to cloth of gold.'

In another of his enlightening footnotes he points out that foodstuffs carried through the streets of an Arabian city are in covered containers, the object of the cover being to protect the vessel's contents from the evil eye of which the people are afraid. This precaution affords protection from dust and flies of which the people are not afraid.

Even in this enlightened, prosaic age, when medical science finds itself baffled by a wasting disease attacking either man or beast, of the nature of which no opinion can be given—and such cases, if not common, are certainly not rare—the patient's friends or the beast's owner will murmur darkly of the evil eye. In 1934 the *Daily Express*, reporting the case of a man pronounced by one doctor after another to be organically sound, but who was, none the less, growing weaker and weaker day by day, did not hesitate

* Vol. IV, p. 37.
† Secret underground cavern.

to give publicity to the non-medical opinion of the man himself and that of his neighbours: namely, he had been 'overlooked'.

'We see likewise the Scripture calleth envy an evil eye,' said Bacon,* hence flocks and herds and transport animals are most particularly susceptible. Cows can be protected by giving the witch some of the animal's milk, but horses and, in Arab lands, camels, need something rather stronger in the form of counter magic. In Judges, VIII, 21 (Revised Version) we read, 'And Gideon arose, and slew Zebah and Zalmunna, and took the crescents† that were on their camels' necks.' These crescents were not placed upon the camels' necks solely as ornaments, but as charms to avert the evil eye. The custom of thus protecting transport animals survived until, in the twentieth century, the internal combustion engine took the place of horse-drawn traffic. Today, horse-brasses are so eagerly sought by collectors that it pays the manufacturers of 'genuine antiques' to employ foundries to cast them by the gross, or even by the thousand.

In *Somerset and Dorset Notes and Queries*, Vol. IV, part XXVIII (December, 1894) will be found, 'Witchcraft in Somerset.—It is hardly credible, but there arises in our day, a belief in witchcraft in some parts of Somerset.

'The following incidents happened during this year. A poor woman, the mother of a large family, had a period of two years of serious misfortunes: her husband was ill, two children were injured accidentally, they were all laid up by a prevailing epidemic. The woman herself, no doubt tired and worn out, came to the conclusion that in this long and bitter trial, which she considered was undeserved, there must be an evil agency at work, and she pronounced herself "overlooked". Once the idea took possession of her, it seemed to spread through the family, her husband and children testifying that they saw strange-looking little black objects sitting on the boxes at night; these little things used to try to pull them by the feet out of bed.

'She became so thoroughly convinced that she was bewitched that she went to interview a wise man who lives at Wells. He took the same view of the case, and said that he would have to pray for her, the point at interest being, who had bewitched her? She had to go through a list of names—names of women; after

---

* Bacon, Essay IX, *Of Envy*.
† The Authorized Version renders 'crescents' as 'ornaments'.

mentioning many, and not the right one among them, as she was turning away, remembering one more, she mentioned her, and that one the wise man pronounced the woman who had bewitched her. He told her that he could break the charm and take away the power of the witch, but it would take a lot of prayer and work. He then gave certain directions which the woman and her husband were to follow, in order to break the spell. About the hour of midnight she and her husband were directed to sit in front of their fire and burn salt, and for the space of one hour no conversation had to pass between them, only they had to repeat the following words:

> 'This is not the thing I wish to burn
> But Mrs—'s heart of Somerset to turn,
> Until thou dost come to me and do my request;
> Or else the wrath of God may fall on thee
> And cause thee to be consumed in a moment.
>
> Amen.

'This accomplished, they were to retire backwards to the foot of the stairs, climb the stairs still backwards, repeating at the same time the Lord's Prayer, also backwards, and then not speak a word to each other until they were in bed; in this way they would break the spell. . . .'

In 1644 or 1645, 'Marion Peebles, a hideous hag, "a wicked, devilish, fearful and abominable curser", had wrecked boats and drowned sailors to whom she bore "one deadlie and venefical malice". She cast her blear eyes upon a cow, and it "crappit togidder till no lyfe was leakit for her". Wretched was the fate of those who came under her malison. Her neighbours pined and languished, and were racked with agues in every limb. But at length they took her, and justice sentenced her to be hanged, the body being burnt.' *

At Flintshire Assizes a labourer named Edward Foulke testified against Anne Ellis, on 6 June 1657. His complaint was that a calf of his had fallen sick and the neighbours said 'God fend noone hath looked on him with an ill heart', and Anne Ellis, being reported an ill-hearted woman, he sent for her. The purpose of the summons was for her to remove the curse, and notwithstanding

---

* Summers, *Geography of Witchcraft*, quoting Samuel Hibbert, *Description of the Shetland Islands*, Edinburgh, 1822.

that the animal was fully recovered before her arrival, she blessed it.

It has been remarked above, in connection with the Throckmorton girls, that accused persons were often, apparently, most noble and generous-hearted in submitting to all the requests of the friends of their supposed victims, notwithstanding that by such behaviour they were often adding fuel to the fire of the accusations against them. Anne Ellis blessed her neighbour's calf, an effort at helpfulness which was likely to be accepted as proof in itself that she had previously cursed the animal. Anne Ellis was acquitted, but she might not have been: on the other hand, had Alice Samuels refused to take up residence in the Throckmorton household in order to sooth the hysterical girls she would not have been subjected to the outrageous abuse and physical attack of Lady Cromwell; and she, her husband and daughter, might not have perished on the scaffold.

Old Alice Samuels in addition to residing in the Throckmorton household where she was ill-treated and offered no food, and patiently enduring the continual teasing and bating of the delinquent girls, permitted them to scratch her face and draw blood; while she was confined in jail there occurred two incidents, both used in evidence against her. One was that the gaoler's assistant, who chained the old woman to a bedpost, was soon after seized with fits of which he died; the second was that the gaoler's son, falling sick, was cured only by having Nan Samuels brought to his bedside so that he might scratch her.

The therapeutical effect of scratching is a belief peculiarly English and theorists put forth the idea that the imp, sent by the witch to harm the victim who had thus become possessed would, upon smelling his mistress's blood on which he was accustomed to feed, voluntarily leave the afflicted person. This belief, which is superficial, may have been held by the uneducated, but it is likely that the underlying principle was sympathetic magic: by inflicting minor harm on the witch her major harm was annulled.

Barrett, in Book 11, Chapter 11 'of Sympathetic Medicines' says, 'In the year 1639, a little book came forth, whose title was "The Sympathetical Powder of Edricius Mohymus, of Eburs", whereby wounds are cured without application of the medicine unto the part afflicted, and without superstition; it being sifted by the sieve of the reasons of Galen and Aristotle; wherein it is

Aristotelically, sufficiently proved, whatsoever the title of it promises; but it hath neglected the *directive faculty*, or *virtue*, which may bring the virtues of the sympathetical powder, received in the bloody towel or napkin, unto the distant wound. ...

'We shall now show some remarkable operations that are effected by magnetism, and founded on natural sympathy and antipathy ....

'Uldericus Balk, a dominican friar, published a book at Frankfurt in the year 1611, concerning the lamp of life; in which we shall find (taken from Paracelsus) the true magnetical cure of many diseases, viz, the dropsy, gout, jaundice, etc. For if thou shall enclose the warm blood of the sick in the shell and white of an egg, which is exposed to a nourishing warmth, and this blood, being mixed with a piece of flesh, thou shalt give to a hungry dog, the disorder departs from thee into the dog; no otherwise than the leprosy of Naaman passed over into Gehazi through the execration of the prophet.

'If women, weaning their infants, shall milk out their milk upon hot burning coals, the breast soon dries.

'If anyone happens to commit nuisance at thy door, and thou wilt prevent that beastly trick in future, take the poker redhot, and put it into the excrement, and, by magnetism, his posteriors shall become much scorched and inflamed ....

'The root of the Caroline thistle being plucked up when full of juice and virtue, and tempered with the mummy of a man, will exhaust the powers and natural strength out of a man, on whose shadow thou shalt stand, into thyself.'

Notwithstanding his verbosity Francis Barrett who was, at the date of the publication of the 'Magnus' regarded not as a quack and cheapjack, but as a seer and philosopher, has made patent what even the learned believed as recently as 1801.

L'Estrange Ewen says,* 'The ridiculous nature of the rites of the witch-cult were equalled in absurdity by the supposed remedial measures .... It is to be observed that the expedients which proved to be effective on one occasion might be quite useless on another. One method most firmly believed in, namely that of scratching or "blooding" the witch, is a case in point. Thomas Darling (1597), although he scratched Alice Gooderidge so that blood "came out apace", did not cease to see the "green cat with

* op. cit.

eyes like flames of fire". Ann Thorne continued to have fits after scratching Jane Wenham, but she had not drawn blood, which want, however, cannot have been the cause of failure, since one of the Throckmorton children, after clawing Agnes Samuels, and drawing only water, had no more seizures. Richard Browne (1653) within a week after scratching Elizabeth Lambe, died. Fitching blood by means of a knife seems to have failed Joseph Weeden (1674), but a pin was effective in the case of the Booths bewitched by Margaret Morton. . . .'

Testimony of an ostler against Elizabeth Stile of Windsor reveals that she 'being displeased with alms given to her, he was taken with an ache in his limbs' from which he recovered after scratching her and drawing blood.

On 1 August, 1606, Alice Stokes and Christiana Stokes (probably mother and daughter), both of Royston, were tried at Hertford, found guilty and hanged. The elder confessed that by use of bones, hair and a parchment chart of the human organs and arteries (all of which had been found in her house), and with the aid of her familiars she could torture any part of a victim's body by sticking pins in the chart at the appropriate spot. One of her victims, who recovered after scratching her, was subsequently sued by her for battery. She won her case. He was fined five shillings and condemned in costs but upon paying the sum he fell sick again and died.

L'Estrange Ewen gives the following transcription of a section of a contemporaneous publication: 'How the Witch Served a Fellow in an Alehouse. There was an honest fellow, and as boon a companion dwelling in Royston, one that loved the pot with the long neck almost as well as his prayers: for (quoth he) as I know one is medicinable for the soul, I'm sure the other's physic for the body. It was this Fuddle-cap's chance with three or four as good malt-worms as himself, and as sure, where the best lap was to be found, together as four knaves in a payre of cards, to be drinking, where this Witch came in, and stood gloating upon them. Now this good fellow (not enduring to look upon a bad face, but his own especially when he is cup-shot) called aloud to her, "Do you hear, Witch, look tother ways, I cannot abide a nose of that fashion, or else turn your face the wrong side outward, it may look like raw flesh for flies to blow maggots in."

'Still as the Witch was ready to reply, he would cross her with one scurvy jest, and between every jest drink to her, yet swear, "God damn him, she should starve ere she should have a drop on't, since the pot was sweet hee'd keep it so, for should but her lips once look into the lid on't, her breath's so strong, and would so stick in the cup, that all the water that runs by Ware would not wash it out again."

'At last the Witch got so much time to call to him, "Dost thou hear good friend?" (quoth she).

' "What sayest thou ill-face?" (quoth he).

' "Marry I say (quoth she) that thou throwest in thy drink apace, but shall not find it so easy coming out."

' "Nay, as for the coming out (answered the fellow) I throwed it in above, and it shall come out beneath, and then thou shalt have some of it, if thou wilt, because I am in hope it will poison thee."

'Then with this greeting, away goes the Witch in a chafe and the fellow sits down to fallow his drink, but as the end of all drunkards is either to ming* or to sleepe. So out goes this fellow, and drawing his Gentleman Usher against a pale side, finds me a top of his nose a red lump as big as a cherry, and in his belly felt such a rumbling, as if the Tower of Babel had fallen about his ears: Oh! the sight thereof drove his heart to an ague, and his tongue to an alarum, and out he cries, "The Witch, the Witch, I am undone, I am undone: O God, women of Royston, help, help, the Witch, the Witch, I am a man spoiled, help, I am undone."

'At that word "help, the Witch", in comes one of his fellows, running in haste, and asked him what they should help the Witch?

' "O! (quoth he) to the gallows, for I am undone by her."

'Well, yet out he runs where for that night she would not be found, but the next morning meeting her in a lane, his pain rather increased than lessened, and there "fasts† his ten-com-mandments‡ upon her", he almost scratched out her eyes, nay, left her not till he brought her to the town, where for this and the rest she was apprehended, and she and her daughter, with George Dell and his mother, worthily suffered death 4 of August.'

* *Ming* [e] : to seek female society : the female pudend, hence, to indulge in sexual intercourse.
† Fastens.
‡ Ten fingers.

Ewen adds a footnote, 'Prof. Notestein "thought it possible rather than probable that the narrative was a fabrication". Except for the names and minor details I do not doubt that the tract gives a fair report. Even the tippler in the tavern incident seems to figure in an indictment as John Rumbold.'

In June, 1650, Anne Wagg of Ilkeston (Derbyshire) was examined before Gervase Bennett, J.P. A local baker, Francis Torratt said, among other things, that 'Mistress Fox falling suddenly sick, and Anne being suspected, Mr Fox brought her to the invalid, who "drew blood on her".'

Rose Cullender and Amy Dury, both of Lowestoft, tried before Sir Matthew Hale in 1664, were charged with bewitching the daughters of Samuel Pacy.* Elizabeth, aged eleven, gave a demonstration in Court by scratching Amy Dury till the blood flowed.

Widow Conron of Great Coggeshall, Essex, refused, in 1699, to pray that Mr Cox's thigh (which she had afflicted) would get well: he scratched her arm with his nails and 'dipping his handkerchief in the blood carried it to his father's house and there burnt it, but it had not the usual smell of burnt linen.'

Perchance it was so revoltingly filthy that the ammoniacal odour of the burning incrustations concealed the comparatively wholesome smell of burning fabric.

In Coggeshall parish register, under the date 27 December, 1699, there is entered, 'The widow Conron, that was counted a witch, was buried.' This might give the impression that notwithstanding her condemnation and ignominious end she was allowed Christian burial, but such a conclusion does not follow from such an entry.

The parish registers had been used, almost from their inception in 1538, as appropriate media for the recording and preservation of local events of outstanding interest, and this usage was confirmed and endorsed by Dr White Kennett, Bishop of Peterborough (1718-28): 'one thing more I would intimate to you, that you are not only obliged to enter the day and the year of every christening, wedding or burial, but it is left to your discretion to enter down any notable incident of times and seasons, especially relating to your own parish, and the neighbourhood of it, such as storms and lightning, contagion, and mortality, drought, scar-

* See p. 29.

city, plenty, longevity, robbery, murders, or the like casualties. If such memorable things are fairly entered, your parish registers would become chronicles of many strange occurances that would not otherwise be known, and would be of great use and service for posterity to know. You have had precedents of this kind in parochial registers within this diocese, and they have been cited to very good purpose by our worthy brother, the author of *The Natural History of this County of Northampton.*'

The register of Youlgrave, Derbyshire, contains a detailed account of a great frost in 1614 followed by drought. Another great frost (1683) is described in the register of Holyrood Church, Southampton; and the tempest (November 1703) to which Addison alludes when comparing Marlborough, at Blenheim, to an angel guiding the whirlwind, is on record in the register of St Oswald's, Durham.

Various references to witchcraft are to be found in the registers: St Andrew's, Newcastle-upon-Tyne, under the date 21 August, 1650, has, 'Thes partes her under named were executed in the Town Mor for Wiches. Mathew Boumer, Isabell Brown, Margrit Maddeson, Ann Watson, Ellenor Henderson, Ellenor Rogers, Elizabeth Dobson, Mrs Elizabeth Anderson, Jane Hunter, Jane Koupling, Margrit Brown, Margrit Moffit, Kattren Welsh, Aylles Hume, and Marie Pootes.' A separate entry, under the same date, states, 'Jane Martin for a wich, the myller's wif of Chattim'. The Newcastle Corporation's accounts for 1650 contain an item, 'paid to the Constables for carrying the witches to gaol, 4s: a grave for a witch, 6d: for trying the witches, 1£ 5s.'

There are, too, in the registers, references to death by enchantment and also to wrecking, of which many were accused. Marion Peebles of the Shetland Isles (mentioned above), had the reputation of possessing, in addition to the evil-eye by force of which she destroyed both men and beasts, the ability to wreck ships and drown their crews. Storm raising by witchcraft seems to be a descendant of benign rain-making by magic; a power vested in the average tribal witch-doctor, but sometimes exclusive to the divine-King. The storms raised by witches, whether by land or sea, were never beneficial: they did not bring rain—even heavy rain—to end a drought that was destroying crops, but they brought hail-stones to destroy the harvest: they did not bring wind—even strong wind—to assist a ship becalmed, but they brought gale and tempest, sudden and violent, often accompanied by lurid lightning and deafening thunder, raising the sea so that between wind and water a ship could not remain afloat, but was overwhelmed with the loss of all hands. The witches themselves seemed to be safe from the perils of ocean travel, which immunity is linked to their inability to sink when put to the water ordeal: they could make successful voyages in sieves, egg-shells, basins and on wooden platters; but so vindictive were they towards sailors, shipowners and merchants, whose goods were carried by sea, that they would, when storm-raising was not convenient, destroy vessels by other means, particularly that of causing un-controllable fires to break out.

This last method was employed by Alice Trevisand of Hard-ness, Devon who (with Michael, her husband, and Peter, the son), was examined before Sir Thomas Ridgway, J.P., in 1601. William Tompson, a sailor of Dartmouth, declared that he and a ship-mate met the accused at about midnight. She was clad in a hooded gown reaching to her feet and the seamen mistook her for a seminary priest. They discovered their error when, upon William Tompson falling down, Alice laughed and William (infuriated as drunken people frequently become when laughed at), struck her with a musket-rod.

She remarked, 'Thou shalt be better thou hadst never met with me.'

William went off to sea again, but his ship caught fire and sank. He was rescued, but was carried to Spain where for a whole year he was held prisoner. Upon his release he returned home and soon fell foul of Alice, who told him he would, before long, be a prisoner once more and, sure enough, on his next voyage he was, for the second time, made captive by the Spaniards.

Elizabeth Clarke (alias Bedingfield) of Manningtree, one of Matthew Hopkins's victims, was asked whether it was she who caused the death by drowning of Thomas Turner, who had, about thirty months before the hearing, been cast away. She denied responsibility, transferring the blame to Beldame West who, said Elizabeth, had raised the storm that sank Turner's hoy.

Another of Hopkins's witches, Priscilla Collet, of Dunwich, who had been allowed only one hour's sleep in seventy-two, con-fessed to a knowledge of the destruction of a vessel belonging to

Goodman Harper of Newcastle, which, she said, had been accomplished by the devil himself.

John Lowes, Vicar of Brandeston, confessed to Hopkins that 'he did much harm by sea and land, especially by sea. On one occasion, being at Langarfort [Landguard Fort, near Harwich] to preach, and walking upon the [sea] wall, he saw a great sail of ships pass by, and bidding his yellow imp go and sink a new vessel stationed about the middle of the fleet, he perceived that craft to be in more trouble and danger than the rest, tumbling up and down with the waves, as if the water had been boiled in a pot, and soon after it sank, the rest sailing away in safety. By this act he made fourteen widows in a quarter of an hour, for which he did not grieve, but rejoiced in realizing the power of his imps.'

Mother Lakeland of Ipswich (1645), displeased with the behaviour of John Beale, sent her familiar to burn a new ship of which he had been appointed master: Elizabeth Harris of Faversham (also 1645), whose son had been drowned on a voyage in a vessel owned by Goodman Woodcot, cursed the ship and it was cast away.

L'Estrange Ewen gives an extract from The Calendar of State Papers (Domestic) 1667. 'Suffolk. Letter from Capt. Silas Taylor to Joseph Williamson. It was related at Ipswich that a ship (Capt. Jonathan Banticke) recently lost in the late storms, having been spoken,* sent messages to friends and stated that "they had long laboured to free their maintop, where sat a couple of witches; but by all that they could do, could not remove nor get them down, and so they were lost people." The witches having been named, were taken and imprisoned at Ipswich.'

Another hag who was accused of having intervened in naval affairs is mentioned in The Calendar of State Papers, but is not named. '27 Feb. 1670. Cornwall. Letter from Thomas Holden at Falmouth to Joseph Williamson. "A woman about Looe is apprehended for a witch. I am informed she has discovered that she was in the fleet when the Duke of York was at sea, and hindered the prosecution of that victory against the Dutch ..."'

Joseph Williamson, to whom both of the foregoing letters were addressed, must have been a collector of witchcraft stories with particular emphasis on maritime manifestations. One is left won-

* i.e. Having exchanged greetings and messages with another ship.

dering how the two witches came to be perched in Captain Banticke's maintop. Were they passengers making the voyage in a unique kind of 'steerage', or did they suddenly materialize after the ship had put to sea? Why could the crew, who must have been accustomed to going aloft to shorten sail in heavy weather, not dislodge them? Surely a brawny sailorman, not timorous, even though superstitious, could have pitched a couple of frail old women overboard?

The woman of Looe might conceivably have been aboard a King's ship: sailors' 'wives' were tolerated in the Navy down to the end of the eighteenth century, but they were packed off below when decks were cleared for action. Holden mentions that she claimed to be 'the cause of the Queen's* barrenness', and concludes his letter, 'Some say she is maze and saith and confesses anything...'

She was certainly ambitious in claiming to be 'the cause of the Queen's barrenness'. Most witches were content to be the cause of barrenness or abortions, of sterility and ligature only among their neighbours or, at best, the occupants of the local 'big house', against whom, for one reason or another, a real or imagined snub, insult or discourtesy, they felt they owed a grudge and had the right of revenge.

This tendency for witches to interfere in sexual life is mentioned in The Bull of Pope Innocent VIII (1484–92), known as *Summis desiderantes affectibus*, from its opening words, 'Desiring with the most heartfelt anxiety ...' which is accepted as the most important document in the history of witchcraft.

'Innocent, Bishop, Servant of the servants of God, for an eternal remembrance.

'Desiring with the most heartfelt anxiety, even as Our Apostleship requires, that the Catholic Faith should especially in this Our day increase and flourish everywhere, and that all heretical depravity should be driven from the frontiers and bournes of the Faithful, We very gladly proclaim and even restate those particular means and methods whereby Our pious desire may obtain its wished effect, since when all errors are uprooted by Our diligent avocation as by the hoe of a provident husbandman, a zeal for, and the regular observance of, Our holy Faith will be all the more strongly impressed upon the hearts of the faithful.

* Catherine of Braganza.

'It has indeed lately come to Our ears, not without afflicting Us with bitter sorrow, that in some parts of Northern Germany, as well as in the provinces, townships, territories, districts and dioceses of Mainz, Cologne, Treves, Salzburg, and Bremen, many persons of both sexes unmindful of their own salvation and straying from the Catholic Faith, have abandoned themselves to devils, incubi and succubi, and by their incantations, spells, conjurations and other accursed charms and crafts, enormities and horrid offences, have slain infants yet in the mother's womb as also the offspring of cattle, have blasted the produce of the earth, the grapes of the vine, the fruits of trees, men and women, beasts of burthen, herd-beasts, as well as animals of other kinds, vineyards, orchards, meadows, pasture-land, corn, wheat and all other cereals; these wretches furthermore afflict and torment men and women, beasts of burthen, herd-beasts, as well as animals of other kinds, with terrible and piteous pains and sore diseases, both internal and external; they hinder men from performing the sexual act and women from conceiving, whence husbands cannot know their wives nor wives receive their husbands ...'

The document continues by strengthening the power of the Inquisition and was therefore condemned as the cause of the horrifying tortures that were daily occurrences on the Continent.

Abortion was induced by the midwives, when they were witches, by the administration of emmenagogic drugs, and if such treatment failed they would, as soon as the head appeared at parturition pierce it with a sharp instrument such as an awl, or a needle. Doll Barthram of Stradbrooke, Suffolk (1599) sent one of her familiars to kill an unborn child by 'nipping out the brains'. The 'birth-strangled babe' mentioned by Shakespeare among the ingredients of the witches' brew refers not to murder, but to cord-strangulation. The witches' object in murdering infants at birth was to provide flesh of the unbaptized for inclusion in the magical brew, and for compounding in ointments. Sometimes cannibalism was practised. Witches tried at both Berne and Lausanne confessed to having eaten their own children. There are three kinds of cannibalism: it may arise from depraved appetite, it may be a cult in which the underlying principle is homoeopathic magic, and it may be resorted to by starving people as, for example, the prisoners in Hitler's concentration camps. 'Savages' who are cannibals are generally practising homoeopathic magic:

by eating part of their enemy they think to acquire his bravery and skill in war: Sir Richard Burton, who never allowed himself to be carried away by popular fallacies, said, 'the dead are in danger from cannibals, not the living'. The cannibalism of witchcraft seems to belong to the category of magic. In France, the standard market price of infants in 1680 was one crown, and La Voisin confessed to the knowledge of two thousand five hundred abortions: she also had a connection with the executioners of Paris from whom she obtained parts of criminals, particularly fat, to be employed in compounding harmful ointments. Continental witches were burned (not hanged, as in England) and there was a brisk business in ashes, which were used as an ingredient of poisons, and for producing an ointment or paste which, smeared on fruit-trees, would destroy them.

In England bodies were (and still are) exhumed to secure parts for magical purposes. Thomas Jefferson of Woodhouse, Yorkshire, was accused in 1657 of 'taking up divers dead men, women and children out of their graves'. There were nine witnesses against him. Dame Chattox* had some human teeth that she used in her machinations.

In 1634 Pendle Forest 'came into the news' again with a second outbreak of witchcraft: on this occasion the witch finder was Edmund Robinson, a delinquent boy of ten years of age. Among those accused by him was Widow Hargreaves who, he said, had 'killed a child in the belly of Ellen Robinson'.

The word 'ligature' suggests to the modern mind a piece of gut-string used by a surgeon performing an operation, to tie severed arteries, but it has a far wider connotation: in addition to its being a noun, it is a verb, the act of applying the gut-string is to ligature the artery; hence, it applies to binding, stoppage or closure, hence to impotence, particularly when caused by witchcraft, or other magical means.

Witches produced ligature by tying knots, usually nine in number, in a length of cord, or in a leather thong, and the victim's condition remained with him until the knots were untied. Since the witch hid the cord after making the knots there was little or no chance of their being undone by any person other than herself, therefore a recommended method of securing relief was to approach the witch in a friendly manner and come to an

* See p. 116.

agreement. Francesco Maria Guazzo, published, in 1608, a book entitled *Compendium Maleficarum*, in which he distinguished seven classes of ligature and broadened its meaning by including marital discord, when the romance has degenerated into reciprocal hatred; and feminine aversion, when the husband remains virile but the wife becomes contracted or totally closed. He put sterility and barrenness in the category of ligature and also the taking of drugs to prevent pregnancy. It was also believed that urination could be obstructed.

Thomas Aquinas distinguished between inherent impotence and ligature: in cases of the former a man was unable to copulate with any woman, in the latter the inability was confined to one woman only, and the matter was of particular interest to the theologians because of wide social implications. Notwithstanding that marriages are made in heaven it would seem that the demand being so great, necessitates the occasional employment of unskilled labour, and some very shoddy work is passed. Anyone with his eyes shut and his wits a-wool gathering could plunge headlong into the matrimonial mansion, but once within the impetuous lover found no exit.

Those who were wealthy, and sufficiently rebellious to desire divorce, could attain to that end by subterfuge: for example, to marry a descendant of one's godparents was a sin which, had the union been contracted in ignorance, could be atoned only by immediate confession and dissolution of the illegal union. Cardinal Ximenez discovered that his province of Toledo was a centre where couples desirous of bringing their marriage to an end could, for a consideration, be introduced to an apparently venerable pious person (both men and women being engaged in the trade), who claimed a pre-knowledge of the antecedents of one of the marital partners and who would 'remember' the name and fame of a godparent and so bring about the desired separation. Ximenez spoilt this very lucrative business by introducing parish registers in which the names of a child's sponsors were entered. However, all was not lost: there yet remained ligature. Impotence was allowed to be a just cause for the dissolution of a marriage.

In the case of the murder of Sir Thomas Overbury,* impotence was the plea on which Lady Essex sued for nullity of the marriage.

* See p. 125.

Although Protestantism was well established in England, the canon law had not been affected, consequently matrimonial cases came before ecclesiastical courts. A Commission, under Archbishop Abbot, sat at Lambeth and received from Lady Essex's lawyers her petition: 'She requireth, since this pretended matrimony is but in fact and not in right, it may be pronounced, declared and adjudged as none and of none effect ... by your sentence and authority.' Notwithstanding that the Archbishop knew the King was in favour of the divorce, he was careful and conscientious; neither convinced by the evidence nor confident of the lawyer's honesty. To strengthen their case they put forward a plea of ligature by bewitchment but, obviously unable to reveal Lady Essex's dealings in the black arts, they could produce no supporting evidence and were compelled to drop the best trick in their bag: particularly as both the Archbishop and the Bishop of London, stated that a case of *maleficiatus versus hanc*—ligature —ought not to be judged by an ecclesiastical commission.

'Sweet Father Forman', as Lady Essex addressed this particular warlock, was a dealer in love potions, and claimed to have ways and means of inducing ligature, in which activities he was comparable with Dr Lambe. The latter, a teacher of English to the sons of the gentry, enjoyed the protection of the Duke of Buckingham, and slowly progressed from teaching to goety. He specialized in finding lost goods by divination, in foretelling the future by some method not stated, but probably astrology, and functioned as a quack-doctor, in which capacity he supplied potions and charms to affect the sexual life of the person on whom they were used. On 16 December 1607, he was charged at Tardebrigg, Worcestershire, with using 'certain evil, diabolical, and execrable arts called witchcraft, etc., in and upon the Rt. Hon. Thomas Lord Windsor, devilishly [he] did use, practise, and exercise, etc., to the intent to consume the body and strength of the said Thomas, Lord Windsor.' Nothing came of this and it is reasonable to assume that the Duke of Buckingham's favour was not without effect.

On 13 May 1608 Lambe was again in the hands of the law on a charge of invoking and entertaining evil spirits. Among the evidence against him was that of a Mr Wayneman, who, having been offered the sight of an angel, brought by Lambe out of a crystal, remained only long enough to hear the warlock say, 'I addure thee, Benias ...' On another occasion Lambe declared that he could intoxicate, poison and bewitch men so that they would be unable to beget children. In these mischiefs he was assisted by the four spirits of his crystal, the chief of whom was Benias. The jury returned a verdict of guilty but Lambe did not go to the gallows. His next trial was for the rape of a young girl. Again he was found guilty and again the death sentence was not executed; however, returning home from a visit to the theatre one evening he was recognized, seized and beaten to death by the outraged public.

The suggestion that victims of ligature should, to effect a cure, come to terms with the witch who had imparted it was a dangerous one. To resort to such an expedient was to compromise with evil, to consort with witches, hence, to become oneself guilty of witchcraft. It was equally dangerous to have recourse to an 'unbinding', or white witch for they, too, were held guilty of consorting with evil spirits to effect their cures. William Perkins in *A Discourse on the Damned Art of Witchcraft* (1608) said, 'Though the witch were in many respects profitable, and did not hurt, but procured much good, yet because he hath renounced God, his King and governor, and hath bound himself by other laws to the service of the enemies of God and His church, death is his portion.'

Anne Bodenham of Fisherton Anger, Wiltshire, had been a servant of Dr Lambe's and in his employ she had, it seems, shewn aptitude and received instruction in the black arts. After Lambe's death she made her living by teaching infants to read and by practising as a 'cunning woman'. In addition to effecting cures by charms and spells she applied divination to the discovering of goods lost and stolen. It would appear that her activities were more white than black, and of her Montague Summers, who is not prone to see innocence where there is a hint of heresy, says* 'she was hanged at Salisbury upon an absurd and unsubstantiated charge of witchcraft .... She was said to have made a particular contact with the Devil, by whose help she could transform herself "into the shape of a Mastif Dog, a black Lyon, a white Bear, a Woolf, a Bull, and a Cat", although it does not appear how such metamorphoses would benefit her, and one might imagine that a black lion, a white bear, or even a wolf must

* *Geography of Witchcraft.*

attract considerable attention if met with in a Wiltshire lane. Such a tissue of absurdities was the evidence, and the whole trial is indeed a glaring example of judicial murder.'

Anne Bodenham's disaster was brought upon her by Anne Styles, an hysteric, a liar and a thief, who, servant to Mistress Goddard of 'The Close', New Sarum (herself anything but a stable character), was sent to the wise woman to discover the whereabouts of a missing silver spoon: this, however, she failed to trace, but the failure did not detract from her reputation, for soon after Anne Styles was again sent for, this time by Thomas Mason, Mistress Goddard's son-in-law, who had lost some money.

Anne Bodenham set up her crystal and Anne Styles declared that she, herself, saw in it all the people in the Goddard household and was aware of their various occupations. However, the missing money failed to show up.

This second failure did not prevent Mistress Goddard who, among her other eccentricities was toxiphobic, from sending Styles again when her two daughters-in-law, Sarah and Anne, had handed her some tarnished coins. It is not on record what Anne Bodenham reported, but it is likely that she declared the coins non-poisonous. She seems to have made no concealment of her magical methods and Anne Styles, on her numerous visits, not only was permitted to crystal-gaze, but no objection was raised to her witnessing other methods of magic: she claimed to have become acquainted with the cauldron and the magic circle; and to have been present at the calling up of Beelzebub, Tormentor, Satan and Lucifer.

Mistress Goddard's toxiphobia led to so many enquiries that Anne Bodenham prescribed a counter-charm: Styles was given money to buy arsenic which was to be burnt; however, it did not go into the fire and was subsequently found under Sarah's bed. Mistress Goddard found (or feared) poison in her ale and Styles was sent once more to the witch to purchase a counter-charm. This consisted of vervain and dill in powder form as well as whole leaves, and nail-pairings. The powder was to go in the broth of the two Mistress Goddards Junior 'to rot their guts in their bellies', the leaves were to be rubbed round the rims of their drinking pots with a view to their teeth coming out, and the nail-parings were to be put in their drink to drive them mad. The two daughters-in-law, Sarah and Anne, feeling there was something afoot, made a journey to town and there discovered who had been buying the poisons. Anne Styles was driven from the house.

It is likely that Anne Bodenham felt sorry for the poor unemployed servant girl, and having noted what a close interest she had, on each visit, displayed in thaumaturgical practice, offered her something between an apprenticeship and a junior partnership. Anne Styles said that the witch thereupon turned herself into a black cat.

Styles, frightened out of the few wits she had, would have run away, but Anne Bodenham detained her, and made her seal a covenant 'not to discover her'. The witch 'forthwith made a circle, and looking in her book, called Beelzebub, Tormentor, Lucifer and Satan appear, then appeared two spirits in the likeness of great boys, with long shagged hair, and stood by her looking over her shoulder, and the witch took the maid's fore-finger in her right hand, and pricked it with a pin and squeezed out the blood, and put it into a pen, and put the pen into the maid's hand, and held her hand to write in a great book, and one of the spirits laid his hand or claw upon the witch's, whilst the maid wrote ... the spirit gave a piece of silver (which he first bit) to the witch, who gave it to the maid ... and bid her be gone. ...'

Anne Styles set out for London but was overtaken by Mistress Goddard's son-in-law to whom she told her story and then, in a state of abject terror at having broken her covenant, she went the way of most hysterics by throwing fits. She was taken to Salisbury, examined and sent for trial on suspicion of attempted poisoning. Anne Bodenham was also taken. She confessed to having the power to cure diseases, discover lost and stolen goods and show the thief in a glass. Taken into the presence of Styles the latter had ease from her fits, and Anne Bodenham began to show signs of distress. However, the improvement was of short duration: Styles became more violent than ever and the witch utterly refused to go to her again, exclaiming 'Ah, whore! Ah, rascall! I will see her in hell first ...'

Anne Bodenham was tried, April 1653, by John Wilde (1590–1669), Chief Baron of the Exchequer, and at the age of eighty, condemned to death. Witch or no witch, her behaviour on the gallows was such that one feels proud to be a countryman of hers: she walked to the place of execution and attempted to

ascend the ladder at once but was restrained. Called upon to confess she refused and roundly cursed those who thus detained her.
At length, when the noose was put about her neck, she attempted
to throw herself off, but the executioner prevented her doing so,
and asked for the conventional forgiveness. Her reply was, 'Forgive thee? A pox on thee, turn me off !'

R. Trevor Davies, in his balanced, dispassionate, copiously
documented, hence, very valuable work, *Four Centuries of
Witch-Beliefs*,* gives incontestable facts that point to the possibility of Cromwell's rise to power having been, at least in part,
greatly assisted by the popular belief in witchcraft, which itself
was bolstered up by churchmen who had returned from Geneva,
to which centre of Calvinism they had fled during the joint
reign of Philip and Mary.

It is often stated that James VI and I abandoned the anti-
witch attitude of mind he had expressed in his *Demonology*, and,
oscillating to the other extreme, became an opponent of the custom of bringing offenders to book. This is, however, an example
of putting a quart into a pint pot. King James had written his
work to protect his subjects and, as King, he had no alternative
but to protect all of his subjects, which included those held in
custody on a charge of witchcraft. Hence, he secured the release
of any who were obviously unjustly accused and he took steps
to expose those who brought such false charges.

His son, martyred Charles, in addition to discouraging witch
persecution, resisted violence of all kinds, with a view to reducing
hooliganism in the streets of London, he devised the body of
watchmen who were, in consequence, nicknamed 'Charlies'. On
receiving the report that there was serious rioting in the city at
the time when Dr Lambe was beaten to death, the King himself
rode out to quell the disturbance. Lambe was already too severely
battered to recover by the time Charles reached St Paul's Cross,
but he dispersed the lingering crowds, and ordered the arrest of
the City constables who had been guilty of neglect of duty in
their failure to protect a subject from mob violence. The Lord
Mayor was summoned before the King in Council and threatened
with the cancellation of the City Charter. A fine of £6,000 was
imposed of which 1,500 marks were paid.

Davies says,† 'much of the power of the Tudor Monarchy

* Methuen, 1949.   † op. cit.

remained in the hands of the early Stuarts. When, therefore,
they had made up their minds that witchcraft was a delusion,
they were able to save from execution most of the victims of
superstition . . . they had in their hands the appointment of all
the great offices of authority and influence in Church and State,
and the great though vague power of the Council in its many
forms, and the censorship of the Press. These they used with
considerable effect in an attempt to turn back the tide of witch-
terror. As vacancies occurred on the Bench of Bishops or the
Bench of Judges they were filled with men opposed to the prevailing superstition, so that it became almost impossible to secure
the conviction of a witch in spite of the fanaticism of her
enemies.'

Censorship of the Press was not the least important of the levers
used by the Stuarts to dislodge witch-mania. The printing of
sensational pamphlets provided a means of informing and inspiring hysterics. Hence, the control of the Press starved the morbid
appetite. None of these undesirable publications was printed in
England 'during the last three years of James I and the whole
of Charles I's reign up to the outbreak of the Great Rebellion
(1622–42). . . . Much of the credit for this deprivation is due to
Laud, who, becoming Chancellor of Oxford University in 1629
and Archbishop of Canterbury in 1633, largely controlled the
University presses as well as the printers of London. . . . Laud
shows himself sceptical in his attitude to alleged supernatural
occurrences without committing himself dogmatically to a total
denial that events can happen sometimes contrary to what is
known of nature. "Shut out all superstition in God's name, the
farther the better," he said in his sermon at the opening of Parliament (19 June 1625), "but let in no profaneness the while."' *

The public was not yet ready to be relieved of its primitive
beliefs: Roundhead leaders were all witch-persecutors: Fairfax;
Robert Devereux, Earl of Essex; Robert Rich, Earl of Warwick;
Sir Harbottle Grimston, who described Archbishop Laud as 'the
Sty of all Pestilential filth, that hath infected the State and
Government of this Commonwealth'; John Wilde, Knight of the
Shire for Worcester, who accused Laud of introducing Catholic-
ism into England 'in a guilded pill, with Baits and pretences of
Reconciliation; . . . This Man's Leprosy hath so infected all, as

* Davies, op. cit.

there remains no other cure, but the Sword of Justice'; Sir William Brereton; Bulstrode Whitelock; Sir Henry Mildmay, the turn-coat; Sir John Barrington; Sir Martin Lumley; Sir John Danvers; Sir Gilbert Pickering; John Hampden, whose mother was Eliza-beth, second daughter of Sir Henry Cromwell and step-daughter of Lady Cromwell, whose death was laid at the door of Mother Samuels; Francis Rous, whose younger step-brother was John Pym; and above all, Oliver Cromwell himself.

It was under the Long Parliament that the Witchfinder General, Matthew Hopkins, carried out his anti-witch campaign and this wickedness was encouraged by Parliament: there is reason to believe that he held a commission from the Government, but there is no documentary evidence in support of this. Such a lack under the Roundheads is not a serious objection: there is no documentary evidence of the sale, in building plots, of Hyde Park (London) and what is more, there is no entry of the receipt of the purchase money in the Treasury accounts. This last means that the money went into Roundhead pockets for there is no denying the sales, which after the Restoration were rendered null and void.

'A study of the death-roll of witches during the Civil War suggests that constitutional questions were by no means the only ones that led men to take up arms against the King. The readiness of the Roundheads to condemn women in hundreds to the gallows on the flimsiest evidence shows that the disaffected parts of Eng-land had long been seething with discontent, and that the dis-content arose not merely from the King's religious persuasion, but largely from the leniency towards witches that was insepar-ably connected with that persuasion. Such an hypothesis is corroborated by the attitude towards witchcraft that persisted throughout the Commonwealth and Protectorate.'*

Oliver Cromwell possesed the diabolical faculty of spreading what might be mistaken for angel's wings when it suited him to do so. He preached religious toleration and practised ghoulish religious persecution; avowedly honest and single-minded, he intrigued with, used for his own ends, and betrayed his friends. During the war he appeared to be a brave, inspired and inspiring soldier, but later he revealed a morbid, miserable cowardice and lived in constant terror of death. This last ambivalence is perhaps

* Davies, op. cit.

the easiest to explain: he was a gleeful, blood-lusting killer, glorying in slaughter and, according to his own declaration, desirous of coming upon the King in person that he might have the pleasure of 'pistoling his Sacred Majesty down the same as any man'. His apparently reckless advances into the thick of the fray were not occasioned by courage, but arose from his know-ledge gained in diabolical compact, that neither shot, sword, nor spear would cause his death.

Davies does not accept Cromwell's bargain with the Devil before the Battle of Worcester, but says 'it is chiefly of interest as one of the many instances of the boundless credulity that affected even the most highly placed officials of Commonwealth England'.*

Cromwell's overt toleration in matters of religion was offset by his diabolical destruction of Roman Catholics, to which passion he gave full reign in Ireland, so that even today the phrase 'the curse of Cromwell on you' is taken very seriously by Irishmen.

In the seventeenth century 'melancholic' was the medical description applied to persons of unstable character, those affected by hypochondria, and by obsessions: witches were included in the category of 'melancholic', and so was Oliver Cromwell. The most important men about him were all strong advocates of witch persecution: Gervase Bennett, a member of Cromwell's Council, was also a member of the Army Committee and a Commissioner of Customs and Excise. He sat as justice of the peace on 18 June, 1650 to take evidence against Ann Wagg, widow, of Ilkeston, Derbyshire, when he admitted evidence of so flimsy a character that his pre-determination to hang the woman was manifest.

Sir John Danvers, a signatory of the King's death warrant, was esteemed very highly by Cromwell, and he made a point of sitting on the bench of magistrates to secure the condemnation of Joan Peterson, known as the witch of Wapping. She was a white witch, and she was neither feared nor hated by her neighbours because of her successful cures of headache. She refused to take part in the conspiracy of some disinherited relations of Lady Mary Powell, who requested her to swear that Anne Livingstone, the beneficiary under the will, had murdered Lady Mary. Dis-appointed at failing to secure Joan Peterson's services, the con-spirators decided that she must be put out of the way in case she

* op. cit.

gave information against them; hence, she was charged with witchcraft. The neighbours who had benefited by her cures were intimidated and dared not come forward in her defence; hence, thanks to Sir John Danvers, she was hanged at Tyburn on 12 April, 1652. There is much to be said in favour of the rumour that Danvers was himself a party to the conspiracy.

Roger Boyle, Baron Braghill, first Earl of Orrery, was a close companion of Cromwell's. He had been a murderous invader of Ireland, which pleased his master so well that the caitiff was elevated to the peerage. It was he who supplied Richard Baxter with much information for inclusion in his witch-baiting book, *Certainty of the World of Spirits* (1691). Of this there is no doubt for Baxter gives full acknowledgments. 'I will begin with that most convincing Instance, which you may have read in a Book called *The Devil of Mascon*. Above twenty years ago, the new Earl of *Orery*, then Lord *Broghil*, a person of well-known Understanding, and not inclined to weak Credulity, told me of much of what is written in that Book, and more; and said that he was familiar with Mr Perreaud, a Reverend Worthy Protestant Minister, in whose house all was done and had his son for his servant in his Chamber for many years; and from Mr Perreaud had the Narrative. Not long after Dr *Peter Moulin*, Prebend of *Canterbury* and son to the famous *Peter Moulin* printed the Book, as having it from his Father, who had it of Mr Perreaud : And Mr Robert *Boyle*, brother of the Earl of *Orery*, a Man famous for Learning, Honesty and Charity, and for also from weak Credulity, prefixeth an Epistle to it, owning it an undoubted Truth, being acquainted with the Author, Mr *Perreaud*, as his brother was. All these three worthy Persons (the E. of *Orery*, Mr *Boyle*, and Dr *Pet. Moulin*) through God's Mercy are yet living. . . . The said Earl of *Orery*, told me of many effects of Witchcraft and Devils (Men carried about near him in *Ireland*, which I shall not particularly recite, though many witnesses were named).'

This is quoted by Davies from *Relation of the Chief Things which an Unclean Spirit did and said in his House at Mascon etc. out of the French by Pet. du Moulin; together with a letter of Robert Boyle Esq., to the said Pet. du Moulin*, 1658. The original (in French) was printed at Geneva in 1653. The Mr Perreaud referred to by Baxter as the author was a Calvinist pastor.

'Cromwell, despite all his efforts to cover up the rule of the

sword, was a military despot supported by a devoted army.*
From the year 1652—if not for many years earlier—till his death
he was in command of greater arbitrary power than any other
ruler of Great Britain, either before or since his time. Had he
disbelieved in the possibility of witchcraft, the trials and executions of witches would soon have become impossible. Had he
seriously doubted the reality of pacts with the Devil, his doubts
would certainly have been reflected in a general slackening of
witch persecutions . . . the imperfect records of the Home Circuit
show that [between 1652 and 1658] at least forty persons were
indicted for witchcraft in the Eastern Counties covered by this
Circuit, and that at least ten, and more probably thirteen or
fourteen, were executed. These figures are lower than those for
the period of the First Civil War; but the wonder is that after
Hopkins's measures of wholesale extermination any possible suspects were left alive in the Eastern Counties. That such suspects
were still being hunted down hardly suggests that the witch
terror was being discouraged by those in authority—especially
when it is recognized that the figures of those indicted compare
most unfavourably with those of any period of equal length
during the reigns of either Charles I (up to the Civil War) or
Charles II.' †

Cromwell and his attendant cut-throats had complete control
of the Press, hence, witch-baiting pamphlets and books might
have been very easily suppressed: we find, on the contrary, that
there was an enormous increase in the publication of such
psychologically and socially dangerous and undesirable literature. Those crawling toadies to Cromwell's tyranny, the Puritan
ministers who had been given the livings of Charles I's clergy,
took every opportunity to terrify their congregations and to
intensify the witch-hunting spirit of the time. Further, they
assisted in the persecutions by extracting from victims their self-
condemnatory confessions. Thomas Ady, the courageous author
of *A Candle in the Dark* . . . (1655) levelled this accusation, in an
unequivocal manner, against the Puritan Ministers: 'It is, and
hath been, the manner of these latter Ages for a Minister to go

* It is said that on one occasion when listening to the report of his agent
of secret police he responded to the statement, 'nine people out of ten hate
you', with the retort: 'Yes. But to the tenth I have given a sword.'
  † Davies, op. cit.

to such, and instead of instructing them [to] urge them to lying Confessions . . . let but any man that is wise, and free from prejudice, go and hear but the Confessions that are so commonly alleged, and he may see with what catching, and cavelling, what thwarting and lying, what flat and plain knavery these confessions are wrung from poor innocent people, and what monstrous additions and multiplications are afterwards invented to make the matter seem true, which yet is most damnably false.'

Ady's work ranks high among anti-persecution literature, and is a noteworthy example of the fighting technique of turning the weapons of the enemy against themselves: Biblical injunction, by which the witch-killers justified their fanaticism and bloodlust, was shown by Ady to be lacking in relation to the prevailing anti-witch beliefs, and customs, in vogue, 'where is it written in all the Old and New Testaments . . . that witches have imps sucking of their bodies? Where is it written that witches have biggs for imps to suck?' He posed the same unanswerable questions concerning the devil's mark, the witches' supposed ability to destroy crops and cattle, their carnal copulation with incubi, their power of transvecton. He shook the ground like an earthquake in his attempt to demolish the edifice of Puritanical homicidal zeal.

The assumption in Christendom that witch-baiting was a religious duty imposed by several Biblical injunctions was false: the misconception being engendered by the distortion of meaning in the process of translation and the limitations imposed by both the English language of the period, the ideas, and the volume of secular knowledge, then current. For example, the ancient Hebrew reference to an animal having one horn was translated as 'unicorn' because this mythical beast was thought to have an objective existence and the rhinoceros was totally unknown in the Western world.

To the Christians the Deity personified infinite and unadulterated good, and all evil was the devil's dominion, hence, they could not conceive of a religious system without this dualism. However, the god of the Old Testament was, in common with other primitive gods, not exclusive, both good and evil were his and there was no devil. Since the European witch was a heretic, one who had entered into a pact with the devil, it follows that none of the Biblical passages which, in translation, referred to witches and witchcraft had, in the original, that signification.

The Scriptural references are as follows: *Exodus*, XXII, 18 (A.V.),
'Thou shalt not suffer a witch to live'. (The R.V. has 'sorceress'
for witch.) *Leviticus*, XIX, 26 (A.V.), 'neither shall ye use enchantment, nor observe times'. (The R.V. pluralizes 'enchantment' and substitutes 'practise augury' for 'observe times'.)
Leviticus, XIX, 31 (A.V.), 'Regard not them that have familiar
spirits, neither seek after wizards, to be defiled by them'. (In the
R.V. the passage begins, 'Turn ye not unto', and in place of
'neither seek . . .' has 'nor unto the wizards; seek them not out'.)
Leviticus, XX, 6 (A.V.), 'And the soul that turneth after such as
have familiar spirits, and after wizards, to go a whoring after
them, I will even set my face against that soul.' (In the R.V., 'unto
them that have . . .' replaces 'after such as have', and, 'unto
the wizards' in place of 'after'.) *Leviticus*, XX, 27, 'A man also
or woman that hath a familiar spirit, or that is a wizard, shall
surely be put to death: they shall stone them with stones.' (The
R.V. differs only in interpolating 'a' between 'or' and 'woman'.)
Deuteronomy, XVIII, 10–11 (A.V.), 'There shall not be found
among you anyone that maketh his son or his daughter to pass
through the fire, or that useth divination, or an observer of times,
or an enchanter, or a witch, or a charmer, or a consulter with
familar spirits, or a wizard, or a necromancer.' (In the R.V., 'with
thee' in place of 'among you', and 'one' instead of 'or' (that useth
divination). 'One that practiseth augury' instead of 'or an observer of times', 'sorcerer' for 'witch', and 'familiar spirits' is
reduced to the singular.) *Deuteronomy*, XVIII, 20 (A.V.), 'But
the prophet which shall presume to speak a word in my name,
which I have not commanded him to speak, or that shall speak
in the name of other gods, even that prophet shall die.' (The
R.V. has 'speak a word presumptuously', and 'that same' in place
of 'even that' (prophet).) *I Samuel*, XV, 23 (both A. and R.V.),
'For rebellion is as the sin of witchcraft.' (*II Kings*, IX, 22 (both
A. and R.V.), 'Is it peace, Jehu? And he answered, What peace,
so long as the whoredoms of thy mother Jezebel and her witch-
crafts are so many?' *II Kings*, XXI, 6 (A.V.). 'And he made his
son pass through the fire, and observed times, and used enchantments, and dealt with familiar spirits and wizards.' (In the R.V.
'to' is placed between 'son' and 'pass', 'practised augury' appears
in place of 'observed times', and 'them that had' is interpolated
between 'dealt with' and 'familiar spirits'. *II Kings*, XXIII, 24

(A.V.), 'Moreover the workers with familiar spirits, and the wizards, and the images, and the idols, . . . did Josiah put away.' (The R.V. differs in 'them that had' in place of 'the workers with', and 'teraphim' in place of 'images'). *Isaiah*, VIII, 19 (A.V.), 'And when they say unto you, Seek unto them that have familiar spirits, and unto wizards, that peep and that mutter: should not a people seek unto their God?' (The R.V. differs only in placing 'the' before wizards, that 'chirp' in place of 'peep'.)

The only important difference between the wording of the Authorized and the Revised Versions is the substitution of 'chirp' for 'peep'. The latter, being a homonym, might refer to the act of looking in a rapid or sly way, and the former clearly indicates a reference to oneiromancy, divination by observing the flight of birds.

The basic, fundamental meaning of all these passages is clear: they express a primitive Deity's unwillingness to share with any other primitive Deity the devotion of his worshippers, because he is himself able to confer all favours and perform all miracles.

Thomas Ady was not alone in English literature aimed at dispelling witch-mania: there are ten or twelve important works of this character. *The Discovery of Witchcraft*, by Reginald Scott, was first published, at the author's own risk, in 1584. It is comparatively light reading, because it is not an ambitious attempt to overthrow the ponderous works of witch-baiting jurists and theologians. It is a simple man's appeal to the common sense of the general public, and its heavy artillery is not logic, but is ridicule. Scott was a Kentish squire whose major interest was the cultivation of hops. His defence of the witches arose out of compassion tempered with indignation at 'what flat and plain knavery is practised against these old women'. He was not a 'giant of intellect' and while he shrewdly rejected witch belief, he accepted sympathetic magic, and had faith in the antitoxic virtue of unicorn's horn. In this last belief he had something in common with King James I, who, regarding the *Discovery* as a dangerous book, wrote his *Demonology* partly to combat it. Notwithstanding the adverse royal criticism, Scott's work is of major importance and it will always stand in the front rank of courageous combat in defence of an unpopular cause.

Apart from the comparative merits of their morality, the standard of scholarship, and the intellectual prowess displayed in each, the *Discovery* as a piece of English literature stands before *Demonology*. Scott's sense of humour shines through the dark fabric of his theme: for example he recounts the experience of a youth who, as the result of over-indulgence, found himself impotent and employed a witch to restore to him his lost powers. 'She brought him to a tree, where she showed him a nest, and bade him climb up and take it. And being at the top of the tree, he took out a mighty great one, and showed the same to her, asking her if he might not have the same. Nay, quoth she, that is our parish priest's tool, but take any other which thou wilt.' He concludes the story with, 'these are no jests, for they be written by them that were and are judges upon the lives and deaths of those persons'.

In 1590, Henry Holland published at Cambridge A *Treatise Against Witchcraft*, which is a warning to 'masters and fathers of families that they may learn the best means to purge their homes of all unclean spirits.' This declaration makes it clear that he did not utterly reject a belief in witchcraft as Scott did. Holland accuses Scott of having reduced witchcraft to a 'cozening or poisoning art', and himself, on the authority of Scripture, supports the belief that witches have 'confederacie with Satan himself'. Notwithstanding this acceptance he ranks among the defenders of witches by his assertion that there was no evidence of the witches of his own time having entered into a pact with the devil.

Next in the procession of defensive literature is George Gifford's A *Dialogue Concerning Witches and Witchcraft*, published in London in 1593 with a reprint in 1603. This work, although his major contribution to the subject, was not his first. A *Discourse of the Subtle Practices of Devils by Witches and Sorcerers* had made its appearance in 1589. The *Dialogue* he dedicated to the 'Right Worshipful Maister Robert Clarke, one of her Maiesties Barons of her Highnesse Court of the Exchequer', declaring his delight at having heard and seen 'the wise and goodly course used upon the seate of justice by your worship, when such have been arraigned.' The material is presented in the form of a conversation between a superstitious rustic who is supported by his wife, a schoolmaster who is on the side of the rustic, and Daniel who is a competent protagonist in favour of cautious doubt. He asserts that an evil spirit as powerful as the devil does not need to ally himself with ignorant old women. He does not deny the existence of witches and witchcraft, but he asserts 'the devil hath bewitched your mind with blindness and unbelief, to draw you from God, even to worship himself.' He declares 'a witch cannot by a familiar, or by any craft, any way hurt or weaken the life, health, or estate of any man by witchery with disease or infirmity . . . because the hogs and the cow died, are you sure the cat* did hurt them? Might they not die of some natural causes, as you see both men and beasts are well, and die suddenly?' A witch's confession, he says, ought not to be accepted because it comes from the devil and 'men must beware that they proceed not upon his testimony.'

Thomas Ady says of Gifford, 'he had more of the spirit of truth in him than many of his profession' which was that of a Non-conformist preacher.

Samuel Harsnett published in 1599 his *Discovery of the Fraudulent Practices of John Darrell.*† He was, at that time, chaplain to the Bishop of London. He subsequently became Master of Pembroke Hall, Cambridge, then Vice-Chancellor of the University. In 1609 he was elected Bishop of Chichester and by 1628 he had advanced to the eminence of Archbishop of York. His literary style was very superior, vivid and forceful; he displayed a withering, sarcastic, mordant humour.

Harsnett's powerful pen is perhaps at its best in the following: '. . . the true *Idea* of a Witch, an old weather-beaten Croane, having her chinne and her Knees meeting for age, walking like a bow leaning on a shaft, hollow-eyed, untoothed, furrowed on her face, having her lips trembling with the palsie, going mumbling in the streetes, one that hath forgotten her *pater noster*, and hath yet a shrewd tongue in her head to call a drab a drab. If shee have learned of an olde wife in a chimnies *end*: Pax, max, fax, for a spel: or can say Sir *John of Grantams* curse, for the Millers Eeles, that were stolne: . . . why then ho, beware, looke about you my neighbours; if any of you have a sheep sick of the giddies, or an hog of the mumps, or an horse of the staggers, or a knavish boy of the schoole, or an idle girl of the wheele, or a young drab of the sullens, and hath not fat enough for her porridge, nor her father and mother butter enough for their bread; and she have a

---

* The witches' familiar.
† See p. 39.

little help of the *Mother Epilepsie*, or *Cramp* . . . with all old mother *Nobs* hath called her by chance "idle young huswife", or bid the devil scratch her, then no doubt that mother *Nobs* is a Witch.

'*Horace* the Heathen spied long agoe, that a Witch, a Wizard, and a Conjourer were but bul-beggars to scare fooles. . . . And *Geoffry Chaucer*, who had his two eyes, wit, and learning in his head spying that all these brainless imaginations of witchings, possessings, house-haunting, and the rest, were forgeries, cosenages, Imposturs, and legerdemaine . . . writes in good plain terms.'

The passage is from Harsnett's *A Declaration of Egregious Popish Impostures*, published in London in 1605. His was the voice of the Anglican Establishment, and his authority gave to his work a weight which that of Reginald Scott (on which his ideas were founded) lacked.

In the matter of witchcraft superstitions the medical faculty had not distinguished itself. The physician, when called upon to give an opinion, merely echoed the theologian, and when they undertook treatment their *modus operandi* was that of the sorcerers and their remedies were counter-magic. The profession's reputation was, however, redeemed by the work of John Cotta, M.D., who, in 1612, published *A Short Discoverie of Unobserved Dangers*, wherein he touched upon the relationship between witchcraft and certain forms of illness: this was followed four years later by his *magnum opus*, on the subject, *The Triall of Witchcraft and the True and Right Methode of Discovery*. In it he revealed his acceptance of the reality of witchcraft, and of pacts with Satan, but he asserted that many condemned women were not witches, and that their innocence might have been established by enlightened medical examination. This would not provide a channel of escape for guilty persons; real cases of bewitchment would be recognized 'whensoever . . . the Physician shall truely discover a manifest trancending power'. His book met with approval which encouraged him to amend and enlarge it, and it was reissued under the title of *The Infallible True and Assured Witch* in 1625. In his introduction he says, 'The Author perceiving that his former Tractate or first edition thereof, either not diligently read, or not truly by many men understood, he hath now, by a second edition thereof offered more ease and light unto such as are willing to search after truth, both by the addition of many things before omitted, as also by this plaine direction unto all the most special points in the whole Treatise.'

His remarks on transvection are, in the light of modern knowledge, most interesting: 'to perform some manner of asportation, and local translation of the bodies of witches and sorcerers, it seemeth in reason a thing to which the Devill is not unable.' After this declaration of faith as it were, he recounts his experience as a medical man: 'Some sick men also have revealed and declared words, gestures and actions done in farre distant places, even in the time and moment of their acting, doing and uttering, as I have known myself in some, and as it is testified to have beene heard, knowne and seene by divers withnesses worthy of credit, in our country, in divers bewitched Sicke people.'

The Rev. John Gaule published, in 1646, his *Select Cases of Concience Conserning Witches*. It was a counter-blow to the vile campaign of murder out of which Matthew Hopkins was doing so well. John Gaule, whose cure was at Great Stoughton, Huntingdonshire, had preached against Hopkins and this brought from the Witchfinder General a bellicose letter to one of Gaule's parishioners: this letter Gaule uses as an introduction to his book wherein he says, 'every old woman with a wrinkled face, a furrowed brow, a hairy lip, a squeaking voice, or a scolding tongue, having a rugged coat on her back, a skull-cap on her head, a spindle in her hand, and a dog or cat by her side, is not only suspected, but pronounced for a witch.'

This is in the spirit of Harsnett but lacks his strength. John Gaule cast doubt upon the 'confession' of witches: was such confession the result of diabolical delusion, melancholia, or maltreatment as practised by Matthew Hopkins? He discredited shape-changing, and transvection, but he did not go so far as to utterly deny the existence of witches and of witchcraft: although the majority of the accused were not guilty there remained the occasional case that could not be denied, and these, he left to the ministers and the magistrates.

Sir Robert Filmer, author of *Patriarcha, or the Natural Power of Kings*, a powerful defence of monarchical institutions, published, in 1653, *An Advertisement to the Jurymen of England, Touching Witches*. . . . The primal object of this work was to imbue jurymen with a sense of their enormous responsibility in reaching a verdict; nevertheless, there is a vast amount of scholar-ship displayed. Filmer clearly has a very sound knowledge of Hebrew, and he criticizes the interpretation of Biblical texts: 'The Hebrew word for a witch properly signifies a Juggler. . . .' A 'consulter with a Familiar spirit' he declares to be a consulter with 'ob' and translates 'ob' as a bottle, '. . . one who speaketh with a hollow voice, as out of a bottle . . . that had his cunning or slight to shut his mouth, and seem to speak with his Belly, which can be done without the help of a familiar spirit.'

Filmer's house was plundered ten times by Roundhead troops and in 1644 he was imprisoned.

John Wagstaffe was 'a little crooked man of despicable pre-sence', notorious for his 'continued bibbing of strong and high-tasted liquors' from which he expired 'in a manner distracted': nevertheless, he attacked witch-mania with sufficient vigour for his book, *The Question of Witchcraft Debated*, first published in 1599, to be reissued in 1671, and translated into German in 1677. He, like Filmer, maintained the inadequacy of the transla-tion of the Bible, and added that the prevailing belief in witch-craft was founded on heathen fables. He pleads, 'Surely the blood of men ought not to be so cheap, nor so easily to be shed, by such who under the Name of God, do gratifie exorbitant pas-sion and selfish ends; for without question, under this side of Heaven, there is nothing so sacred as the life of man.'

There appeared, in 1677, *The Displaying of Supposed Witch-craft*, the author of which, John Webster, was another 'character'. He had been an Anglican clergyman, a schoolmaster, and even a chaplain to the Roundhead Army. This last was, however, an expedient that went very harshly against his grain, and he re-signed, for which his property was seized, and he was very fortunate to escape with his life and freedom. His next adventure was the study of metallurgy, from which he migrated to medicine. Webster believed in apparitions and other supra-normal manifes-tations, but he laid emphasis on the unlikelihood of the accusa-tions, against witches, being admissible. The work has a long explanatory annexe to the title, namely, 'wherein is affirmed that there are many sorts of deceivers and imposters, and divers per-sons under a passive delusion of melancholy and fancy. But that there is a corporeal league made betwixt the devil and the witch, or that he sucks on the witch's body, has carnal copulation, or that witches are turned into cats or dogs, raise tempests or the like, is utterly denied and disproved. Wherein also is handled the existence of angels, and spirits, the truth of apparitions, the nature of astral and sidereal spirits, the force of charms and philters with other obstruce matters.' Such an annexe to the main title of a work was, at the period common: such clarity in setting forth the contents and the author's aims, very uncommon.

A late contribution, but by no means too late, was *The Historical Essay conserning Witchcraft* by Francis Hutchinson, perpetual curate to St James's Church, Bury St Edmunds, who later (1721) became Bishop of Down and Connor. His work was published in 1718 and, being the outcome of sound historical research, paved the way to a law reform which prohibited the condemnation to the gallows as a punishment for witchcraft. Hutchinson, like Filmer, criticized the translation of the Bible: 'the translation of our *Bible* ... hath made some Phrases that favour the vulgar Notions ... of a *Familiar Spirit* tho' the *Hebrew* hath no Epithet at all, and should rather have been translated into some of those Words that signify a cheating Ventriloquist.'

The foregoing is a goodly crop of humane literature; it is, however, counterbalanced by the other sort, and, perhaps at the head of the list, stands the work of William Perkins who, an example of hysterical conversion, changed from a drunken profligate to what is accepted as the leading Calvinistic preacher that England produced. He died in 1602 and his book, *A Discourse on the Damned Art of Witchcraft, so far forth as it is Revealed in the Scriptures*, was seen through the press by Thomas Pickering, minister of Finchinfield, Essex.

Perkins was a smug killer: 'and now I proceed to the second point considered in this text, the punishment of a witch, and that is death.' His reason is the assumed pact with the devil 'whereby they covenant to use his help for the working of wonders. ... Hereby they renounce the Lord that made them, they make no more account of his favour and protection, they doe quite cut themselves off from the covenant made with him in Baptism, from the Communion of Saints, from the true worship and service of God. ... For this cause Samuel told Saul that rebellion was as the sinne of Witchcraft: that is a most heinous and detestable sinne in the sight of god.'

Perkins's homicidal mania is not satiated by persecution of

malefic witches: his net spreads wide and includes the white witch. '... though the Witch were in many respects profitable, and did no hurt, but procured much good; yet because he hath renounced God his King and Governor, and hath bound himself by other lawes to the service of the enemie of God, and his Church, death is his portion iustly assigned him by God; he may not live.' Perkins's passionate blood-lust made so great a demon of him that he went to the very unEnglish length of advocating the use of torture: 'touching the manner of Examination, there be two kinds of proceeding; either by a Single Question or by Some torture ... when besides the enquirie in words, he useth also the racke, or some other violent means to urge confession. This course hath been taken in some countries, and may no doubt lawfully and with good concience be used. ...'

He closes by insisting on the coverage of witchcraft: 'For this must alwaies be remembered, as a conclusion, that by witches we understand not those onely which kill and torment: but all Diviners, Charmers, Juglers, all Wizzards, commonly called wise men and wise women ... and in the same number we reckon all good Witches, which doe no hurt but good, which doe not spoil and destroy but save and deliver. All these come under the sentence of *Moses* because they deny God, and are confederates with Satan. By the lawes of England the thiefe is executed for stealing, and we thinke it iust and profitable: but it were a thousand times better for the land, if all Witches, but specially the blessing Witch, might suffer death.'

Equally venomous but less vigorous was James Mason, a Cambridge M.A. (as was Perkins) and Vicar of Teversall, Nottinghamshire. His book, entitled *The Anatomie of Sorcerie, Wherein the wicked Impiety of Charmers, Inchanters, is discovered and confuted*, was published in 1612 by John Legatte, Printer to the University. His angle of approach is that the witches themselves do not work their spells but simply act as mediums for the devil.

This was followed in 1616 by the work of Alexander Roberts, a Fellow of Caius College, Cambridge, Headmaster of Lynn School, and Rector of West Lynn. His book, known by its short title as *A Treatise of Witchcraft*, has an 'Epistle Dedicatorie' addressed to the municipal authority, and the citizens of King's Lynn. In it, he declares his book to be directed against two categories of people: 'The first of these mentioned are slie and masked Atheists, the second be Sorcerers, Wizards, Witches, and the rest of that rank and kindred.' He accepted the full orchestra of the witches' performance, they could destroy men and beasts, and trouble the elements by virtue of their contract with Satan. 'For they endamage both in body and mind : In body for *Danaeus* reporteth of his owne knowledge, as an eye witnesse thereof, that he hath seene the breasts of Nurces (onely touched by their hands) those sacred fountains of human nurishment so dried up that they could yield no milk; some suddenly tormented with extreame and intolerable paine of Cholicke, others oppressed with Palsie, Leprosie, Gout, Apoplexia etc.

'In minde, stirring up men to lust, to hatred, to love and the like passions. . . .

'Now conserning beasts they doe oftentimes kill them out right . . . or pine and waste them little by little . . . .

'For the elements it is an agreeing consent of all, that they can corrupt and infect them, procure tempests, stirre up thunder and lightening, move violent winds. . . .' In short, he restated the Calvinistic doctrine.

The other University has its black sheep too. Thomas Cooper M.A. (Oxford) was the incumbent of Great Budworth, Cheshire. His book, published in 1617 bears the title, *The Mystery of Witchcraft, Discovering the Truth, Nature, Occasions, Growth and Power thereof*. Having previously written a work on the Gunpowder Plot, he says, 'hath not the Lord enabled me to discover the practice of Anti-Christ in the *hellish Plot of Gunpowder Treason?*' He emphasizes his own righteousness by confessing to an interest in the occult when he was an undergraduate. 'Was there not a time when I admired some in the University famozed in this skill? Did not the Lord so dispose of mee, that my *Chamberfellow* was exceedingly bewitched with these faire shewes . . .? And did not the Lord so arme his unworthy servant, that not onely the snare was gratiously espied; but, by the great mercie of my God, the Lord used me as a means to divert my *Chamberfellow* from these dangerous Studies?'

So be it. Thomas shall have a front seat in heaven. His book was re-issued in 1622 under a new title, *Sathan transformed into an Angell of Light* . . .

Michael Dalton published in 1619 his *Country Justice* which, by 1630 was in its fourth edition. It was he who laid heavy emphasis on 'the little teat or pop' and is largely responsible for its discovery assuming such importance in the trials: he especially recommended the examination of children who could generally be relied upon to give evidence against their parents, and he asserted that 'voluntary confession' ought to be given precedence over all the accusations against the witch.

Richard Bernard was Vicar of Balcome, Somerset, and published, in 1627, *Guide to Grand Jurymen with respect to Witches.* He was a Puritan of the most puritanical kind, who thought that those who became witches were 'superstitious and idolatrous, as all Papists be ... for Sorcerie is the practice of that Whore, the Romish Synagogue. ... Secondly it is found true, that healing Witches doe use many of their Superstitious Ceremonies, Lipprayers, Ave- Maries, Creeds and Paternosters by set numbers. Thirdly when Poperie beare sway heere, then Divels and Spirits often appeared, and at that time there were many more witches than now. Fourthly, they allow of coniurers and Diabolicall Exorcismes ... lastly, wee may reade in the *Admirable History of a Magician*, set out by Papists, and dedicated to the Q Regent of France, that the Divell, called Verrine, justified most of the superstitious and idolatrous practices of that Church, as *Transubstantiation, Worshipping the Host, Invocation of Saints and Angels*, with the rest: Is it not likely then that there the Divel can have power over the Professors of that Religion, which be so well liketh and approveth of?'

The foregoing passage is a complete revelation of the man, his motive and the deplorable state of his mind.

John Brinley wrote *Discovery of the Imposture of Witches,* which was published in 1680. That these models of rectitude, so ready to hang their neighbour, were themselves not without flaw and blemish is indicated in the fact that Brinley's book is an unblushing plagiarism of Richard Bernard.

Joseph Glanville stands out among those who believed in the reality of witchcraft because he sought to put the whole conception on a scientific basis. His book, *Saducismus Triumphatus, or full and plain evidence conserning witches and apparitions*, was published in 1681. He was a Fellow of the Royal Society, and he believed that science (then very young) could explain the supernatural. In this he was probably right, but it must be confessed that in the three hundred years of advancing knowledge since his time, science has succeeded only in establishing the supernatural, not in explaining it. Glanvill was himself very far from being scientific: he built his theory of the reality of witchcraft on the unsound foundation of twenty-six accounts of manifestations, and he received only one of these at first hand. He was no genius living in advance of his time: he was, in the spirit of the age, credulous, but his aim was to be objective. He is sometimes described, unjustifiably, as 'the father of modern psychical research'.

In the same year as *Saducismus Triumphatus* came out, Henry Hallywell—another minister—published his *Melampronoeia, or a Discourse on the Polity and Kingdom of Darkness*, which has neither savour nor salt: it is not lacking in logic, but is lacking in originality and punch. It consists of proofs of witchcraft argued from Bible texts. Three years later another minor advocate of wholesale murder, Richard Bovet, produced *Pandaemonium* which is a dilute solution of Glanvill tinctured with venomous anti-Catholicism.

The spate was drawing to an end: John Beaumont published in 1705 *Treatise on Spirits*, and, in 1715, Richard Boulton came out with *Complete History of Magic*. The former makes it manifest that the author was well read in the literature of witchcraft, and that he was so lacking in critical ability as to accept it all: the latter was a piece of journalese, a pot-boiler.

The subject of printed books both for and against the witches cannot be left without a brief reference to Continental publications. Johann Weyer's work, imprinted at Basel, 1563, entitled *De praestigiis daemonum et incantationibus ac veneficiis*, which was thought by King James to be contrary to the public weal was, in part, the cause of the King's own authorship in the subject. In his *Demonology* he says the work is 'against the damnable opinions of two ... whereof the one called Scot an Englishman, is not ashamed in publike print to deny that there can be such a thing as Witch-craft. ... The other, called Wierus, a German Phisition, sets out a publick apologie for all these craftesfolkes. ...' Of course, nothing so humane as Weyer's work could have come out of Germany. Weyer, who was born at Gran in North Brabant (1516) was what we would describe as a Dutchman. He became court physician to Wilhelm IV, Duke of Julich, Cleves and Berg who, after the publication of Weyer's book (which was dedicated to him) protected the author from the wrathful vengeance of the Inquisition.

Weyer drew a line of distinction between simple old hags who did, and were capable of doing no harm, and those who were deliberate devil's disciples making a profession of magic and murder by poison. He was a simple man and compassion was his mainspring. He was no sophisticated unbeliever: he acknowledged the power of the devil, did not deny the ability of magicians, and had no doubt of the truth of the legend of the Pied Piper. He exposed the cruelty and wickedness of the witch hunters, emphasizing how prisoners were 'constantly dragged out to suffer awful torture till they would gladly exchange this most bitter existence for death' and he asserted that they would 'confess' to 'whatever crimes were suggested to them rather than be thrust back into their hideous dungeon'.

Weyer's work made its impact and became a restraining influence: further, it paved the way for the later Jesuit humanitarians: Fr Tanner, Fr Laymann, Fr Loos and Fr Spee.

On the other hand, *Malleus Maleficarum* (the hammer of witches), first printed in 1486, the joint work of Jakob Sprenger, Dean of Cologne University, and Heinrich Kramer, Professor of Theology at the University of Salzburg, and both of them Dominican Inquisitors, is perhaps the most dastardly incitation to mass murder ever printed. The purpose of the book is 'that the Judges, both ecclesiastical and civil, may have a ready knowledge of the methods of trying, judging and sentencing'. The diabolical cruelty of these judges, and the people's pleasure therein is illuminated by the book's having run to sixteen German editions, eleven French, two Italian, and one or two in English. It teaches terrorism in horrible detail; was the well of wickedness whereat other authors filled their buckets, and it remained the supreme source of inspiration for witch-baiters even after more up-to-date works had, in the course of time, been produced from the powerful pens of influential authorities.

Notwithstanding their eminence in the world of learning, the joint authors display a very suspicious ignorance: it required no very high standard of scholarship to be aware that the etymology of the word 'femina' is not 'fe' (faith) and 'minus'; that 'diabolus' is not derived from 'dia' (double) and 'bolus' (death), implying the utter destruction of both body and soul. The book is a long one containing about a quarter of a million words, which gives it scope to handle its theme in grim detail. Although witchcraft is heresy, say the authors, Christians who do not believe in it are guilty of heresy: they declare that there is no such thing as hallucination, the appearances before the eyes of affected persons are true demons who can manifest themselves to as many or as few as they wish.

They dealt, in lascivious detail, with the various aspects of ligature, of carnal intercourse with the devil, with the activities of incubi and succubi. Witches they declared slew babies in the womb, secured abortion. 'What are we to think of men who are sometimes devoured by wolves and children who are thus snatched from their cradles. May not this not unseldom be wrought by black magic?'

Instructions on how to proceed against a witch are given in minute detail: how to commence the process, what kind of witnesses and how many of them shall be called, what questions shall be put, what lawyers briefed; what searching, unanswerable, confusing, and self-contradictory questions put to the prisoner, what torture was to be applied to extract the confession 'by the bitter Tears which Our Lord Jesus Christ shed upon the Cross for the salvation of the world, and by the burning tears of the Most Glorious Virgin, Saint Mary, His Mother, which when evening had come She shed over His Most Precious Wounds', thus adding blasphemy to the enormity of the crime they committed in advocating torture.

It is noteworthy in passing, and at the risk of repetition, to point out that the Puritans, who put all Catholics in the category of witches, accepted and approved of every word in this wicked book which they revered as second only to the Bible.

After *Malleus Maleficarum* the anti-witch works of Jean Bodin, Henri Boguet, Pierre De Lancre and Nicholas Remy, each sufficiently horrifying, pale into insignificance. Remy, a lawyer, proudly boasted of having burnt nine hundred witches: De Lancre, another lawyer, burnt only six hundred: Boguet, also a lawyer, is not notorious for the number of his slain, but for the fact of his having included little children in his witch hunt. He expressed the wish that all witches might 'be united in one single body, so that they might all be burned at once in a single fire'. Bodin, another lawyer, said 'I confess it is far better to absolve the guilty than condemn the innocent', but he took great pains to prove the innocent guilty. He maintained that the rules of prosecution must be abandoned in witch-trials for 'proof of such evil is so obscure and difficult that not one out of a million witches would be accused or punished if regular legal procedure were followed.' In order to make condemnation of an accused person certain he advocated false promises of immunity in exchange for information; the forcing of children to give evidence against their parents; agents might be used to wheedle confession from suspects and, on suspicion only, torture should be applied; the accused was never to be acquitted unless the falsity of the accusation was so strongly manifest that even the most stupid of laymen would not accept it. Bodin's own treatment of suspects exceeded in its brutality that of all other brutes. He tortured both children and invalids, including in his list of torments burning with red-hot irons. He said that execution by burning a witch quickly was a mild form of punishment as the period of pain seldom exceeded half an hour.

For sheer, cold, calculated, deliberate cruelty the jurists seem to exceed the theologians, but this may be merely an impression: no standards of comparison have been laid down. Anti-witchcraft law has not left a large legacy of literature: the earliest condemnation of the practice of witchcraft in this country is *Liber Poenitentialis* of Theodore, Archbishop of Canterbury (668–690). Between 690 and 731, an anti-witch clause appears in the codex of King Wintraed: Ecgbeorht, Archbishop of York (735–766) in his *Confessional*, made mention of penalties for witches, and under Guthrum the penalties were made more severe. King Aethelstan (925–940) also enacted against witches, and King Edmund (940–946) included in the category of witchcraft the compounding of philtres: King Edgar (958–979) in enjoining priests to promote Christianity instructed them to diligently suppress heathenism which included all forms of magic. King Canute (1014–1038) also forbade the practice of magic.

Duke William of Normandy, who successfully invaded England in 1066, mentioned, in a summary of law, punishment for *veneno* which might refer to venom—venomous behaviour—or to poison, but as *maleficium* and poisoning were so closely related, there can be little doubt that the reference is to witchcraft.

King Henry I (1100–1135) passed ordinances against *malefi-*

ciis, and in 1290 (A.R. x John) a case was heard in *Cura Regis* and the accused acquitted by ordeal. In 1406 King Henry V instructed the Bishop of Lincoln to enquire into witchcraft practised in his diocese. The first witchcraft Act of King Henry VIII (Act 3, Cap. 11), was directed against persons claiming to effect cures, prohibiting the activities of all persons who were not qualified. This was followed in 1542 by a further Statute which was more clearly directed against witches, but it was repealed in 1547 under Edward VI.

Under Queen Elizabeth I, witchcraft was allied to high treason, and noblemen rather than peasants were proceeded against. In 1563 an Act was passed which like that of King Henry VIII, made witchcraft a capital offence. In 1604 (A.R. i. James I) the Elizabethan Act was broadened and strengthened. It remained in force until 1736 when, under King George II, it was repealed, but the public was protected by Clause IV of the substitutional Act, 'And for the more effectual preventing and punishing any pretenses to such arts and powers ... whereby ignorant persons are frequently deluded and defrauded ... if any person shall from and after the said 24th day of June, pretend to exercise or use any kind of witchcraft, sorcery, enchantment, or conjuration, or undertake to tell fortunes or pretend from his or her skill or knowledge in any occult or crafty science ... every person so offending, being thereof lawfully convicted ... shall for every offense suffer imprisonment by the space of one whole year without bail or mainprize ...'

Under Queen Victoria this Act was modified: for example, punishment by standing in the pillory was removed from it: and in 1951 it was repealed, hence, so far as the witches were concerned, 'they all lived happy ever after'.

Chapter Six

THE repeal of the Witchcraft Act would have been hailed by the daily press (supposing that at the time there had been a dearth of rape, murder and arson, thus releasing space), as a piece of 'enlightened legislation' notwithstanding that it arose out of abysmal ignorance, namely the idea that there was no such thing as a witch. 'Our wise legislators' were, it seems, restrained by a minority consisting of those who were not one hundred per cent cock-sure materialists. This is suggested by their having substituted the Fraudulent Mediums Act which made it criminal 'fraudulently to purport to act as a spiritualistic medium or to exercise power of telepathy, clairvoyance, or other similar powers'.

In these days when Spiritualism has not only attained to respectability, but its devotees have been accorded the status of a minor religious sect, it may seem out of place to align it with witchcraft; nevertheless, a connecting link is manifest, and although the modern Spiritualists are not witches, many of the ancient witches were spiritualists.

The movement that led to the repeal of the Witchcraft Act may have been stimulated by the case of 'Rex *v* Duncan and others', heard at the Old Bailey before Sir Gerald Dodson, the Recorder of London, in March 1944. The scene of Mrs (Helen) Duncan's activities had been The Master Temple Psychic Centre, registered as a church, in Portsmouth, but it was a church where one paid for admission—as at a music hall. J. Maude, K.C. was the prosecuting counsel, and the charge against Mrs Duncan and her three assistants was that they had 'conspired together to pretend to exercise conjuration that spirits of deceased persons should appear and communicate with living persons present in the hall.'

C. E. Loseby, for the defence, juggled with words: 'conjuration', he contended, referred only to the invocation of evil spirits, which art required in its performance a magic circle, incantation, and certain mathematical calculations, with none of which the prisoners were charged. More than forty witnesses were called to attest how marvellous Mrs Duncan's mediumship was: all had recognized their departed relations in her materializations, some went so far as to claim to having kissed the ghost.

Witnesses for the prosecution declared they had seen and touched nothing more ethereal than stockinette and butter-muslin. It was also revealed that Mrs Duncan had, in May 1933, been fined £10 in Edinburgh on a charge of fraudulently having obtained £4 by pretending to be one through whom the spirits of the dead could materialize. The Old Bailey jury brought in a verdict of guilty and no appeal was allowed.

This trial attracted a great deal of attention, and even the blindest, most obtuse and ignorant legislative body could not have failed to note the public concern. Whether there are or are not spirits of the dead, willing and able to be 'called from the vasty deep', whether there is or is not such stuff as ectoplasm, and whether or not Mrs Duncan's materializations were of this diaphanous link between matter and spirit, or were of stockinette or butter-muslin matters not at all. The major point at issue was whether it was or was not wise in a disbelieving, materialistic age to keep the Witchcraft Act (which had suffered some distortion and strain during the trial of Helen Duncan) on the Statute Book. The decision reached makes it clear that its retention was considered not wise, but the substitution of the Fraudulent Mediums Act reveals a doubt as to whether the decision reached was, after all, itself wise.

By mid-twentieth century extra sensory perception—known by the initial letters, ESP—had become accepted by even the most sceptical as an undeniable fact. Every human being has a 'sixth sense': the ability to cognize without the aid of the five senses. In most people this power is but vestigial, in a few it is highly developed and subject to conscious control. The nature and the method of the functioning of ESP is unknown and likely to remain so. Sir Richard Burton, in a footnote on page 426 of Volume IV, of his *Supplemental Nights*, in relation to 'the flying carpet' and with reference to the passage, 'then, at the mere will and wish of Prince Husayan the twain were at once transported to the Khan', says, 'among Eastern peoples, and especially adepts, the will of man is not a mere term for a mental or cerebral operation, it takes rank as a substance; it becomes a mighty motive power, like table-turning and other such phenomena which, now looked upon as child's play, will perform a prime part in the kinetics of the century to come. If a few pair of hands imposed on a heavy dinner-table can raise it in the air, as I have often seen, what must we expect to result when the new motive force shall find its Franklin and be shown to the world as real "Vril"? The experiment of silently willing a subject to act in a manner not suggested by speech or sign has been repeatedly tried and succeeded in London drawing-rooms; and it has lately been suggested that atrocious crimes have resulted from overpowering volition.

'In cases of paralysis the [Medical] Faculty is agreed upon the fact that local symptoms disappear when the will-power returns to the brain. And here I will boldly and baldly state my theory that, in sundry cases, spectral appearances (ghosts) and abnormal smells and sounds are simply the effect of Will which has, so to speak, created them.'

Sir Richard Burton's confidence in the expected achievements of 'the century to come', namely, this one, arises from his being unaware that he was living on the crest of the wave of Western culture which was soon to break over the beach of mechanically-minded materialism. In place of the solution to the mystery of psi-phenomena, the twentieth century has produced the internal-combustion engine, and all cultural advance lies mangled beneath the ruthless wheels.

ESP in its various departments, clairvoyance, clairaudience and precognition; healing by the laying-on of hands; second-states in which a person having nothing more than elementary education can read and recite (for example) ancient Hebrew, or ancient Greek poetry, can account satisfactorily for supernormal abilities and the power to perform miracles, as recorded in Biblical, and other archaic texts.

Some of the activities of witches, revealed in trials, may safely be explained as the working of ESP. 'Death's brother, sleep'–'a blessed thing, beloved from pole to pole'—with its dream-life, has been accepted from earliest times as a portal into prophecy, and even today 'Dream Books' in which standard recurrent dreams are interpreted, sell in huge quantities: 'to dream of the dead is to hear of the living', 'to dream of excrement means money is on your path'. Such publications, containing such definitions, make their appeal only to the less intelligent members of the community; nevertheless, modern psychology has revealed the importance of dreams: Freud's definitions of the dream as 'the disguised fulfilment of an unconscious wish', so ably demonstrated in the works of Wilhelm Stekel, has proved a pathway to the relief of psycho-neurosis. Prophetic vision has been sought by magicians, soothsayers, and witch-doctors in all parts of the world by inducing sleep, or else trance, through the use of narcotic drugs. Another method employed in the attainment of this end is auto-hypnosis. The medium in trance is sometimes able to reveal matters concerning which reason insists he or she could not normally be aware, and mediums also become capable of performing acts which, in the normal state, would be far beyond their physical capabilities: for example, D. D. Home's astounding feats of levitation.* An interesting difference between a person put in a state of hypnosis for therapeutical or for experimental reasons, and a medium in an auto-hypnotic trance is that the former becomes possessed of an abnormal sense of time. He will perform an act of post-hypnotic obedience exactly (say) eight hundred and ninety-nine seconds after the suggestion has been made to him by the hypnotist, but the latter is without even normal time sense. There appears to be a relationship between auto-hypnotic trance and hysteria, but authorities disagree sharply on this possibility. There is more agreement on the relationship between hysteria and religious ecstasy with its attendant physical manifestations, such as levitation and stigmata. Witches who anointed themselves with the 'flying ointment' (highly narcotic) fell into a trance state in which their dream was of transvection and, at the sabbat, high feasting and sexual orgies, being, in the estimation of modern psychology, compensation phantasy for malnutrition and sexual repression. It is on record that some witches have, in the trance state, exhaled 'a bluish vapour': this is better attested ectoplasm than that of Mrs Duncan, which may, after all, have been butter-muslin. This misty exudation from the body of a medium seems to be the stuff that ghosts are made of and, much as we would like to write it off as illusion or worse, namely, butter-muslin, we are prevented from doing so, and

* See p. 113.

forced to accept its objective existence, by the fact of its having been investigated by scientists using the microscope and reported on as a fluid containing epithelium and fat-globules.

The object of psychical research is to observe and probe, criticize and record the abnormal abilities of the mediums in the séance-room. Many conscientious, sober-minded gentlemen have been cruelly hoaxed by conjuring tricks performed with the aid of the curtained 'cabinet' (which is always present) and in the dim light demanded. Spirit demonstrations of the materialization of apports, and in telekinesis, have ultimately proved the outcome of prestidigitation and contortionism (the German, Rudi Schneider, who had been making a very good thing of his magical powers was finally and utterly exposed through the ingenious apparatus devised by Harry Price) but much that was genuine also appeared, and some of the supernormal feats of mediumship are to be found, expressed in a different idiom in the witch trials.

L'Estrange Ewen points out* that the victims of witchcraft, more often than the witches themselves, manifested symptoms compatible with aspects of mediumistic trance.

Rigor, inflexibility of the limbs, is sometimes experienced by the mediums, and was also a symptom of the fits of bewitched persons: in both, the state may be an aspect of hysteria. The present writer, while serving in the London Fire Brigade during the Second World War, and engaged on training recruits to the Auxiliary Service, was confronted by a case of fear-rigor which seized a man half-way up a fifty-foot escape. His body was not only rigid but was hard to the touch, as stone. In addition, he appeared to have become deaf and dumb: no amount of coaxing or reassurance seemed to penetrate to his consciousness. The situation was desperate, and something had to be done to resolve it. A change of tactics seemed worth trying. In place of gentle coaxing, stern orders, and a threat to sling him in a double bowline and rope him down had the immediate effect of causing the sufferer to run up the rest of the ladder and leap into the open third-floor window to which it was pitched. Later in the afternoon, chatting over tea, it was revealed that the man had no recollection of the incident. It was a clear case of hysteria.

* *Psychic Phenomena in the Witchcraft Cases*, published by the author, 1947.

Bewitched persons might suffer a weight change in either direction: becoming so heavy that a team of strong men were unable to lift them, or so light that they could be easily raised by a not notoriously muscular person employing one hand only. Weight change is common to mediums: Eusapia Palladino, the Italian medium, could rest her head on a table and extend her body in a horizontal position for several minutes on end, thus combining loss of weight with rigor. 'Col. Rochas, the French psychical investigator, has noticed, on the authority of three eye-witnesses, an ecstatic of Grenoble, whose body became stiff and "so light that it was possible to lift her up like a feather by holding her by the elbow."'* Sir W. Crookes found that when his medium conjured up a spirit she lost half her weight, and Dr W. J. Crawford, of Belfast, claimed that during the séance his medium lost fifty pounds in weight.

Apart from weight, girth may be affected. A Roman philosopher (Iamblichus) writing in the fourth century A.D. said that an inspired person might either increase or diminish in girth. Anne Ashby, at Maidstone Assize, in 1652, 'swelled into a monstrous and vast bigness'. William Sommers† 'extended to the height of the tallest man': Eusapia Palladino could increase her height by four inches, and D. D. Home, measured by Lord Adare, extended from five feet eight inches to six feet five and a half inches.

Another inexplicable change is that of temperature. William Sommers's 'pulces and temples did not beat, he lay for dead, cold as ice'. The temperature of mediums often falls very considerably, and their pulse-rate slows. Mediums, witches and bewitched persons may become immune to fire: D. D. Home on one occasion pressed his face into the fire, and he frequently demonstrated his ability to lift red-hot, flaming coal with his bare hands, and place them against his chest inside his shirt. Mary Glover, tried in 1602, felt no pain when a lighted taper was held beneath her hand till it blistered. William Sommers, in one of his fits, fell into the fire without its affecting him. In India, fakirs will gladly walk through fire to secure a few coppers from European spectators, and one, Kuda Bux, gave a demonstration in England, before Harry Price. He walked bare-footed over a veritable furnace of

* Ewen, op. cit.   † See p. 40.

oak logs from the surface of which all ash was brushed away by the spectators.

In 1847, in the home of John D. Fox, farmer, of Hydesville, U.S.A., mysterious knocking, or rapping, occurred. His two young daughters, Margaretta and Catherine, took over the investigation, declared the sounds to be produced by a disembodied spirit with whom they established a signal code to enable them to receive answers to their questions, and so established this popular method of communication with ghosts and, indeed, set the seed out of which modern Spiritualism has grown. The general public of the period were not convinced of the innocence of these juvenile mediums and in 1850 an angry crowd gathered outside a house in which Margaretta Fox was lodging, and shouted angry imprecations against the 'witch-woman'. Knocking by spirits was not something new: an outbreak in Fulda Abbey, Mainz, as early as 858, is on record. Such knocking was, in England, considered to be one of the manifestations of witchcraft. These sounds were heard in the vicinity of William Sommers, and they troubled John Mompesson, J.P. of Tedworth after he had sentenced an itinerant drummer in 1661. The case of the Drummer of Tedworth is accepted as an example of poltergeist phenomena: the experience of the Fox sisters is accorded, 'in this enlightened age', a far different status.

What little enlightenment we really have achieved in the study of ESP enables us to prove, under scientific control, that thought-transference, or telepathy, is a fact of occult communication, not merely a superstition bolstered up by the occasional coincidence. Between successfully selected pairs, a powerful 'sender' and a sensitive, affectible 'receiver', thought-transference can be solidified into a kind of hypnosis so that the 'receiver' will perform some act thought into him by the 'sender' several miles away. That this power was known to and used by witches is indicated by the fact that Dr Lambe* on one occasion when entertaining friends caused a woman passing by 'to lift her coat above her middle'.

On the same occasion (Dr Lambe was entertaining his friends while he was in prison in Worcester Castle, in 1608) he is reported to have caused bottles of wine to materialize which carries the suggestion that the bottles were apports, brought in from

* See p. 161.

outside by Lambe's power of telekinesis: the ability to move matter without touching it, and of causing matter to pass through matter. There is, however, another report of this prison party in which Lambe conjured up a 'boy in green' who was sent to the tavern to buy the wine. In numerous witch-trials there is a passing reference to the magical appearance of some object but so apparently minor an act of magic was not given much attention. The stones which many victims of witchcraft vomited may have been apports, brought in from outside by themselves unconsciously while in their hysterical fits. In the modern séance room it is not uncommon for apports to arrive under conditions of control that preclude the possibility of the explanation being that a more than normally skilful conjuring trick has been performed. Genuine apports are likely to be hot—even very hot—indicating friction engendered on their journey. In 1682, stones that came into a closed room were reliably reported to be 'as hot as if they came out of the fire', and in a report printed in *Psychic Science* (25 January 1925) a lost finger-ring that suddenly dropped on to the séance table was too hot to hold.

Materialization of hot apports could be accepted, in the days of witchcraft persecution, only as the work of the devil who brought them out of hell and, unseen, threw them about; in these days of nuclear fission even a schoolboy can understand that stones, being composed of atoms, could pass through bricks, also composed of atoms, for in both substances the spaces between the electrons in orbit are proportionately as great as are the spaces between planets in orbit in a solar system. The mystery that remains is what is the power that can push or pull the stone through the brick with sufficiently accurate timing to prevent major atomic collisions.

Outbreaks of poltergeist phenomena have, in the past, sometimes been attributed to a witch's malice, the accused being found guilty and hanged. 'Racketing spirits' are still with us, but we now know that these mischievous (sometimes dangerous) sprites indulge in their fun only in houses where there is a pubescent boy or girl. Why that particular phase of development has that effect on some children who remain unconscious of their responsibility for the tricks is not yet discovered, but what has emerged out of scientific investigation is that some of these patients become aware of their part in the drama when the attack is receding, whereupon they try to produce the same effects by simulation and invariably fail.

In these days, when even children no longer believe in fairies, or in Father Christmas, it follows that only the feeble-minded will give credence to the idea that an old woman could, by urinating in a hole in the ground and blowing upon the surface, raise a ship-wrecking storm at sea, or that she could send her cat to kill a neighbour's cow, or that by glancing at a child she could cause it to suffer convulsions and death. Therefore all the witches who were in England hanged, and elsewhere burned, were innocent victims of the superstitions of the age.

To exonerate uncritically is one of the superstitions of this age. Although a witch could not raise a storm there were among the accused those who believed that they could, who did not refrain from maliciously going through the motions, and taking credit for being the creator of the next storm that broke in the neighbourhood. If a shipmaster, while ashore, had an altercation with an old crone bearing a bad reputation, and she had retorted with some cryptic remark, such as it would have been better had he not crossed her, that shipmaster might, if confronted with sudden unexpected heavy weather when making his next voyage, be reminded of the witch's 'curse' and in a panic give a wrong order that cast the vessel away with the loss of all hands. The cause of the disaster was the fear of the power of witchcraft, but the fear was stimulated by the altercation with a witch, hence the hag, who, on hearing of the disaster chuckled and jibbered with delight, was guilty by intention.

This is holding no brief for the persecution of witches. The torture and torment and brutality to which the prisoners were subjected makes of their persecutors demon-possessed servants of Satan far more guilty than were the most iniquitous of the accused: it is simply an endeavour to temper with reasonable caution the modern, materialistic conviction that 'witchcraft is all nonsense'.

The links that exist between ancient witchcraft and modern Spiritualism are of a sufficient strength to show that witchcraft was not all nonsense, and this holds good even when we assert it is most likely that modern Spiritualism does not deal with disembodied spirits. Nothing so far has been revealed by mediums, or by any manifestations that have spontaneously occurred in the séance room, justifying the assumption that spirits are causative, or even that spirits exist. The extremists, those who belong to the Spiritualist movement, have no better argument to support them than their own belief, and that of such outstanding persons as Sir William Crookes, Sir Oliver Lodge, and Sir Arthur Conan Doyle, who have, in the past, been strong adherents to the cult. Without wishing to stir up any mud that has long since settled, it is asserted on good authority that Sir William Crookes's beliefs were dictated to him by the medium with whom he worked and whom, for personal reasons, he did not dare to defy or denounce. Sir Oliver Lodge's grief at the loss of his son, Raymond, in the 1914–18 war was so keen, and cut so deep, that his experiences in Spiritualism caused his intellect to be overruled by his emotions. Sir Arthur Conan Doyle, in his maturity, mentally fatigued by a long life of literary work, accepted evidence that Sherlock Holmes—in fact, that Lestrade—would have rejected.

Whether there are spirits or whether there are not spirits, extra-normal feats are accomplished in the séance room and precisely the same kind of extra-normal feats were performed by, or in the vicinity of, witches. There are many people today who, without being either supporters of or adherents to the Spiritualist cult, are satisfied that mediumistic manifestations are of the spirits, but who are, quite illogically, equally satisfied that the maleficia of witches were not of the devil.

The theologians and the jurists who led the anti-witch movement were sincere, believing they were serving God, and protecting the public: and the public itself, at all cultural levels, was credulous. In this credulity there is not a pin to choose between then and now. The average person, without being particularly interested in the matter, and very unwilling to become involved would, if cross-examined, reveal a vague belief in the disembodied spirits with whom the medium claims to be in touch, and with other spirit entities who are the heroes of hauntings: such persons do not consider that the 'best authenticated ghost-stories' are works of fiction, and they read into the vague, reversible pronouncements of astrologers and other soothsayers whose formulae fill a column or two in otherwise serious newspapers, prophecies relating to their own careers. Mankind is no less superstitious today than it was in the witchcraft period and back into the Old Stone Age. The difference is that today, superstition is rationalized: the man who does not believe in ghosts will not volunteer to sleep in the haunted room because, by disuse, it is cold and damp. If reassured that it is kept warm and dry, the bed well aired, and that he will be fortified by hot-water bottles, he finds some other plausible reason, but he does not sleep in the room. One does not pass under a pitched ladder: this, we assure ourselves, is not connected with superstition: it is a wise practical precaution because the workman aloft might drop a tool, or a splash of paint. However, we refrain from passing under a ladder when there is no workman above. One does not organize a party whereat thirteen persons will be present, and most certainly not on Friday the thirteenth of the month. This is, of course, merely a form of courtesy: one of the guests may be superstitious.

That little brass figure which auntie gave to us 'for luck' when we first went out to work we continue to carry not because we believe in its positive power to induce good fortune, or in its negative power to avert evil—we are not superstitious—but we keep it with us because we are used to it, or out of respect for the memory of auntie, or for divers other good, practical reasons. We may leave home in the morning having forgotten the documents vital to our day's business activities, we may leave home in the morning having forgotten our artificial dentures, but never do we leave home having forgotten our talisman: it is the first object to be transferred from the pocket of this suit to the pocket of that suit.

The difference between superstition in (say) 1575 and in 1975 is that today we possess the intellectual case-hardening of objective knowledge that makes us ashamed of our superstitions because we recognize in them the curious human ability of believing what we know to be untrue, and we rationalize to conceal from ourselves the folly of our ways.

Superstition was (and is) a pathway along which the cultus of the left hand, the black art, demonism, witchcraft and fortune-telling, several facets of the same evil, makes progress, for witchcraft was (and is) a diabolical force moving of its own volition, casting its spells and committing murder by enchantment, as well as in more obvious and objective ways.

Reports of trials, and other records of the past, suggest a stratification in witchcraft. There are the educated warlocks and the degenerate nobility, such as 'Sweet Father Forman' and Lady

Essex. The most lenient, the most tolerant, the most merciful and rational of modern apologists, cannot but agree to the guiltiness of this stratum. Next are the uneducated practitioners, the compounders of poison, the vendors of philtres, the mumblers of incantations which, though meaningless, they believed to be fraught with magical power generated by their master, Satan. At another level will be seen the white witches: people who had, perhaps, the occult power of healing, who far from being malicious were often benefactors of a local community, but who, nonetheless, suffered and died ignominiously. In a further group we may place the senile hags, so well described by Harsnett. They knew nothing of magical practice or of occult lore, but were sufficiently cunning to use the reputation their neighbours gave them as a threat, and as a form of superiority behaviour. Last are the wholly innocent multitude who barely knew of the existence of either white or black magic; often worthy citizens of superior spiritual awareness, filled with rectitude and good-neighbourliness, who were seized and ultimately sentenced to death, having been included in a tormented witch's list of accomplices, which all too often, particularly under Continental torture, contained names of persons with whom the witch was not even acquainted.

It is the penultimate category that commands most attention, and medical interest has been stimulated by the modern speciality of geriatrics. Miss Sona Rose Burstein, M.A., former assistant curator of the Wellcome Historical Medical Museum, summarizes the modern movement in a clear, concise exposition entitled *Aspects of the Psychopathology of Old Age, Revealed in Witchcraft Cases in the Sixteenth and Seventeenth Centuries*, which was published in the *British Medical Bulletin*, Vol. 6, numbers 1–2, in 1949. Miss Burstein says: '... at the height of the witch-trials ... the vast majority of the accused were old women. Of this we have overwhelming evidence. ... There is an undoubted challenge to those concerned with mental and social welfare in the question why, for two and a half centuries, suspicion of, and prosecution for witchcraft constituted a major hazard of female senescence.'

After numerous references to writers who had described the witches in much the same way as Harsnett had done, and mentioning the fact that in the dominions governed by William Duke of Cleves, 'foolish old women were not put to death, and were punished only if there was a proved case of poisoning', Miss Burstein says, 'An occurrence quoted by Westphal in a book called *Pathologia daemoniaca*, published in Leipzig in 1707, indicates that the tradition of Weyer had taken some hold in the medical world, even in Germany, the stronghold of the belief in witches. The story is of an old woman who, in 1674, a century after Weyer was writing, confessed to congress with an incubus. She was handed over for medical examination; this in itself marks an enormous advance. Dr Michael Ettmüller, in a long opinion given with much detail of symptoms, pronounced her insane and declared her intercourse with demons imaginary, and her "progeny" nothing but faecal discharges after severe constipation. . . .

'Not least evidence in the narratives is that type of senile psychotic behaviour arising from lack of comprehension of immediate reality or danger. Eighty-year-old Temperance Lloyd, we are told in a contemporary pamphlet, went to the gallows "all the way eating and was seemingly unconcerned" . . .'

The old woman, deprived of her erstwhile agility and strength, no longer able to box an ear, slap a face, or tug a neighbour's hair, is driven to lash with her tongue in self-defence, and deeming attack the best means of defence will be continually calling her neighbours by unpleasant names so as to be on the safe side. This aspect of the psychopathology of old age does not escape Miss Burstein. 'Over and over again it is this loud, aggressive behaviour which brings the woman into trouble. Numerous instances in support of this are adduced from our own records, and the following from Württemberg where, early in the seventeenth century, the mother of Johann Kepler the astronomer, was accused of witchcraft (by a neighbour whom she had insulted), and was defended by her son.

'The "Keplerin", as she was called, deserted by a thriftless husband, soured and embittered by misfortune, made morose and eccentric by solitude, was described by Kepler as "small, thin, swarthy, sharp-tongued, quarrelsome, of evil mind." He added that she was the disturber of the local community, and in a letter said ". . . this suspicion spread at once among highly superstitious folk, since they based their argument on the seventy years' age of my mother and on several of the faults with which my mother is burdened, which are lying, prying, violent anger, cursing, persistence in complaints ..." '

Several quotations of this kind follow, among them Reginald Scott's *Epistle Dedicatory*, 'in which he covers a whole range of senile psychotic behaviour and makes some acute observations on cause and effect. He pleads, ". . . they, which are commonly accused of witchcraft, are the least sufficient of all others to speak for themselves; as having the most base and simple education of all others; the extremity of their age giving them leave to dote, their povertie to beg, their wrongs to chide and threaten (*as being void of any other waie of revenge*), their humour, melancholical to be full of imaginations, from whence cheefly proceedeth the vanity of their confessions ..." '

Burton, in his famous work *Anatomy of Melancholy*, says, 'This natural infirmity in old women, and such as are poor, solitary, live in most base esteem and beggary, or such as are witches.'

Miss Burstein says, 'a Johann Weyer could blaze a trail for the modern alienist. Yet doctors of later times have tended to relegate the whole matter of witchcraft to the antiquarian and the folk-lorist. . . . Nevertheless, there is not complete silence. Alienists of the later nineteenth century such as Hack Tuke and Maudsley make reference, albeit briefly, to the witchcraft records as of some value in their work with the insane. Tuke declares that "it is impossible to read the narratives of some of the unfortunate hags who were put to death for witchcraft, without recognizing the well-marked features of the victims of cerebral disorder".

'A series of articles on the *State of Society Past and Present, in Relation to Criminal Psychology* appeared in 1881–3 from the pen of David Nicolson, deputy-superintendent of Broadmoor Criminal Lunatic Asylum. This contribution . . . attempts an assessment of the social implications of the persecutions.'

We extract the following from Miss Burstein's quotation:
' "Sometimes the eccentric or insane appearance or conduct of the individual will be found to have given rise to an accusation founded on a *bona fide* belief in the individual's actual or potential guilt. Sometimes the insanity will reveal itself in wild and ecstatic utterances of the individual at whose instigation or upon whose evidence a charge is sustained against a reputable and

unoffending neighbour. Sometimes the mixture of hysteria or epilepsy with a malicious or criminal disposition will mask the real character of the case and give, as in any form of criminal charge, grounds for the expression of honest though contradictory opinion on the two sides."'

In 1904 a controversy concerning the 'memorial-worthiness' of a doctor of the past broke out in the *British Medical Journal*. The protagonist for the 'againsts' was an Irish alienist, Conolly Norman, whose main, in fact, only objection to the memorial was that the doctor to be commemorated had given 'expert testimony' in 1664 that had led to the execution of two witches. When this bonfire burned down, 'in the following year, Norman published an interesting study on the reappearance among modern paranoiacs of notions having the closest connection with old witch-craft delusions.'

Quoting a German writer* 'concerned with child psychology in relation to the witch-beliefs and trials', Miss Burstein points out that he 'also draws attention to the type of ragged, hunch-backed, dishevelled, emaciated old woman presented to child-belief as a witch. One or two other authors have referred the suspect behaviour of supposed witches to schizophrenia and epilepsy, to trance-mediumship or essays in extra-normal experi-ence, or to unrealistic symbolism ...'

Miss Burstein concludes her masterly and most enlightening article with a brief review of recent literature relating to, and an examination of the sociological and medical mental relationship to the problems of old age: 'it is only within the last decade that the mental state of old people, and the happiness or unhappiness of their reciprocal relations with the community, have come to be realized as a factor to be reckoned with in communal welfare.'

No one who is himself reasonably sane will contend against the theory so ably put forward by Miss Burstein, namely, that the witch trials reveal the bulk of the accused to have been sick with senile dementia. There were, however, also to be reckoned with those who were neither senile nor demented in the way the old women were, and no sweeping judgement in the matter can be reached except, perhaps, if one may be permitted to purloin

---

*Tramer, M. (1945) *Kinder im Hexenglauber und Hexenprozess des Mittelalters*. Z. Kinderpsychiat, 11; 140; 180.

a witticism from the average schoolboy's repertoire, 'mad and bad are two-thirds the same.'

In the two decades that have passed since Miss Burstein wrote her study, 'Psychiatry' has taken command of the good ship Psychotherapy like the main-mast over the side.

Psychiatry is youthful, objective, forceful, glutted on a diet of its own apparent success, and is a short cut to the cure of mental conditions that it does not permit common sense to call insanity. This blustering newcomer calls both madmen and criminals 'mentally sick' and sets out, by a kind of 'brain-washing' and reflex-conditioning, to return to the bosom of his family, labelled 'cured', that member of it who had dominated and induced despair and misery into all the others, and who, dumped back again, will doubly dominate, but in a different way, from behind the label 'cured'. Psychiatry will cut another notch on its gun: the mother of the afflicted family may commit suicide. The noble psychiatry has pandered to the patient's welfare, but has considered the life of the sufferer—his or her next of kin—not at all.

Today we have neither lunatics nor lunatic asylums. They are replaced by the mentally sick patient, and by mental hospitals, hence, the beds are filled by people who are under treatment voluntarily. No matter how dangerous to the community the patient's condition may be, he has freedom to walk out at any hour of the day or night and continue his dangerous insane obsession where he left off. The reason why this does not occur may be that in place of the padded cell we have the hypodermic syringe: the doctor protects the public against a possible result of 'enlightened legislation'.

'She is maze and will confess to anything,' said Thomas Holden in his letter to Joseph Williamson concerning the witch who was supposed to have been with the Duke of York's fleet,* thus indicating that the average person was not totally unaware of there being a substratum of insanity in witchcraft, but insanity—other than feeble-mindedness, idiocy, imbecility and the like—was believed to be merely the expression of demoniac possession which, if the host was not deliberately harbouring the demon—might be relieved by exorcism. The medical profession has, in our time, done manfully in its dealing with madness, but so did the exorcists

* See p. 156.

in their own day and so do they now when they are called to a case. Protestantism, taking over witch-beliefs from Catholicism also took over, as a sort of accessory, exorcism, and they have not abandoned it, as the following report in the *Daily Express*, 28 May 1968, reveals. 'Three pastors claimed last night to have exorcised evil spirits from a woman after police were called to the "purifying" service. . . . The drama started when the pastors, with the permission of the woman's husband, dragged her scream-ing and shouting, into a big, stone-built chapel in Treharris, near Merthyr, Glamorgan. . . . Ten hours after she was taken to the chapel the woman walked out . . . she was quite calm. Her long hair was done up in a neat pile, and she was wearing ear-rings . . .' The pastors, on being interviewed, said, ' "the woman has been ill and violent . . . she was possessed by evil spirits or demons. We used the power of prayer to drive out the spirits, just like it says in the Bible." '

It will be recalled that Lady Essex was, in later life, pronounced mad.* Today, the particular form of insanity from which the worst of the witches suffer is named paranoia: it would seem that witch-work has a rebounding quality, and the demon within ulti-mately destroys the vehicle.

Lombroso, the great Italian anthropologist, said in one of his works that if no radical change took place, the entire population of Central Europe would, in about a hundred years from the time of his writing be mad. His prophecy was fulfilled, the elapse of a century saw the rise of Hitler who, ably supported by satellites such as Hess, Streicher and Goebbels, implemented Satanism to the applause of the German nation. One of the first acts of the Nazis was to ban all forms of occult practice. By so doing they cornered the market as it were and kept magic in their own hands. Hitler's deputy, Hess, was a devotee of the black arts, and he excelled in astrology. The whole truth concerning his sudden dramatic departure will never be known: it was probably part of a very complex Nazi plot that failed. In the Fatherland the reason was given as due to the machinations of occultists and astrologers. This gave an excuse for a further purge, known as 'Action Hess': the least of the practitioners was roped in.

One of the earliest Nazi uses of black magic is connected with

* See pp. 124–35.

the Reichstag fire. A stage-performing clairvoyant who, if a mere mountebank in his clairvoyant demonstrations, was a powerful hypnotist, was given an unstable youth to work upon. This cats-paw was conditioned to enter the building at a certain time, proceed through specified corridors, and start the blaze. He was also conditioned to forget, utterly, all that he did. In a state of post-hypnotic obedience he carried out his instructions but, having no experience of, and probably in his normal state, no particular taste for arson, he started a fire that was quickly and easily extinguished. Goering's agents, however, stepped into the breach and the building was thoroughly gutted. The subsequent trial aroused world-wide interest: steps were taken to prevent the lifting of the post-hypnotic amnesia, and afterwards the boy's body was found in a wood near Berlin. He was not the only victim of German thoroughness: everyone else who had been privy to the plot was murdered.

Another outstanding magician was one Krafft: no cheapjack, but a scholar, accepted as an expert on Nostradamus. He was wellknown for his prophecies based on astrological calculations, and he wrote, warning Hitler that there would be an attempted assassination. There was. Himmler, the Secret Police Chief, concluded that the astrologer was himself in the plot, and arrested him, but Goebbels, less crude than Himmler, had Krafft released, gave him a 'cover' post as a translator in the News Bureau, and employed him to translate Nostradamus, and interpret his prophecies in favour of a German victory. Pamphlets, in divers languages, were spread far and wide.

A special department was set up with, at its head, a high-ranking naval officer, where water-diviners, pendulum-sensitives, and others of that kind were kept busy determining the positions of British surface ships and submarines: the Nazis apparently believed that the British had such an organization which accounted for the increasing number of U-boats destroyed. (The simple and obvious explanation of British superiority could not occur to a German.)

There is, too, good reason to believe that the Nazis coupled black magic to their espionage system. During the war, some boys playing in a wood near Birmingham, found, hidden in a hollow wych-elm, some human bones. The local police were informed, a careful search was made and there came to light semi-rotted remains of clothing and a shoe.*

The remains were sent for investigation to a forensic laboratory and their research revealed that the bones were those of a woman. Her height, the colour of her hair, the details of her teeth, and even the style of her clothing, were discovered. She had been killed and, while the body was still warm, lowered into the hollow tree.

Every effort was made to identify the woman: her garments and her shoes were described to local vendors of such articles but none could give information: no dentist responded to an advertisement describing her teeth. At length an identity card was found, sodden and defaced, under a bush near the hollow tree. The police called at the address and interviewed the person named on the card. She was unaware of having lost it, and had never been anywhere near the wych-elm.

The next development was that wall-chalking started over a fairly wide area surrounding the scene of the discovery: the general theme was, 'who put Bella down the wych-elm?' Sometimes the name was extended to 'Lubella'.

A local journalist who was writing a series of articles on the 'Bella' murder received a letter, signed with a pseudonym, saying '. . . the person responsible for the crime died insane in 1942, and the victim was Dutch and arrived illegally in England about 1941 . . .' The writer was traced and interviewed. What emerged was that 'Bella' was probably Dutch, and almost certainly a Nazi spy. The Nazis had organized a very efficient spy system based on Holland. Hess had an organization through which he set up Nazi cells in England. One of Hess's agents was a certain Lehrer, who had a Dutch mistress. She had lived in Birmingham and spoke English with the local accent. From documents secured after the war it is known that among spies sent into England in 1941 was a woman—code name 'Clara'—who was dropped by parachute in the vicinity of Birmingham.

Lehrer's Dutch mistress was described as 'well educated, intelligent, attractive, and about thirty years of age . . . her teeth were slightly irregular . . . she claimed to be Dutch [but was] German

---

* The Lower Quinton and Hagley Wood Murders: *Birmingham Post*, (numerous reports). See also *Murder by Witchcraft*, by Donald McCormick, (John Long, 1968).

on the side of one of her parents . . . The last time I saw this young woman must have been about the end of 1940. . . . She read horoscopes . . . she might have been killed in an air-raid, or rounded up in *Aktion Hess*.'

Further information from Holland revealed that a person answering to 'Bella's' description, 'was a very serious student of astrology' and, what is most significant, she wore a garter of green snake-skin, a symbol of witchcraft. Proof may be lacking, but who can doubt the identity of the skeleton in the wych-elm? The 'Bella' incident came to light because of the murder without which complication it is unlikely that anything would have been known, hence, it ought not to be regarded as an isolated case. It is probable that there were dozens, if not hundreds, of such spy-witches at work in our midst. They, being the servitors of Satan, were dedicated in their devotion to the system that established Satan's temporal power in Central Europe.

The foregoing activities, and others, similar, in connection with the prosecution of the war, were not the only fields of diabolism entered by the Nazis. Among their organized wickedness was the inversion of psychotherapy, partly in order to undermine resistance and secure confession from persons suspected of anti-Nazi sympathies, and partly to produce 'synthetic' neurotics who, carefully placed in the various departments, would act as disturbers and so bring out latent anti-Nazi tendencies in their colleagues: it was not only Jews who went to the concentration camps.

Hitler himself did not resort to soothsayers, astrologers and other advisers claiming occult power: he was satisfied that guidance came direct to him from occult powers, and that he was alerted to receive a forthcoming revelation from below by a preliminary rushing sound in his ears.

Since diabolism was so deeply enmeshed with Nazism, it is almost amusing to read that the English witches, by what they call 'Operation Cone of Power', opposed Hitler and saved us from invasion. Gerald Gardner, 'King of the witches', gives details:

'We were taken at night to a place in the [New] Forest, where the Great Circle was erected; and that was done which may not be done except in great emergency. And the Great Cone of Power was raised and slowly directed in the general direction of Hitler. The Command was given: "You cannot cross the sea. You cannot

come; you cannot come." Just as we were told was done to Napo-
leon, when he had his army ready to invade England and never
came. As as was done to the Spanish Armada, mighty forces were
used, of which I may not speak. Now to do this means using one's
life-force; and many of us lived a few days after we did this. My
asthma, which I had never had since I first went out East, came
back badly. We repeated the ritual four times; and the Elders
said: "We feel we have stopped him. We must not kill too many
of our people. Keep them until we need them."'

It is good to know that we were saved again by a party of
prancing nudists, some of whom evidently caught cold and died,
and that the Navy and Air Force had nothing whatever to do
with it.

This Gerald Gardner, who spent many years in an official post
in Malaya, could not fail to observe native witchcraft, but there
is no reason to suppose that he had, at that period, discovered that
he was himself a witch. The discovery does not seem to ante-date
his reading of the works on the subject from Margaret Murray's
pen. Having made a collection of weapons and native odds and
ends he set up, in 1950, his Witchcraft Museum in the Isle of
Man.

Opinions concerning Gardner are mixed. He is the author of
two books, *Witchcraft Today* (1954) and *The Meaning of Witchcraft* (1959). Both of these works are, apparently, directed to a
'popular' readership. It is certain that neither of them reveals
scholarship, nor esoteric knowledge. He was personally abnormal:
a flagellant, and an exhibitionist: he also painted very bad pictures of voluptuous witches being burned to death. His flair for
self-advertisement enabled him to attract attention to himself,
and to gather together numerous social and sexual misfits who
organized themselves into covens of thirteens and pretended to
be witches. A few of them had read a little in the realm of
black magic and other occult practices, others of them were
herbalists and astrologers; there were to be found in their ranks
hysterics, and folk with semi-developed mediumistic powers.
Exhibitionists and nudists, they were not witches. They considered themselves rather superior to ordinary folk: they were
far too enlightened to believe in the devil: they were the rem-
nants of that pre-Christian European paganism of which they

had never heard before Margaret Murray's work brought it to their notice.

The eccentrics who became organized under 'Doctor' Gardner's influence, did no harm: they did not even try to do harm. Gardner himself was, at the time of the present writer's meeting with him (about five years before his death), a mild, garrulous, rather boring old man whose constant theme was the problem he experienced in settling the future of his Witchcraft Museum. He confided that he had offered it, gratis, to the British Museum and it was with great regret that they had been unable to find space to house it. This is a monument to the diplomacy of B.M. officials. The problem was evidently finally solved to Gardner's satisfaction and his collection is now one of the holiday sideshows of the Isle of Man.

Gardner and the motley collection of social and intellectual oddities who formed the 'covens' were very far from being witches; the harm that their play-acting (in the nude, of course) wrought was to provide an organization (for want of a better word) to which the really evil diabolists could attach themselves. They did not compare with the devotees of the 'Silver Star', the devil-worshipping dark brotherhood of malefic, anti-human beasts set up by Aleister Crowley, who delighted in being described as the most wicked man in the world and who was overjoyed that his own mother, a pious if narrow-minded woman, had come to the conclusion that she had given birth to the Great Beast 666 of Revelations. Crowley, drug addict and sexual pervert of the most revolting kind, performed ritual at which he 'murdered' Jesus of Nazareth, and set himself up as the Messiah. Whether Crowley's following was or was not numerous is a matter that will never be revealed, for his worshippers could not, like himself, come out into the open. What effect his death in 1947 had on his organization is also unknown, but members of his cult certainly survived. That Gardner would have welcomed these diabolical characters in his 'covens' also seems obvious, for he had met Crowley and entertained a great admiration for him.

If Crowley's organization crumbled into its component parts on the death in 1947 of 'the Great Beast', Gardner's, bolstered up by the Crowley crumbs, did not dissolve on the demise of the 'Doctor' in 1964. On the contrary, witch groups have grown from strength to strength, and have, in the last five years, become a menace to society. They openly practise sexual excesses, crave the fullest publicity and they do not deny their capability of causing disease and death by enchantment.

In 1954 Gardner asserted that witchcraft was not associated with the Black Mass: he was probably speaking the truth from the point of view of his own mild manifestations of witchcraft, but the Crowleyites would have known better. He further denied that witchcraft was a cultus of the left hand and devoted to the worship of the devil, and he contended that witches do not believe in the devil.

However, in spite of 'Doctor' Gardner, the Press published early in February, 1969, an interview with a renegade priest, a member of the Dominican Order, who had been ordained as a first-degree witch, and had taken part in nude rites at the meetings of two covens. When his extraordinary double life was discovered and he was confronted, he was busily preparing to conduct the most horrific of all witchcraft ceremonies—the Black Mass. The priest admitted that he reaches an 'intensity of dedication to the dark ones', and that inspiration came 'from the Father Below'.

The first requirement in the celebration of the Black Mass is a virgin, naked, spread-eagled on the 'altar' and the climax is reached when the officiating priest performs the sexual act with her. This priest, having been introduced to a young lady who it was thought would serve his purpose, 'interviewed' her, and during the course of the conversation made disparaging remarks concerning the Holy Father and advised the young lady to go on the birth control pill in order to avoid an undesirable result of his performance of the ceremony. The result of this exposure was that the priest went across to Ireland and there disappeared, but the Press did not cease to investigate and reveal what was dis-covered. They interviewed a 'high priestess' of witchcraft at her home in London who said, 'By the turn of the century witchcraft will have overtaken Christianity.' She was a woman of middle age who has been a witch since she was a girl, but her husband had never found out. All devotees to the witch-cult keep the matter secret, and some apparently very ordinary people are deeply involved. The lady being interviewed claimed to be only a white witch: she said, 'I have come across the black ones. But I did not stay with them long enough. I would not stay with anything black. . . . I am not even one per cent Christian. I cannot see that being nude or not, or the use of phallic symbols in witch-craft makes any difference one way or the other . . . the phallic symbol comes in everywhere . . . the steeple of a church . . . the only difference really is that paganism is a natural and beautiful religion and Christianity is a frustrated one.' It is noteworthy that to the witch the spire is a phallic symbol, but to the Christian it is pointing 'as with silent finger to the sky and stars' (S. T. Coleridge). The same thought is expressed by Wordsworth: 'And spires whose silent finger points to heaven.'

This cesspool uncovered, the Press continued to expose to public view the revolting contents. Investigators, posing as recruits, journeyed to the Isle of Man, a veritable hotbed of witchcraft, and made contact with the proprietors of the Witches' Mill (previously held by 'Doctor' Gardner) who had initiated their own daughter, Yvette, into the Wicca (their brand of witchcraft) when she was only four years old. Now at the still tender age of eleven she is a first degree witch and no stranger to nude rituals. She has been given the witch-name, Morven.

After the child had gone to bed her father, in conversation with the 'recruit' said, 'She has only gone through the first degree so far. We will wait for another year to put her through the second and then hope that she will choose a nice witch [boy] by the time she is eighteen so she can go through the third [which involves the sexual act] on a Friday and then have a church, or register office wedding, on the Saturday.'

The next move in the game was for the child's parents to strip naked; later they asked the 'recruit' if he'd like to see the 'altar-room' into which none was permitted to enter unless he, too, stripped naked. In the middle of this room was an altar bedecked with candelabra, knives, incense-burners, a blue-tinged figure of a naked woman, a lectern and several small bowls. The hostess asked the 'recruit' to hand her one of these and remarked on what a good witchcraft omen it was that he had used his left hand. She then dipped one of her fingers in 'anointing-oil' and touched him three times on the body. Afterwards she pressed her body against his, pulled his head down and kissed him on the lips. This was but a preliminary canter. The initiation ceremony was not held until a few days later, and the 'recruit' had to take a pre-liminary bath in salt-water, and was told, 'We take everything seriously. From the time a ritual starts and we are all within the circle we are in the presence of the gods of black magic. We always act in a respectful manner and with sincerity towards them.'

Later a ceremony involving walking round inside the magic-circle in the altar-room, anointing with both oil and water, the burning of incense, and scourging, which lasted about twenty minutes, ended in all sitting down to enjoy a glass of sherry. Shortage of glasses launched the host and hostess into a far from magic domestic quarrel, brought to an end by one of the guests pointing out that such behaviour was 'disrespectful to those we worship'. This incident revealed to the 'recruit' that there was backbiting and spite between the witches and intrigue between 'covens': the guest, who had invoked the gods to close the crisis over the sherry glasses, had a circle of her own to which the 'recruit' was invited, and where he was informed that this was the only true coven on the island, the one centred on the Mill being very inferior.

The 'recruit' being from London, was put in touch by telephone with a London witch, whom he subsequently visited, and from whose lips he gleaned a little more of the inter-coven scandals: the London witch said, with reference to the child having been initiated, 'I think it's quite wrong, and in any case I'm thoroughly disenchanted with people in the Wicca. I just cannot be bothered with the whole thing now—there is all this bickering and cattiness....'

While interviewing another London witch the same investigator asked, 'Could you cause people physical harm by willing it upon them?' The reply he received was, 'On one occasion I did attempt it on somebody ... he died in a matter of about three or four years.' It was at this witch's flat that the 'recruit' ultimately went through the initiation ceremony. He was blindfolded, kissed, and whipped, after which the blindfold was removed, revealing, at four points representing north, south, east and west, candles burning. On a small table were various swords, a magician's wand, the scourge, a phial of oil, a small cup of red wine, a black-handled dagger and a white-handled one, and a reel of pale green cotton, which last had been used to measure the 'recruit's' height, head and chest. He was told, 'your measure has been taken so that if you ever betray the secrets of witchcraft the cotton will either be burned or buried in a hole in the ground and left to rot. Whatever the fate of the cotton will also be your fate.'

About three months later the 'recruit' declared himself to be a newspaper man and was warned, 'Remember that you yourself are a witch, and nobody can ever take that away from you. You still come under the rules. Your measure has been taken and that measure is the most significant and secret thing in the whole of witchcraft. You will never see it discussed in any books. When your measure has been taken it is the length of your body, your head, and your chest. In the old days if you did anything wrong they just got your measure, dug a hole in the ground and just stuck it in there. As it rotted so you did.'

At this point another renegade minister of religion comes into the picture. This time it is a Church of England Rector. His wife said, 'I imagine my husband's disappearance has something to do with this witchcraft thing. He hasn't been in touch with me.' During his 'missing' period he was in Ireland. His behaviour in leaving his parish was extremely puzzling, but even more strange were a series of letters he wrote to one of Britain's witches. The first said, 'You say that the path you follow could be called Satanic . . . some time back I came to venerate Lucifer as the god of light. I found that this helped me a great deal, it enabled me to become sexually uninhibited. I therefore have my feet on the left-hand path. You ask me what I really seek . . . it is to go further, much further. Can you please help me to do this? Can you send me invocations and rituals that I can use?'

In the second letter he wrote, 'First you say that you are very glad to know that I venerate Lucifer—but the point is, how much? Your asking me this has made me think a very great deal about Lucifer. I had to admit that, up to the point of getting your letter, I did venerate Him but, at the same time, He hardly ever came into my mind. Now, my thinking about Him has brought about a great difference. I find that I have become conscious of His power and His greatness. The black mass—yes, I would much like to be there if it is possible.'

It is gratifying to learn that the Bishop of his diocese is conducting an investigation. Doubtless the appropriate Cardinal will deal with the renegade Catholic priest when, and if, he is discovered in Ireland. The preparations he had made to celebrate the Black Mass seemed to be confined to his having obtained black candles, and his attempt to procure a virgin for the altar. There is no suggestion that he anticipated performing human sacrifice during his celebration of the obscene rite, but this ultimate crime did, and still does, occupy an important place in the extreme ritual.

During the investigation made by the Press more than eighty witches were interviewed, among them a male who stated that he was no longer connected with the black arts but he is still believed by many witches and occultists to be a master Satanist with incredible powers of evil. Everywhere, the mention of his name evoked either abject fear, or bitter hatred. Many mysteries surround his man: but certainly he has been no stranger to the Black Mass. Sometimes blood sacrifices are made. He said he had once attended a ritual in Rome whereat the officiating 'priest' was to sacrifice a child. His story continues that he saved the infant by attacking the priest with a ceremonial sword, and the priest died a few days later of a 'heart attack'.

Such heroism seems out of character, and there is no information concerning the subsequent fate of the 'sacrifice'. Had it been carried to a place of safety the hero would, surely, have given full details so that confirmation could have been obtained. As nothing of the kind emerged we may conclude that the 'priest' was attacked only to fulfil a private grudge, and the infant was left in the hands of the Satanists to be sacrificed at the next celebration.

This 'reformed' Satanist possesses, as some of the witches of old, fire-immunity: this he demonstrated by licking a red-hot poker. In the witches' circle he is invariably dressed in a blood-red robe. No other robed witch can override his authority in the circle without a sign of anger being given by the 'God of Fire'. Later at a West London coven the 'resident' high priest insisted on being similarly robed. The 'reformed' Satanist who, notwithstanding his reformation, was present, argued fiercely against this. The 'resident', who insisted on retaining his scarlet vestment moved, during the rites, too near a candle and his robe caught fire. Coincidence? In these materialistic days far too many effects of black magic are dismissed as 'coincidence'.

Doubtless there are many people who will lightly dismiss this exposure as 'sensationalism'. Sensationalism it is indeed: and more than that. It is arresting. Further, it is true. The Press did not hesitate to state names and, very often, addresses: this we have herein avoided, and furthermore we have given but a fraction of what was revealed. A tribute is due to the reporters and other investigators who undertook and fulfilled what they must have known before starting was a dangerous mission. Witchcraft cannot harm anyone who is not afraid of it, and these investigators were certainly not lacking in courage but, when spells fail, there are to be found in the covens those who glory in committing objective murder most foul.

Perhaps the majority of the members of the Gardnerite covens are merely nudists, exhibitionists, and the like, who lack the intellectual ability to study deeply the arcane mysteries of magic: who are not malefic, and who possess neither the will nor the power to cast spells with a view to bringing disaster, disease and death by enchantment to their neighbours. They are, in fact, not witches, and in so far as their behaviour is private, and performed only for their own gratification it might be contended that no one has the right to interfere.

Taken at their weakest and meekest, merely as local congregations of abnormal, perhaps even undesirable people, their existence is more than a mere social evil: it is a source of grave danger because, having an organization, a place of meeting, and impressive pieces of bric-à-brac picked up cheap in street-markets and 'junk' shops, they are enabled the more easily to seduce adolescents to become partners in their orgies.

Further, it is reasonable to suppose that some of the Gardnerite covens have become lurking holes for Crowleyite criminals: black magicians who, in addition to sharing the general degeneracy of the other members of the group, possess superior intellectual powers, have acquired esoteric knowledge, are malefic, and can and do dispense death by enchantment, and if that fails will not hesitate to commit (as we have said) most brutal murder. Witchcraft killings, when recognized as such, are so described in the Press, but for every one such incident that is revealed by *modus operandi*, there are ten or a dozen so cunningly concealed that they can be reported only as 'motiveless'.

Such a motiveless, but clearly witchcraft murder, came into the news when, on 14 February, 1945, an elderly farm labourer was found dead. His own hay-fork had been used to pin him to the ground like a fly to a card, and his throat bore a cruciform cut.

The body was found on Meon Hill, near Lower Quinton, War-wickshire, where there were strong local traditions in the matter of witchcraft. The murdered man was somewhat 'fey'; for exam-ple, he, like St Francis, could talk to birds. He was rather solitary in his habits, but, on the whole, not disliked, and the villagers agreed that he was not the sort of man to have created enemies. The local police called for the aid of Scotland Yard and no less a personage in the detection of crime that Inspector Fabian was put in charge of the case. In spite of the most careful and thorough investigation, the killer was never discovered. There was, how-ever, no reason to doubt that this was a witchcraft murder. Such a conclusion cannot always be officially reached in cases of mysterious violent death: murders without apparent motive. Assuming, however, a witchcraft background, then motive is not far to seek: the darker and deeper Satanic cults call for human sacrifice. Among the methods employed by Satanists to encom-pass the death of a victim the use of the puppet was, and still is, a favourite one. Old Mother Demdike* said, 'the speediest way to take a man's life away by Witchcraft, is to make a picture of clay, like unto the shape of the person whom they meant to kill ...' The following was published in the *Daily Mail* on 26 July, 1968, 'A life-size effigy of a woman found on a lonely common yesterday may have been used in a pagan fertility rite. The effigy, made of straw and dressed in trousers, blouse and scarf was [found] near Newbury ...' The report continues, 'An expert on Witchcraft and black magic, said last night, "it seems that a rite to help a woman bear a child has been carried out".' This wiseacre, a local 'expert', did not, apparently, explain how the figurine had func-tioned as a parturition charm, to which end, in days gone by, the practitioners employed holed flints, known as 'hag-stones'. It is a pity that news reports do not permit of a leisurely investigation: some other local expert, had there been time to trace one, might have explained that the effigy, exposed on the common and there left to rot, was a black magician's means of committing slow murder.

The opinion that modern witches are, without exception, persons of unsound mind is a generous one: far too generous, because it is an aspect of the modern tendency to unload guilt from the criminal. Today, the rapist and the murderer are des-

* See p. 116.

cribed as 'deviated', the ever-growing throng of juvenile delinquents are 'deprived', and in place of punishment they are
sentenced to a course of 'treatment'. To thus pamper criminals,
to relieve them of the responsibility for their anti-social behaviour
and to confer upon them exemption from a knowledge of good
and evil is not symptomatic of increasing civilization, but of the
contrary. It is the pathway to the German philosophy of the
non-moral overman, and that thing is a monster more savage and
destructive, and far lower in the scale of Creation than is the
least of brute beasts. The crime of witchcraft, which today is not
even indictable, comes high on the list of disruptive causes. Even
allowing that the modern witches are persons of unsound mind,
they are not so mad as to be unaware of their having deliberately
chosen to pursue their path of evil, of atheism, of pagan—if not
actually Satanic—adherence.

It cannot be denied, even by the broadest minded of excuse
finders, that the Gardnerite groups are a menace to public morals,
or that they form a matrix for the Crowleyite minority and it is
probably these who are responsible for the numerous outrages
of profanation of churches and desecration of graveyards. When
reports of either appear in the Press, and they do, all too frequently, the general public's reaction is to attribute them to
'hooliganism'. It should be born in mind that hooligans are not
heroes. They will cut telephone leads, they will attack young
girls or old women, they will tar and feather a war-memorial,
they will board late buses (preferably when a woman is conducting the vehicle) and terrorize the passengers, but they will not
enter a burial ground by night, and even if a more than usually
courageous gang did so, to disinter a corpse would be much too
much like work for them to embark on the enterprise: after all,
their outrages are merely fun—they do it for 'kicks'—as they
tell the magistrate if they are arrested, and they pay their 5/-
fine with tears in their eyes. No. It is not hooligans who violate
the dead, it is Satanists. This fact is not disguised by the Press. In
the *Evening News* on Thursday, 6 February, 1969, the following
appeared: 'Fears of a dramatic revival in witchcraft in Kent and
Sussex increased today with the discovery of three more acts of
desecration in isolated cemeteries. In most of the cases gravestones
had been smashed, stone crosses pulled to the ground and signs
daubed in green paint on the graves.

'Tunbridge Wells police think the damage was caused after dark on Sunday which was Candlemas Day for the Church and also an important date in the witches' calendar. There was also a full moon. At Rustall burial ground, near Tunbridge Wells, more than £500 worth of damage was found by the gardener, ... when he visited the area ... many of the gravestones had been daubed with green paint.

'Green has always been regarded as a colour with magic properties. Many of the signs, especially a witch's staff and an entwined serpent, play an elaborate part in Black Magic. Further acts of desecration were discovered today at Pound's Bridge, Groombridge and Fordcomb, all villages near Tunbridge Wells; the same signs were daubed in all the cemeteries, and at Pound's Bridge special signs were printed across the church door and crosses placed against it.'

In the foregoing example no graves were opened: in the following, published in the *Evening Standard* on Friday, 1 November, 1968, the activities were far more heinous: 'Graves disturbed, coffins dug up and prised open, crosses broken and the remains of a midnight Witch's Sabbath—that was the scene today at a London cemetery where devil worshippers held Hallowe'en rites last night. The superintendent, who is a clergyman, and is also chaplain, said, "I've never seen anything like it. It isn't just ordinary vandalism. Everything has been carefully done, and arranged according to some evil rite. There's more in this than meets the eye. I believe some kind of Black Magic ceremony has been held here—and it's not the first time."

'The main drive of the seven-acre private graveyard [was] strewn with dead flowers, inverted crosses and broken urns which had been pillaged from graves. The objects were arranged in a pattern, with arrows leading to graves where recent burials have taken place. At the new graves, earth had been dug out, and scattered in heaps. In a large hole was a coffin which had been broken open and the body in it had been disturbed. Near by was a tiny coffin of a new-born baby, which had been unearthed and thrown aside. A third coffin in the grave had been stood on end and was broken so that the shrouded feet of the body were exposed. Through the coffin had been plunged an iron stake in the form of a cross.

'The damage was discovered by the graveyard foreman . . .

who lives in a cottage [on the ground]. He returned home from the cinema at eleven p.m. ... the iron gates ... were locked and everything was in order. He heard no disturbance at all in the night ... "this isn't the first time it's happened—it's about the sixth—but never so bad as this ... The graveyard is supposed to be haunted; but this has been done by humans."'

On 2 November, 1968, the *Evening News* added, 'an expert in Black Magic visited Tottenham Park cemetery, [he said] that desecration occurred at the same time at two other cemeteries both in East Anglia. "Black Magic is far more widespread than many people imagine ... as soon as I am in a position to provide definite proof I shall hand over my dossier to the police."' This would be a most laudable public service, and the expert should be encouraged. It is, however, unlikely that the police are totally in the dark—they are fools only in detective novels—but knowing who is responsible and being able to prove it are two very different things. We may expect more and more of such outrages for there is now no law to protect the public from witchcraft.

'Doctor' Gardner's groups of nude dancers, and misfit cranks whom he dignifies by describing as 'the Wicca', devotees of a non-Christian religious cult who do not believe in the devil, who are, therefore, not supporters of the Black Mass, and who, far from their being evil, think no evil and do no evil, are revealed by what is printed in the press to be other than how their champion represents them. The twentieth century has flung wide the flood-gates of restraint and even 'respectable' people are candid with regard to their immoralities: what is called 'freedom of the individual' is in fact the rising tide of Satanism. Vice has become legalized: homosexuality between consenting male adults is permitted: on a dozen doorsteps in thoroughfares between Shaftesbury Avenue and Oxford Street stands a slimy southern European shouting to passers by that the show is now on: a bevy of beautiful girls are prancing and parading in full view stark naked; prostitutes display electrically illuminated notices calling would-be clients to walk up to their apartment; narcotic drugs are sold to school-children; churches are attended (in so far as they are attended) not by Christian congregations, but by people who having nothing to do, and (in some cases) smoking is permitted during the service.

The devil, booted and spurred, is riding Western civilization to eternal death while the broad-minded steed declares there is no devil. The conception that vice made manifest is 'healthier' than the same sins committed in secret is dictated by the devil and is itself as evil as the legalized crimes, and the candid indecencies complacently tolerated in modern society. If there had existed in the nineteenth century groups of witches such as those championed by 'Doctor' Gardner, and had they found a 'public relations officer' such as he, it is quite certain that the books would not have been issued by a self-respecting, dignified publishing house and, if printed at the author's risk and offered for sale to the general public they would have been banned and burned.

It would be interesting to know whether the general laxity has increased the number of, and enhanced the activities of the very dangerous 'lone' witches labelled 'paranoid' by medical science, but even modern mechanized statistics would fail if the computers were applied to the problem. These sinister devotees of the devil succeed in displaying an exterior sweetness, kindliness, helpfulness, friendliness and social desirability notwithstanding that within they are as black as the pit, malefic, and perpetually plotting the destruction of all who befriend them and accept them at face value. They do not gravitate to groups, would be loud in their condemnation of the Gardnerite covens but, on the principle of like attracting like, they aften associate with one or two characters of their own kind. Being evil by nature they need to make no study of the mumbo-jumbo of classic witchcraft, but some of the time-honoured tricks, such as the use of puppets, and the employment of the left hand in gestures of malediction become known to them.

At this juncture it may be wise to point out, even if only in self-defence, that every neurotic, socially maladjusted person whose reaction to life is moulded on hatred rather than love is not to be condemned as a lone witch. The neurotic's inability to lead a normal social life, and his tendency to regard all with whom he comes in contact as potential enemies is involuntary: on the other hand the lone witch can, and generally does, pass herself off as the most desirable of companions, behind which façade she, unsuspected, deliberately contrives disaster—even death—for her associates.

The behaviour pattern of a number of lone witches observed by the present writer has proved to be uncannily alike. Careful, planned questioning has revealed that each of them, as a child at school, was unsociable and quarrelsome, victimized by the other children, all of whom were common and stupid, persecuting the embryo witch because they were jealous of her social superiority and her mental brilliance which invariably placed her, without any special effort, at the top of the form and caused the teacher not only to love her, but to cite her as an example of perfection. In this fabric of early history there is to be found one thread of truth: namely, their excellence of learning, which served them only as a means of causing the discomfiture of the rest of the class. They passed no scholarships. The mental brilliance was superficial, and so it remained through life: they give the impression of having a huge fund of learning but by its aid they achieve nothing.

Their unpleasantness as children and, it seems, lack of parental control, makes of them appropriate vehicles for the conveyance of a demon which, entering at about the onset of menstruation, guides them along the path of witchcraft and inspires them with evil to their teleological termination in both physical and mental degeneration.

At an early age, sometimes even before leaving school, they select with unerring accuracy a gentle-natured sensitive youth on to whom they batten, whom they hypnotize into the conviction that he is deeply in love and, in spite of opposition from the youth's friends and sometimes, even his own growing reluctance, they trap him into an early marriage not by the comparatively honest (though immoral) feminine trick of getting themselves made pregnant by him, but by working on his sympathies as, for example, pretending to be deeply unhappy at home among their brothers and sisters who, of course, are jealous of either their superiority, or their intellect, or their possession of a beloved, or any other heart-breaking situation they can, in their cunning, contrive. Having thus achieved marriage they rejoice exceedingly, for by this success they have graduated in their witchcraft ideal: they have secured their first victim. The young husband is, in signing the register of marriages, attaching his signature to his own death warrant.

These witch-worked alliances appear to be sexually unsatisfactory: there is often no issue, and (in this writer's experience), never more than one who, whether boy or girl, invariably proves to be what our wise ancestors described as a changeling: an imp out of hell put in the place of the human child. They are abnormally destructive, take no interest in toys, display cruelty to in place of love of animals and, almost as soon as they can talk they manifest a revolting precocity, the ability to give tongue to spiteful and hurtful utterances, as well as a sexual sophistication beyond the knowledge of many an adult, which delights the obscene mother but horrifies the gentle father who, by that time, having been subjected to the character-undermining activities of his malefic wife, does not dare raise his voice in protest. These changelings, allies of the mother, take an active part in the persecution of the father whom they defy, scream at, punch and kick.

The slow murder of the man commences immediately the marriage knot is tied. The first move seems to be that of estranging him from his friends of bachelor days by slowly conditioning him to form the opinion that they are, behind his back, making a laughing-stock of him; or that they are socially inferior; or that they were, on such and such an occasion, deliberately insulting to his wife, or any other story that will take effect on a sensitive young man who is still being indoctrinated with the idea that he is deeply, passionately and most romantically in love. The next move in the death-dealing game of the lone witches is to cause a rupture between the husband and his family. The method employed varies with circumstances. Whenever it is possible it is done by telling barefaced and most wicked lies as, for example, to a sister, 'John told me in confidence that you and your boy-friend went to the seaside for a week-end as Mr and Mrs, and I said to him, "Well, most girls aren't as particular as I was before we were married, but you've no right to have told me, anyway!"' There is no need to explain the consequences and the complications, the insulted girl's tears to the mother, the mother's tears to her husband, the heavy father's 'words' to his apparently dishonourable (and untruthful) son, the son's spirited denial and his own wife's sympathy: her reiterated wonderment at who could possibly have said so wicked a thing, and her assurance 'Well, Johnnie dear, you've got *me*, so it does not really matter if you never see your family again, now does it?'

Without friends, without family ties, his next vital loss will be his hobbies, out of the indulging in which he will be both ridiculed and bullied: 'Ha, Ha! Little Johnnie plays with his postage stamps. Shall I buy you a little clock-work railway-train?' or, 'Hm! Nice thing! My devoted husband sits playing with post-age-stamps, and I with my varicose-veins [or weak heart, or delicate chest, sensitive stomach, or any other imaginary disease] have to go out and dig the garden!' The stamp collection is ulti-mately sold. The sensitive youth has developed into the nervous young man, pallid, and with a perpetual strained expression de-pressing the corners of his mouth, and furtive, sidelong glancing eyes. His temper is quickened, he is no longer popular among his colleagues at work because his dear wife, so full of solicitude and anxiety for his welfare, has convinced him that they sneer at him 'behind his back', and are plotting to push their way past him in promotion precedence. Although he was, before marriage, a boy with the average equipment of both physical and moral courage, he has become, under the incessant spiritual bludgeon-ing of his witch-wife, an abject coward who, although he is unaware of it, lives in fear of her and, at all times, and under all conditions conforms to her will, even to the extent of acting in a manner contrary to his nature by, for example, writing on her behalf aggressive and insulting letters to his neighbours. He slowly but surely grows depressed and introverted, loses appe-tite, loses weight, loses his grip on life, outside the prison he calls home, and ultimately loses his employment. Then begins the last phase in the process of murder. Unable to obtain fresh employ-ment, he hangs about the house, never at rest, nagged and dis-paraged night and day by his witch-wife.

At length, aware of the evaporation of his romance, conscious of the fact that his wife has hated him bitterly since the ever-to-be-damned day on which they first met, overwhelmed by depres-sion and deep grief he settles down to die, and although the doctor declares him to be organically sound, die he will, another unrecognized victim of the maleficium of witchcraft.

In the days of the witchcraft trials, those found guilty and condemned to death were hanged. There are, however, to be found in the records a number that were sentenced to be burned. This was not the capital punishment for practising witchcraft, but was the death prescribed for those found guilty of 'petty treason'; that is, the killing of a husband by a wife, or a master (or mistress) by a servant, no matter what the means of murder may have been: the knife, the poison cup, or the malignant spells cast by a witch.

The foregoing composite picture can be bolstered by a number of examples, the progress of each of which will be recounted in chronological order, although the details of the early history were unknown until the case had been under observation for a considerable time.

A young craftsman of abnormal ability had, at an earlier age than is normal, been put in charge of a section of the factory wherein he was employed and, because of his responsibility, was obliged to report to, and consult, the chief-engineer several times a week. These visits to the office-block brought him in contact with the chief-engineer's secretary in whose presence he was at first rather shy and withdrawn. However, the period of waiting for his interview with the chief was sometimes prolonged which, most likely, was arranged by the secretary, who took advantage of the occasions to engage the craftsman in conversation. This softening-up process was successful, and in about three months they were engaged and, before a year had expired, married.

The first move made in the process of destruction was the woman's perpetual reminder that she had married beneath herself: her husband belonged to the 'overalls' class whilst she had been among the most exalted of office workers. This persistent pin-pricking became intolerable and the craftsman made up his mind to 'better himself'. With this end in view he attended evening-classes, was accused the while of neglect, but succeeded in passing an examination in theory, and became a black-coated worker, at a lower rate of pay than he had customarily received as a craftsman. This laid him open to ridicule from his wife, and his reaction was to point out that he had made the effort to please her. He soon learned that to please her was impossible, and that every word he uttered was turned to a weapon against him, hence, he grew estranged, stopped trying to please, and spent all his spare time on his hobby of model-making. This led to further ridicule, more accusations of neglect, to the 'accidental' destruction of his work.

After this, he would often find, upon arrival home, a scribbled note to the effect that the wife was visiting friends and he must fend for himself; a tin of this, or that, or the other was in the cupboard. Where the wife went and who the friends were never emerged, but the absences became more frequent, the customary notes were no longer left, and the husband found, on investigation, that there were no tins of anything in the cupboard. On these occasions he would go out for a meal, but such comfort for him did not please the wife who, having in pleasant conversation extracted from him the name of the restaurant he patronized, would, at irregular intervals, turn up unexpectedly, insult the waitress, complain of the service, even assert, in a loud voice, that the food supplied to her was bad. After such demonstrations the husband was forced to find another eating-house, and invariably he would ultimately suffer the same humiliation.

At length he found consolation in alcohol, and became an inveterate drunkard who went straight from his work to the public-house, and arrived home at near midnight in a state bordering on stupor in which he was deaf to the torment of his wife's envenomed tongue.

This is not simply the story of an unsuccessful marriage: it is an account of a marriage deliberately destroyed by a lone witch who, not fully successful in driving her sorrowing husband to death was herself ultimately admitted to a mental hospital.

Another case in which the husband had qualities of resistance was that of a middle-aged couple, Swiss in origin, with one daughter, aged about twenty, who had been born here. The husband, a watch-maker, was employed in the watch-repairing department of a big store and, being more interested in his work than in the money he obtained by it, his hours were irregular. Although he came home for his mid-day meal, he might arrive at any time between twelve and three. The wife, who had been born in the same village as her husband, and who had, as a child, invariably awaited his emergence from school so that he never had a chance to form friendships with other boys, or to develop an attachment to any other girl, incessantly complained that his irregular mid-day habits made life very hard for both herself and her daughter who, since leaving school had never sought work, but lounged idly at home declaring it to be her duty to help her mother, which she did not do.

The minimum amount of effort was put into the preparation of the husband's mid-day meal: a pot was kept simmering into which was dropped odds and ends of meat, or fish. When the husband arrived he uttered not a word, sat at the table and there was placed before him a soup-plate into which some of the stew had been ladled and a loaf of bread. While he was ingesting (it can scarcely be described as 'eating') this dismal concoction, the wife perched herself against the edge of a small side-table behind him, folded her arms, and incessantly mumbled. From time to time she croaked, 'Mind the little bones! You'll choke!' What did not at first appear but, when ultimately observed proved to be an invariable accompaniment, was that her left hand was closed in malediction.

This gesture, which seems to be Continental, consists in flexing the two middle fingers and holding them down with the thumb, and extending the index and little finger, thus creating a representation of the devil's horned head. It is believed by witches to be a most potent charm, and an ambivalent one. It is used both in directing a curse (by pointing the horns at the intended victim while uttering the destructive formula) and in fending one off. In this last usage many superstitious peasants, who fear malefic spells and the evil eye, protect themselves and their children when passing a person who is suspected of evil power and intention.

Having finished the meal the husband would smoke, through a cherrywood holder, a cigarette, and then depart without having spoken a single word: he might have been dumb. The moment he shut the door behind him the wife hurried to the window and apparently waved 'good-bye'. This was false observation: what she was doing was brandishing the left hand in malediction.

This man, silent and withdrawn, was very difficult to get to know, but when at length the barrier was broken, he proved talkative enough. His knowledge of the history of time-pieces, and the biographies of famous makers was encyclopaedic. His pathological silence when at home was due to his having learned the adage 'least said, soonest mended'. His delight in his work fenced him round protectively from the malicious hate of both his wife and his daughter, whose idea of helping her mother did not extend beyond assisting to cause distress to her father, whom she persecuted by incessant demands upon him for money: she never had a shoe repaired, she never darned a stocking, and seemed to have an abundance of frocks, costumes, coats, hats and umbrellas. Her ruthless demands were, to a very large extent, due to the mother having implanted in her mind, from childhood, that the father was a miser with a secret huge hoard of wealth.

This fleecing of the poor man was always staged to take place in the evening: his custom was to sit down to another plate of stew immediately upon arrival home, hurry through it to the accompaniment of the suggestion concerning choking through swallowing bones, and then go to a club where he played chess at which game he was a minor champion. The daughter's demand for money was timed to fall upon him the moment he had finished the meal. His spirit being already ahead of him at the chess-club, he invariably curtly refused, and so brought forth a tirade from the two witches to escape from which, and seek solace in chess, he invariably gave in, handed over the sum demanded or the bulk of it with a promise to give the balance at the week-end.

On Sunday morning he went to the chapel where he was a person of consequence and, after the religious service took part in a vestry meeting, returning home—to another ladling out of the stew—at about two o'clock. At this meal he sat, as usual, alone and silent, the two witches having enjoyed an early lunch of an appetizing nature, such as a mixed grill, steak, or fried liver. Having once more come to the end of the plate's contents without having choked himself with a bone, out came his cherrywood cigarette holder and he would chain-smoke until, becoming drowsy, he extinguished the cigarette and fell asleep. While he thus dozed the plate was removed and the table cleared with the result that his cigarette holder invariably rolled on to the floor and became crushed underfoot. He was so accustomed to this 'accident' that he kept a supply of new ones (at this time they cost only a penny each) in his pocket.

On some occasions he smoked less, and sat concentrating on a printed chess-problem cut from a newspaper which he quite often solved and replaced in his pocket before dozing off. On a few occasions, the solution not appearing, he fell asleep with the cutting still on the table and it invariably was cleared away with the cloth. On these occasions his rule of silence was broken and he displayed a violence of table-thumping temper that seemed unnatural to so mild, sensitive, religious a man. It was as though his wife's demon left her and leapt upon him: she became silent, trembling and tearful. The daughter, if present, always hurriedly dressed and went out. During these outbursts the tormented man would shake his fist in his wife's face, but kept sufficient control not to strike. He finished up either by going to bed, or going out.

The wife, in her wickedness, lacked the ability to refrain from destroying these press-cuttings, and so bringing upon herself the fright caused by her husband's rage. He, knowing what to expect, seldom made the mistake of leaving one on the table, but now and then sleep would overtake him. The climax was reached one Sunday when he awoke to find the problem gone, and his much-treasured pocket set of chess-men on the floor, trodden upon and broken. His rage was understandably and justifiably so great that he did not dare give reign to it. Instead, he dashed from the house without either hat or coat (and it was mid-winter) and little more than two-hundred yards from his own front door fell down dead from attack of *angina pectoris*.

This disorder is not, as is popularly supposed, primarily an affection of the cardiac. The condition is caused by the contraction of the capillaries of the coronary artery, and death is due to suffocation, the heart failing from lack of oxygen. A small bone swallowed and lodged in the wind-pipe would have precisely the same effect. Nothing more need really be said in this terrible tragedy, but it is significant that the two witches were delighted, until the daughter, after a most exhaustive search, discovered that there was no secret hoard, whereupon mother and daughter almost came to blows, and in the matter of but a few months they parted company. The mother went into a home for old people (where she caused chaos), the daughter disappeared and it was rumoured that she had found a weakling youth and married him.

Another lone witch who had, at the age of seventeen, seized upon a gentle and rather dreamy youth, began persecuting him to bring about marriage while he was still a minor. This move failed, but only a few months elapsed after his twenty-first birthday, when the net was successfully cast. His parents did not attend the register office wedding and they never became reconciled. At that early age the youth's earnings were very small and life in a furnished room was hard. However, the wife made no effort to go out to work and what was more declared herself unable to cook, hence, the youth, upon arrival home, donned an apron, prepared the meal, and afterwards washed up. Notwithstanding this unnatural and exacting life the youth believed himself to be happy, his sole regret being his estrangement from his parents. In about six months his area of regret was expanded by his wife having very successfully driven away his two friends with whom he had been on almost brotherly terms since his schooldays. In their place the witch imported friends of her own —people entirely after her own heart—who blatantly insulted and ridiculed the easy-going and not very understanding young man. He thought the sneers were simply a form of fun that he had not hitherto encountered. The wife, however, employed the situation as a means of inducing misery.

After every meeting she picked a quarrel: her husband had said the wrong thing, or had not said the right thing. The more he strove to explain, the more fuel he added to the fire, for his wife had a way of inverting the meaning of everything. Accusation and cross-examination would continue till the youth was mentally exhausted and near to tears, but the witch, who knew full well that the marriage was not yet sufficiently firmly set to enable her to carry the persecution beyond a certain point, would suddenly change: smile, throw her arms about him, overwhelm him with endearments, and become the epitome of charming young womanhood. After the storm came sunshine, but on each occasion a little of the damp of depression was left behind and it became cumulative. The young man, who had always had a tendency towards day-dreaming, spent morbid hours in self-examination struggling to discover what major fault of character he possessed that caused his wife displeasure when he strove incessantly to please her.

His introversion increased and his dread of innocently precipitating an attack caused him to become furtive and apprehensive. He tried to be casual, to keep both mentally and emotionally from under his wife's cloven hoof, but his attempt at avoidance opened a wider front for him to weakly barricade.

The witch brought her heavy artillery to bear by asserting that his withdrawn behaviour was a defence mechanism to hide the fact of his sexual philandering while at work. Whether she knew it or not (and she probably did) there was nothing in her armoury of malice and venom more lethal than this, for her husband, who had been strictly brought up, was convinced that there was no greater sin than an extra-marital sexual relationship. It was manifest that this new line of attack was rapidly destroying his mental and physical health, hence, the persecution was intensified. The witch began calling at his office, demanding in a loud, rude manner to see him and would, on his emergence, make some insulting remark such as 'Who's that painted slut with dyed hair —eh?' in a voice loud enough to be heard.

This kind of intrusion occurred two or three times a week and after a few months the victim found himself unemployed.

The reason for his dismissal was clear to everyone except himself. He complained miserably to his wife—the only person with whom he was now intimate—of his bad and unjust treatment. She, knowing herself to be the sole cause of the disaster, pretended to be mystified and sympathetic: she made the matter a subject of conversation continually and, soon after her husband was established in another job, began planting in his mind the idea that he would not keep it long because he was sure to be caught again in sexual intimacy with one of the women. Her cruelty in the use of this weapon was diabolical: she never let it rest, and would even wake him up in the middle of the night, pretending that she felt ill, declaring the cause to be his infidelity, and continuing the bombardment until it was time for him to go off to his office. Because of incessant mental depression, and frequent loss of a night's sleep, his work became inferior, and he knew himself to be far from secure. He was haunted by the dread that his wife would, in her suspicion, intrude upon him during his working hours. One can imagine, therefore, what terror overwhelmed him one week-end when his wife, who had been being particularly sweet and charming, suddenly announced her intention of travelling to the City on the following Friday so that they could have lunch together. It is quite certain that he would not have made an attempt to dissuade her, for to do so would have precipitated a verbal bludgeoning on the declared assumption that his unwillingness arose from his being involved—'as usual' —in a sexual intrigue: nevertheless, the threatened luncheon party did not take place. On the preceding Wednesday he was knocked down and killed by a motor vehicle.

Nothing is to be gained by the multiplication of examples such as these: the modern materialist will still contend that these witch-wives were persons of unsound mind, and that the victim-husbands were sub-normal, effete, lacking in masculinity and unable to assert their authority as masters in their own houses. This, being the opinion of the qualified medical fraternity, cannot be contested by the unqualified layman, who can but mildly proffer the previously quoted schoolboy's witticism: 'mad and bad are two-thirds the same.' There is not to be found in this wide, over-populated world, a mind that can be universally accepted as sound. The problem will never be solved by the mind-healers no matter how benign, compassionate and scientific they may be, for the line between rectitude and wickedness is scored across the spirit.

The people in whom madness and badness mingle are, as it were, the visible spectrum of abnormality: there is left the ultra-violent of unadulterated madness, and the infra-red of unadulterated badness. The wholly insane cannot be held responsible for their actions, but the partially insane, the abnormals and the 'deviateds' can be, and ought to be. They generally do not lack the ability to distinguish between rectitude and wickedness and they deliberately select the latter. The dominant females and the sub-masculine males did not come together because of a biological urge beyond the control and outside the consciousness of both parties, but by the calculated machinations of the female. This is indicated by the declaration of one such witch-wife that she hated her husband as soon as she saw him, and made up her mind to marry and destroy him.

Another lone witch, who never married, developed, when in her early 'teens', a diabolical speciality. She sought for, and found, young men, happily married, over whom she cast her spell, inducing in them an abnormally intense sexual attachment to herself. When she had them inextricably enmeshed she forced an acquaintanceship with her victim's wife to whom she revealed the true situation. This fiendish female confessed that she was happy only when involved in an intrigue, and that she experienced peaks of exultant joy in connection with each case: the first, when her intended victim yielded to her, and the second when she precipitated the disaster and saw the grief and despair that her revelation brought to the wife.

Lone witches invariably take pleasure in causing grief and distress; they often work very hard, paying calls, spreading scandal, writing letters, telling lies, tendering bad advice to achieve their end. There is no occupation more pleasing to them than breaking up a marriage even when they are themselves not playing the part of 'the other woman'.

When the supporters of the 'unsound mind' idea are asked why the patient has, all her life, served an evil end and never a good one, they conceal the flaw in their front with a fence of technical terms, but the fact remains that none of these devotees of the devil have ever been known to write their letters and tell their lies in order to strengthen and repair a marriage showing signs of disunion.

That admirable modern social service, the Marriage Guidance Council, does not countenance witchcraft among the causes of the disasters it conscientiously struggles to avert but, to quote an Arabic proverb, 'were it graven with needle-gravers upon the eye corners it would stand as a warning to those who would be warned.'

It is a curious and quite illogical fact that the Christian West, where mankind is attributed free-will and personal responsibility, has by the application of psychological theory exonerated the criminal, but the Mohammedan East, where the doctrine of predestination rules, does not exonerate, but will sometimes piously forgive, the criminal.

In the European Middle Ages, in spite of ignorance, mankind could distinguish between the mad and bad. The former, possessed of a demon, might be relieved by the exorcist. The world was relieved of the latter via the court house and the gallows.

Doctors today do not deal in demonic possession and they explain the successes of the exorcists as cases of hypno-therapy applied to hysterical patients.

Science has shut the door on Satan and achieved the fusion of good and evil which is so satisfying in this hedonistic age, but 'Be sober, be vigilant; because your adversary the devil, as a roaring lion, walketh about, seeking whom he may devour.'*

* I Peter: 5, 8. (A.V.).

Acknowledgements

For permission to quote from the following books, thanks are due to:

The Hutchinson Publishing Group Ltd. (*Witchcraft and Black Magic* by Montague Summers), Associate Book Publishers Ltd. (*Four Centuries of Witch Beliefs* by R. Trevor Davies), Routledge & Kegan Paul Ltd. (*The History of Witchcraft and Demonology* and *The Geography of Witchcraft* both by Montague Summers, *Medicine, Magic and Religion* by W. H. R. Rivers), Mrs Katharine Jones and The Hogarth Press Ltd. (*On the Nightmare* by Ernest Jones), the *Evening News*, London and the *Evening Standard*, London, Alfred A. Knopf, Inc. (*Life in a Haitian Village* by Herskovitz), Faber & Faber Ltd. (*The Murder of Sir Thomas Overbury* by William McElwee), Mr Eric Partridge (*A Charm of Words*, Hamish Hamilton Ltd.), Crown Publishers Inc. (*Encyclopaedia of Witchcraft and Demonology*) and *The British Medical Bulletin* (Vol. 6, page 1, article by E. Slater, 1949; Vol. 6, page 63, article by S. R. Burstein, 1949).

In addition, the author particularly wishes to express his great appreciation of the most generous assistance given by the staff of the Department of Ethnography of the British Museum.

Index